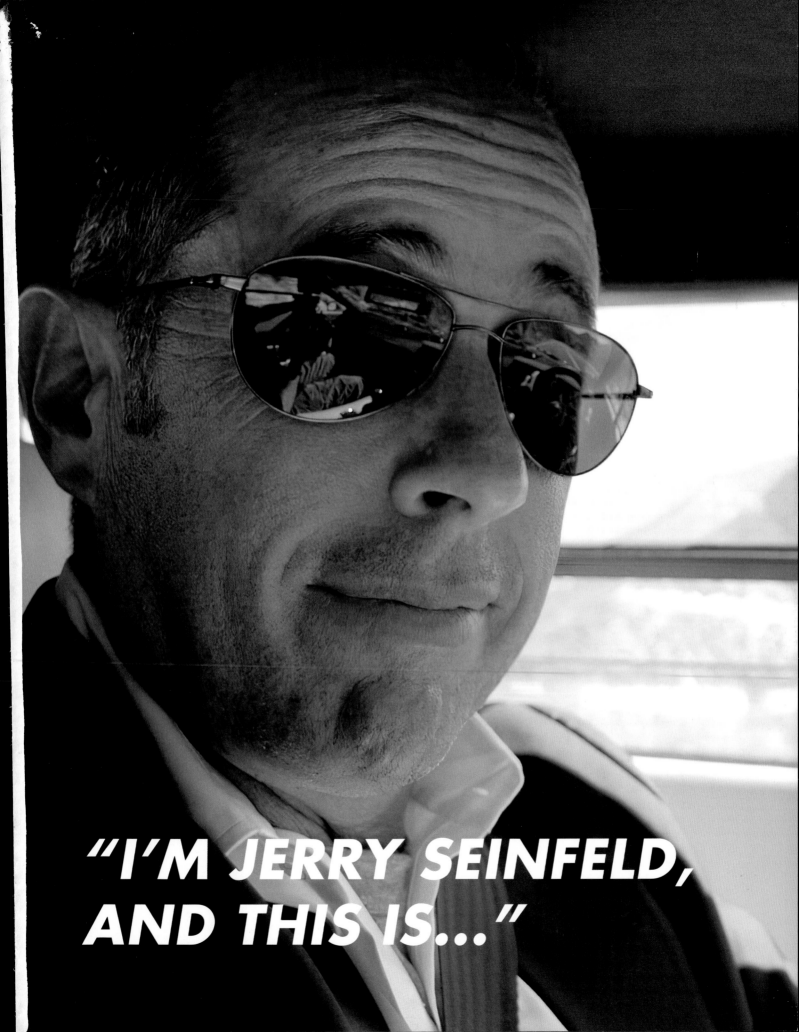

"I'M JERRY SEINFELD, AND THIS IS..."

"THE COMEDIANS
IN CARS GETTING
COFFEE BOOK."

# JERRY SEINFELD

### Simon & Schuster

NEW YORK    LONDON    TORONTO    SYDNEY    NEW DELHI

Simon & Schuster
1230 Avenue of the Americas
New York, NY 10020

First Simon & Schuster hardcover edition November 2022

SIMON & SCHUSTER and colophon are registered trademarks of Simon & Schuster, Inc.

For information about special discounts for bulk purchases, please contact Simon & Schuster Special Sales at 1-866-506-1949 or business@simonandschuster.com.

The Simon & Schuster Speakers Bureau can bring authors to your live event. For more information or to book an event, contact the Simon & Schuster Speakers Bureau at 1-866-248-3049 or visit our website at www.simonspeakers.com.

Book design: Brian Conery, bricondesign.com

Manufactured in the United States of America

10  9  8  7  6  5  4  3  2  1

Library of Congress Cataloging-in-Publication Data is available.

ISBN 978-1-9821-1276-9
ISBN 978-1-9821-1278-3 (ebook)

# CONTENTS

viii    **INTRODUCTION**

xiv    **UNDER THE HOOD: AN ORAL HISTORY OF COMEDIANS IN CARS GETTING COFFEE**

025    **GROWING UP**

039    **GETTING STARTED**

087    **RELATIONSHIPS**

099    **TV & MOVIES**

117    **OTHER COMEDIANS**

169    **FOOD**

185    **FAMILY**

195    **MUSIC**

211    **THE ART OF COMEDY**

247    **MONEY**

259    **SPORTS**

271    **SEINFELD: THE TV SHOW**

281    **GETTING OLDER**

301    **MISCELLANEOUS WISDOM**

317    **EPISODE INDEX**

330    **ACKNOWLEDGMENTS**

333    **CREDITS**

# INTRODUCTION

I almost feel like I should apologize for the idea of *Comedians in Cars Getting Coffee* because it was really just a very personal concept of something I enjoyed doing. I had no idea at any point if it was even really a show. Even the way I announced the show at the top, "I'm Jerry Seinfeld . . . and this is *Comedians in Cars Getting Coffee*," I was actually kidding, just pretending it was a real show. So many times after we would spend a couple hours shooting this nonsensical talk between me and a favorite comedian of mine, driving around in some marvelous, idiosyncratic car, and just going for coffee, I would ask one of the people on the crew, "Does this seem like an actual show to you?" Or, "What is this? What are we doing?" Even after people started imitating the idea—which I never had any problem with, I loved it—I was never quite sure about it. And of course, that is the whole fun of a new idea. You don't know what it is exactly or where it's going. Just as the song says "the world will always welcome lovers," the world is always starving for a new idea.

The most important word I used in putting this thing together was "valentine." Most significantly, it was a valentine to the comedians I have been so fortunate to have surrounding me in this lifetime. I thought this aspect of a life in comedy was somewhat unreported in a lot of what is written about comedy. And it is a very, very large part of the comedy aquarium in which I live. Comedians never, ever stop making fun of absolutely every single detail of every aspect of the human life travail. So my idea was, how can I show what this part of comedy life is? Many shows have tried to examine and understand comedians in various ways, and it's really pointless, unenlightening, and, most egregiously, no fun. What if I figured out a way to bring the viewer along on a bit of comedy hang time but filtered it down to mostly the jokes and whatever else has some thought value? I'm not much for podcasts. I think virtually everything in life could do with a good edit. Your closet, your diet, your conversation, everything. That's what a beautifully put-together stand-up set is. It's "I have a lot of funny and interesting thoughts. Here's the best ones." I'd use a classic car because they have more personality, like comedians do, and I also just wanted to see what some of them were like to drive. And the activity would be going to get coffee because that has a certain meaning and meaninglessness that gets comedians thinking and talking.

I always thought "Getting" was an important part of the title phrase. It wasn't "Having" or "Drinking" coffee. We're "GETTING" it. I think that's a real distinction. Someone handing you a coffee is not at all the same as them saying, "Hey, would you like to go get a coffee?" That question is really a way of saying, "I like you enough to do absolutely nothing with." No higher compliment, to my way of thinking.

The other odd thing is I only started drinking coffee a few years before I started doing the show, and that was only because I had young kids and didn't have time to have meals with people anymore. But there was always time to grab a coffee. All the coffee shop scenes in the *Seinfeld* series, I never knew anything about coffee or why people drank it. Now 90 percent of my existence revolves around the wondrous brown-gold liquid, and I've never been happier.

The magic of coffee is the complexity of growing it, farming it, transporting it, grind-

ing it, brewing it, pouring it, and assembling it to your personal liking. I love all the ingredients and tools necessary. Try to have that first taste of coffee in the morning and not make an audible sound of gratification. Can't do it.

Similarly to the way I see the cars in the show, I don't view coffee as an inanimate. I see it as a companion. I never feel alone if I have a coffee in front of me. It has so many life-affirming properties. I once said in an interview, "We want to do a lot of stuff but we're not in great shape, didn't get a good night's sleep, and we're a little depressed . . . coffee solves all these problems in one delightful warm cup."

Okay, the cars. I'm not going to talk too much about the cars because if you're not an automotive enthusiast, cars are an unbelievably boring subject. I try to keep the impressions of the cars very brief at the front of the show for this reason. How a person could not be interested in cars, I'll never understand. They're such large, important, fascinating objects. They have so many difficult complex functions they must perform perfectly 100 percent of the time or people hate them violently. They're a perfect fit with the comedians and the coffee. The reason I love cars is each one's personality always

expresses a moment in mechanical history and culture. People did really seem to enjoy how I would match the car to the guest comedian. That was so easy. Every car is so unique to me. And so much like a person. Always trying to please, so often failing . . .

Discovering and describing the world is the only reason I can see for trying so hard to continue living. Because those perceptions are the entryway for loving the world and the life in it. And again, a car is an inanimate object that makes me feel not alone. I've never felt lonely in a car. I'm with something that's got a lot going on.

Now, the comedians. As humans go, comedians are as close to inanimate objects as you can get. The ability to perceive and describe the human experience in such an entertaining way does not by any means make the comedian a part of that experience. The thing I notice about every comedian is they do not seem to be part of the terrestrial world. They move perceptually like an alien spaceship—like quickness and unpredictability. They flit and spark in unexpected directions at unexpected moments, and if they're any good, you can never quite track what direction they're going to go next. Good comedy bits are short, dense, and always catching you a little off guard. People cannot move this adroitly on the ground, only in the air. This is always what we seek to capture in an episode of *Comedians in Cars Getting Coffee*.

Since I know so many comedians and most people don't know any, I felt perfectly positioned with my video butterfly net to try to show them in their unpackaged, natural state. That's the other weird thing about the work of creating these shows. What you are seeing is incredibly raw and totally manufactured at the same time. The video footage of course starts out raw, but by the time we edit, shape, reorder, and, in a couple of very rare cases, fake what you are hearing and seeing, it has become a very polished piece of whatever the hell this thing is. I swear to God sometimes I still don't even know.

I do know I loved making every single one of them. I love and am so appreciative of every comedian who joined us for a nice drive and a coffee. And also so want to thank my production team who did whatever I asked every time, even when there really was no way to do it. To all of them and to you, our loyal, generous audience, thank you for letting us give you this very special valentine.

**Jerry Seinfeld**
New York City

UNDER THE HOOD:

# AN ORAL HISTORY OF COMEDIANS IN CARS GETTING COFFEE

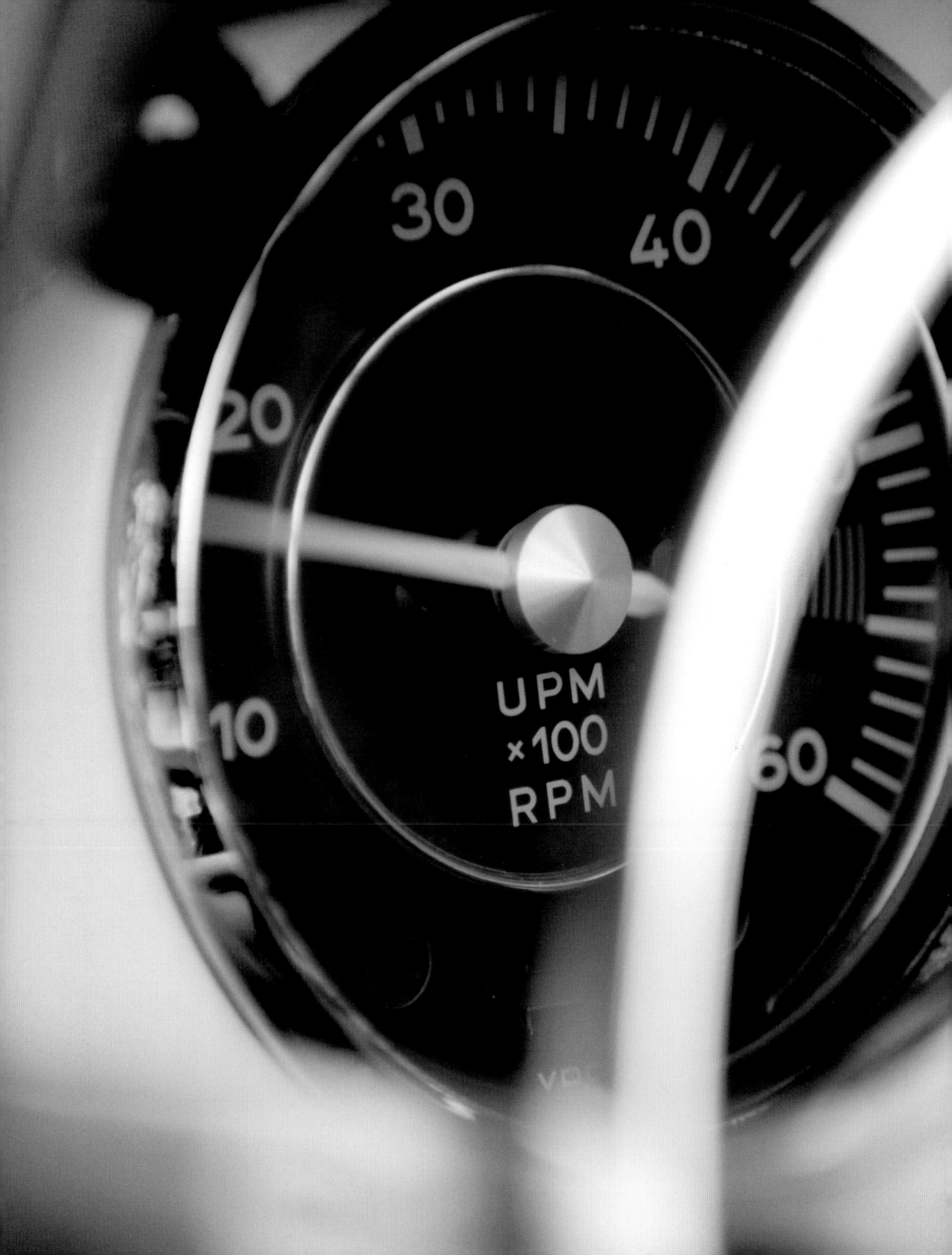
30
40
20
10
UPM
×100
RPM
60

# I. ORIGINS

**George Shapiro** (manager): If Jerry is at a party or any kind of event, and if he sees another comedian, he'll run across the room to them. That's the basis and the passion for *Comedians in Cars Getting Coffee*.

**Ted Sarandos** (co-CEO and CCO, Netflix): He's a brilliant observer of what is funny about people. And that is at the heart of what the show is: What's funny about funny people?

*Jerry: Being funny doesn't have that much to do with what a great comedy act is about. A great comedy act is a machine that's built. Being funny is the fuel, but you've got to have a whole machine to burn it, and that's the act.*

**Amy Schumer** (episode guest 502): Comedians are different. There's something different that drives them. I always think of Chris Rock. He said, "If ignorance is bliss, what's the opposite of that?" Comedians notice every little thing. It's kind of hell. But you've lived that way your whole life, so it's fun to meet someone else who's trapped in this hell with you.

**Barry Marder** (episode guest 107 and 1110): If you're a comedian, you've probably been a comedian since you were born. I have to tell you, we're strange people. Comedians are the greatest sitters and do-nothings and talkers that I've ever seen. They sit there, and anything is a premise. Everything to a comedian ends up as a joke. "Is anything here?" Everything is a bit, because we all want that potential to come up with the next joke.

So a comedian is always looking for material. That is the experience. It's always just a couple of guys in a coffee shop, in a diner, ordering regular food. A tuna sandwich or something. Nobody's looking for a huge steak. And then just talking about mostly comedy. You talk to another comedian, and you say something funny, they'll come back, and then it's ping-pong.

In the early '90s, Jerry and I would drive around and just talk and laugh and have fun. I remember him saying to me one day, "This is the show." And I said, "What's a show? Driving around with me?" And he said, "Driving around with comedians is a show. I think it would be funny to drive around with comedians and they just talk, because they're laughing and joking around and they'll see something funny on the street and they'll say something funny."

When *Seinfeld* ended, he said to me, "I bought a car in Albuquerque. Do you want go to Albuquerque and then drive across the country?" I said, "Okay, I'm up for that." My agent at the time told me to get a video camera. We drove across the country in that car—just chatting, being friends. And that was the genesis.

**George Shapiro:** Starbucks passed on *Comedians in Cars Getting Coffee*.

**Barry Marder:** Jerry was telling me, "I just had a meeting with Starbucks."
I said, "How did that go?"
He said, "The guy goes, 'Jerry, I don't see the connection between Starbucks.'"

" 'This show with the name coffee in the title? No connection at all? You sell coffee. We're doing a show about drinking coffee.'

" 'Sorry, Jerry, I just don't get it. I don't know how we fit in.' "

**Ted Sarandos:** In 2012, Netflix was not what we are today, of course. We hadn't even launched *House of Cards* yet. The fact that Jerry was pitching us original content before we even launched original content speaks volumes about his foresight and his level of innovation.

At the time that he came into our offices in Beverly Hills, he was one of the only stars who'd ever been inside the building. One thing the Netflix office is famous for is the espresso machines. Jerry immediately goes straight to the kitchen and starts making espresso for everybody. It was quite a thrill for everybody to have Jerry in the building.

He had a very broad vision for what the show was going to be. When I say "broad," I mean he had no idea what the show was going to be.

I said, "Are there going to be episodes?"

He goes, "Yeah, I guess so."

I'm like, "Well, how long are they going to be?"

"I don't know."

"Uh, what's it going to cost?"

"I don't know."

"How many are you going to make?"

"I'm not sure."

He wanted to drive around in cars and talk to comedians and get coffee. The title is remarkably descriptive of what the show is.

Jerry respects the art form of comedy so much. He could talk about it with anybody for as long as they want. That's what we connected on, right away, and we've been friends ever since. The history of the art form, the people who do it, the different styles, what works, what doesn't, what we like, what we don't like—Jerry and I have those conversations without the cameras and the coffee sometimes.

I wish that at the time we had been a little deeper into producing original content. I would have taken bigger swings with something like this. But it was just too broad a concept for us then.

**Steve Mosko** (CEO, Village Roadshow/former chairman, Sony Pictures Television): In the meeting about *Comedians in Cars Getting Coffee*, Howard [West, George Shapiro's business partner who died in 2015] tells me how all the big guys are coming after this, and Jerry proceeds to give the pitch. He goes, "I get a nice car, I call up my comedian friends, we go for a ride, and we go have coffee somewhere."

I go, "Great, I'm in."

**Tammy Johnston** (executive producer): This is the only project that I ever worked on that there were zero network notes. There was no notes process whatsoever. We shot the episode, we cut the episode, and we delivered the episode. It's the only time in my career that that has ever, ever happened.

**Denis Jensen** (producer): That's unheard of in this business. I remember a couple of times receiving some kind of gently worded recommendations from Crackle [the original platform]. My response could always easily be, "Jerry doesn't want to do that." And that's where it would end.

**Tom Keaney** (publicist/advisor): I remember him saying, "The problem with where I am in having had *Seinfeld* and the success of that show is that when I get behind something, the expectation is that it's going to be as big as anything I've ever done."

**Steve Mosko:** He wanted this to be like somebody finding a wallet on the sidewalk.

**Ted Nelson** (technical supervisor): Jerry's line was, "Let's make it like a wallet on the sidewalk." We had that conversation. "Let's not promote it. Let's not tell anybody we're doing it."

**Tom Keaney:** He really wanted this to feel like the cool thing that people were talking about but it wasn't being shoved down your throat. We thought that it would have a better shot at success if it didn't feel like Jerry was telling everyone, "You got to see this."

He built a great trailer. There weren't any words. It was just shots of him and the guests quietly sitting in the car. And at the end it says, "Talking soon." We did almost nothing with it. We loaded it to YouTube—just dropped it into the water. The *New York Times* emailed me saying, "What is this thing? Is it a show? Is it not a show?" It totally worked. It built a really good ripple of interest.

## II. PRODUCTION

**Ted Nelson:** Jerry wanted to figure out a technological way for people to do a TV show without them realizing that they were doing a TV show. So we started kind of just chiseling away at it. Can the camera operators hold their cameras under their arms? Can the

> "He wanted this to be like somebody finding a wallet on the sidewalk."

audio guy be sitting at a bar in a café with headphones on and not looking at anybody and not have a boom? Can my camera operators be so far away that waitresses will walk in front of them and break shot? We just started spitballing how all that stuff would work.

**Peter Holmes** (editor): I had worked on some previous projects with the company that was producing *Comedians in Cars Getting Coffee*. I was slated to work on something else for them, but then they said, "Sorry, the project has been delayed for a month and we don't have anything for you to edit. But we have this other secret project that we need some help on. We know that you're a car guy, but do you like *Seinfeld*?" Like most people with a learner's permit in the '90s, the show *Seinfeld* had a big impact on me. I remember thinking: "Oh man, it's like I was trained my whole life for this." When you meet him, within five minutes you realize how he became *Jerry Seinfeld*. He's incredibly hardworking, focused, disciplined, and very well-organized.

**Gio Lima** (audio supervisor): He was always very cool and down-to-earth and talked to every crew member, knew everyone. He'd bust our chops and joke around. He was not dropped off on set with a handler. There's nothing like seeing Jerry ride up for an episode on his bike.

**Jill Penuel** (production manager): He's very nice to the crew.

**Denis Jensen:** It's funny, when I tell people I work on the show, I'll get the question "Oh, have you ever met Jerry?" And my response is, "Yeah, he's in the office three days a week." He saw every minute of footage taped—literally every minute—and was intimately involved in the creative decisions. He's very hands-on.

**Tammy Johnston:** There's not an element of the show that Jerry is not involved in, that he doesn't sign off on.

**Jill Penuel:** Jerry picks the car that he wants for the guest, what he thinks fits their personality.

**Tammy Johnston:** I would say 98 percent of the car ideas all came from Jerry. Once we identify the guest, we identify the car. And then it's all hands on deck. It's myself, the production manager/line producer, maybe a PA—we start researching that car. What are the options to get that car? Where are they? What kind of condition are they in?

**John Taggart** (director of photography, seasons 5–11): The car is a character—it's another character in the show.

**Denis Jensen:** There are two outcomes for dropping Jerry's name. Either you get carte blanche permission to do whatever you want, or all of a sudden the price jacks up because they're just seeing dollar signs.

**Josh Ricks** (line producer): If we found the best car ever and the owner would say, "You have to pay me," I'd be like, "Okay, next." I knew I would find someone who is a hobbyist. This is what they love. They just want to show it off. They don't want money. They're just like, "Jerry gets to drive my car?" You would send them an autographed photo or something. That was their payment, and they loved it.

**John Taggart:** B-roll day was my day to shine and try to put my stamp on what *Comedians in Cars Getting Coffee* was. I'd make these crazy rigs where I'd put the camera ten feet off the car, shooting back on it. I'd put a GoPro on a wiper as it was moving back and forth. I'd put a GoPro on the ground and have the car drive over it. I remember driving through the streets of New York with the minivan door open, shooting this incredible footage of Jerry in a yellow Ferrari. I was laughing to myself and thinking, "What are we doing? This is amazing!"

**Ted Nelson:** I used to say to people, "You can't text and drive. That's really dangerous. But you can do a talk show and drive. That's fine."

**Denis Jensen:** Jerry would often express that there were no rules. He was always looking for ways to do things differently. I think a lot of really successful things in any area are the result of people not knowing they can't do something. And then they just do it. Maybe that's a secret to Jerry's success, in that he's somebody people don't say no to very often, so he thinks everything is possible, and you have to make things happen 'cause he doesn't know that it can't be done. People get kind of intimidated by Jerry, but one thing he said—which I repeat often—is, "I like to hear all ideas, even if they're bad."

**Tom Keaney:** He had such a sense of curiosity about this new way of doing a show. He wanted to surround himself with people with ideas.

**Tammy Johnston:** He's very collaborative.

**Ted Nelson:** One thing that was really crazy about this show was the amount of passionate, creative people involved in it who wanted to push the envelope—and leading that charge was Jerry. Any suggestion that he had, we tried, and any suggestion that we had, he tried. I'd say, "Hey, try this," and Jerry would just do it. It didn't matter what it was. There was never "No."

I remember when we were shooting the Zach Galifianakis episode with the Volkswagen Thing. We're all standing around and we've got the car in this off-road kind of area.

Jerry says, "I want to make it look like I've been away, but now I've come back."

I say, "Why don't you tear up your shirt and come out of the woods like you've been living with Bigfoot for the last year?"

He grabs his Ralph Lauren shirt and he starts ripping it apart and messing up his hair and walking up into the woods. And then he walks out. It was a great opening sequence.

Another time, for the Will Ferrell episode, we were at a racetrack shooting a 1970 Plymouth Road Runner Superbird. It was a car built for NASCAR originally, and then they decided to sell it to the public. It had this huge rear wing and spoiler.

I said to Jerry, "It'd be really cool to get a shot of you hanging on to this wing and the car driving really fast—so that you're flying behind it like Superman."

He said, "Well, how would we do that?"

We found a spare tire and put that between the bumpers of the car and one of our SUVs. I pushed the Road Runner with the SUV while Jerry lay on the hood holding on to the spoiler. We shot it at such an angle where you wouldn't see the SUV or it could be taken out in post.

I don't think we ever ended up using the shot. There was a point when Tammy looked over and saw me giving a hand to Jerry to climb up on the hood and hang on to the wing. She said, "What the hell are you doing? You can't drive the talent around on the hood of a car."

**Gio Lima:** Jerry would say, "We already did that shot. We've done that already. We need something different."

**John Taggart:** One of the first episodes I did, we missed something. Jerry made a joke about a piece of pie or something. It was a funny joke, and we missed it. And I could see Jerry, you know . . . So we learned that we need to be ready.

**Jill Penuel:** We really just are following them around, and whatever happens and whatever they do, we try to get it on camera.

*Jerry: I want you to feel like you're just hanging out with us. I take out the celebrity reaction so that it has this kind of accessible vibe of "Yeah, I would like to hang out with those two guys for twenty minutes . . . but I don't want the show business stuff."*

**Denis Jensen:** We couldn't go back and say, "Jerry, we missed you guys walking through the door. Can you do that again?"

**Josh Ricks:** There was never stopping and redoing.

**John Taggart:** I've done shows where an audio guy would run up to the guest and try to fix the microphone. You can't do that. Jerry doesn't want that. He just wants the flow of the conversation.

**Denis Jensen:** It's essentially a live show.

**John Taggart:** That's what we tell all the cameramen: don't put the camera down on the ground. When you're moving your shot, don't point it to the ground. It's basically a live show for five hours.

**Peter Holmes:** There are no breaks in filming on guest day.

**Denis Jensen:** One of my favorite lines from the show is Brian Regan noting how many times his coffee had been refilled. He said something like, "If you want good service in a restaurant, just bring in four cameras."

**John Taggart:** Listening to the conversation and trying not to laugh is hard. It is a challenge to stay focused when you're witnessing Jerry interviewing these comedians and seeing his enthusiasm. Martin Short and Will Ferrell both had me giggling. But you try not to because if the mics pick it up, we won't be able to use it.

**Denis Jensen:** During the Tracy Morgan shoot, I was in the follow van with Tammy and Tracy Morgan's assistant and several other people. Tracy Morgan is going on about something and kind of loses focus. And he says to Jerry, "Do you remember Kramer from *Seinfeld*?" There was an awkward pause, and Jerry looks at him and says, "Do I remember him?" The whole van erupted in laughter.

**Jill Penuel:** I assume one of your questions is: "What's the most difficult episode you've ever worked on?" And I assume the majority of people answered, "Steve Martin."

That was the most difficult episode of any television I've ever worked on. And that was my very first episode on this show. In fact, I had only been working on the show for two weeks when we filmed it. So not only was I just nervous for that episode anyway, but this is Steve Martin.

It started off with Jerry following the wrong SUV over the George Washington Bridge. Which was not the plan. The diner wasn't even in New Jersey. Then the car broke down.

**Ted Nelson:** We found the Siata, which is a car that was built in such a small production few people even knew it existed. It was elegant and beautiful. Perfect for Steve Martin, who's one of a kind.

**Jill Penuel:** It broke down on the side of the highway. Normally when a car breaks down, we can get it working at some point. But that car was never going to start again.

**Tammy Johnston:** Jerry Seinfeld and Steve Martin standing on the side of the road for forty-five minutes. We finally put them in one of the production vehicles and drove them to the diner.

After the shoot, some of the guys came back to the city and stopped to have lunch before they took all of their gear back to our staging location. Do I know why? No. Absentmindedly, they put one of the cameras in the coat closet. And when they came back, the camera wasn't there.

**Denis Jensen:** It's not an uncommon thing in New York. There are people who follow productions around waiting for a slipup, just waiting to steal something. Waiting for somebody to go to the bathroom or whatever window of opportunity they see. It's a racket in New York. It's really sketchy.

One of the most surreal parts of working on the series as a whole was walking into Tom's Restaurant [the diner exterior used in *Seinfeld* episodes] with Larry David [for the series' Super Bowl halftime "The Over-Cheer" taping] and him saying, "Wow, I've never been in here."

**Marshall Rose (director of photography, seasons 2–4):** The same with Jason Alexander. He said, "It's smaller than I thought." That whole day existed outside of reality. It took place in some other netherworld.

Anyway, we were a block north of Tom's Restaurant, and we had a Steadicam and were about to get the two-shot of Jason and Jerry walking down the street together, and somebody walks by and sees Jason Alexander. He stops and says, "Jason, I just have to tell you, you have made such an impact on my life. Like, I can't even tell you."

Then an assistant director or somebody came over and said, "Can you come over here, please?" And then we were like, "Okay, ready? Action."

Everyone kind of goes through that a bit with Jerry. He's not just some famous person. His comedy has changed how we think. With most comedians, you remember a joke or two. And of course you remember jokes that Seinfeld told. But he also changed how we think of comedy. He has altered the way we look at things.

> "He's not just some famous person. His comedy has changed how we think."

**Denis Jensen:** We shot a promo for Crackle with Michael Richards. When we wrapped, I rode in the elevator with Jerry and Michael out of the office building. I was standing behind them. We stopped at a floor, the door opened, and there's two women. And they essentially see Jerry and Kramer in the elevator. Their jaws just dropped to the floor. Michael doesn't miss a beat. He says in a very Kramer-esque style, "We work here." It was a really surreal experience, seeing these two people essentially walk into the *Seinfeld* set on an elevator and having their minds blown.

## III. THE WHITE HOUSE

**Tammy Johnston:** The first time I had ever seen Jerry nervous was for President Obama.

**Josh Ricks:** It was the only time I ever saw him nervous—like visibly nervous.

**Ted Nelson:** It was the first time he admitted to me he was a little nervous.

**Tammy Johnston:** They had met before, because Jerry had done a performance in the East Room when Paul McCartney got some award.

**George Shapiro:** In 2010, Jerry appeared at the White House for the Gershwin Prize ceremony honoring Paul McCartney. Jerry had to work in front of Michelle Obama and Barack Obama and two hundred people in the East Room. That had to be the toughest gig of his life. He scored beautifully, did an incredible job. We got that feedback from the president.

**Tammy Johnston:** But they certainly had not spent any time together or had any sort of conversations or anything like that.

**George Shapiro:** Shooting *Comedians in Cars Getting Coffee* at the White House was one of the greatest days in Jerry's life. It was initiated by Tammy Johnston.

**Tammy Johnston:** One of the other projects I do every four years is the general election debates. I had done two debate cycles with President Obama, so I knew people from his team. Jerry joked every now and then about the president. He was very much a fan. One time I made the comment, "Do you want me to call the White House?" And he said, "Sure, go ahead."

I called a friend of mine who worked for the president. I said, "This is what we want to do. What do you think?" Several weeks later I got an email back saying,

"Okay, let's do this." I called Jerry. He was actually at a car show, I think the Concours in Pebble Beach [California].

"Do you have a minute?" I asked.

"Sure," he said.

"If you're serious about doing an episode with the president, we're in."

I think he was a bit floored. He just started laughing. And he laughed and he laughed.

**John Taggart:** Jerry was nervous. We were all nervous.

**Josh Ricks:** I remember there being a very specific conversation about who's allowed to be there. The Secret Service permitted a very limited amount of people. Tammy had a really difficult decision of who got to be there, because she knew how important that would be for the team.

**Tammy Johnston:** They did background checks on everybody. Then we started the process of really drilling down on what we could and couldn't do, what the Secret Service parameters were going to let us do. It was the only episode in which we knew what the format had to be. "Act one is this, act two is this, act three is . . ." Beat by beat.

**Denis Jensen:** It was planned out a lot more than other episodes.

**John Taggart:** He had asked if a *Mad* magazine and a folder that said TOP SECRET could be placed in the Oval Office as props. They were like, "Sir, this is the White House. We can't do that." But the night before, we were going through a White House brochure and Jerry saw a bowl of apples. He goes, "If the brochure is correct, I think there might be apples there." I could tell he had an idea.

**Tammy Johnston:** For the car, we knew we wanted something that reflected the uniqueness of the guest: a trailblazer but someone who was a classic, calm yet strong, not overly flashy but had muscle and gravitas. We thought briefly about a number of sports cars that reflected a really strong presence. It didn't take us long to come around to the idea we needed an American classic. The split-window '63 Stingray fit the bill.

**Ted Nelson:** They bring the dogs over to sniff through the car. They don't find anything. Then they open the second gate and say, "Take it over to the stables." John F. Kennedy built stables for his daughter, Caroline. She liked to ride horses on the lawn. Now those are a garage, a kind of field house where they keep lawn mowers and stuff.

Tammy and I leave the car there so the Secret Service can continue their inspection, and we start back over to the East Gate to meet the crew and bring them in. As we're walking, a dude comes down from a tree dressed all in black with an M16 across his chest and starts walking right next to me—scares the hell out of me. He says, "Oh, you guys are here to do *Comedians in Cars*! I love that show!"

I look over to Tammy and I say, "You know those times when we all sprint into the bushes to hide from being on camera? We might not want to do that on this one."

> *"He's going to knock on the window. Don't shoot him."*

At some point, I was able to take a picture of the Corvette in front of the White House from afar, with all the foliage. I sent it to my mom and she responded, "Are you at a country club?" We weren't allowed to say what we were doing. So I couldn't tell my mom, "No, that's the White House."

**Gio Lima:** I was sweating. I was not brought into the White House as a reporter who just plugs in and stands twenty feet away. I was standing six inches from the president, and I had to invade his private space. My hands were shaking. Normally I conceal the mic, but I just clipped it to his tie. Easy to remove, easy to put on, guarantees we can get it. He's like, "Why don't we just tuck this in. Let's do this the right way." I was like, "You're absolutely right, let's do that."

**Tammy Johnston:** We had talked about how Jerry was going to enter the Oval Office. We decided he'd just walk up and knock on the door—like he had decided to pop in. But when we got there, we realized the door was sort of invisible. You couldn't really see where the doorframe was.

**John Taggart:** One of the Secret Service guys said, "You should knock on the window." That was his idea: to have Jerry come through the bushes outside and knock on the window.

**Tammy Johnston:** We did the phone call first. The president was like, "Yeah, come on over." After Obama hung up the phone, he said to the Secret Service agent who was in the office with him, "He's going to knock on the window. Don't shoot him."

**John Taggart:** It's just amazing how all this happened. There were no rehearsals. I have an earpiece in, and I can hear Jerry's microphone. I hear all this rustling—the bushes rustling. Then, all of a sudden, he appears outside the window. He knocks on it. The president waves him in. Jerry takes a seat on the couch.

**Josh Ricks:** The two of them are sitting in the Oval Office. They're bantering.

**John Taggart:** Then Jerry sees the bowl of apples.

**Josh Ricks:** Jerry looks at the bowl of apples and says, "Are these washed?" It's one of my favorite Jerry lines from any episode. "Are these apples washed?" I lose it every single time.

**Tammy Johnston:** We could not show a side shot of the doors of the presidential limo or how thick the doors are or certain angles that would show what kind of material it was made out of.

**John Taggart:** It's armored, so it's pretty small in there. There are four seats facing each other—two looking toward the front and two looking toward the rear. Jerry gets in and sits across from me. I thought the president was going to go around to the other door, but he comes in the same way, actually puts his hand on my knee and slides over me to get to the other seat.

That two-shot in the limousine is just this Osmo [a small handheld camera]. I'm getting incredible footage of them interacting inside the limousine, and I'm just sitting there thinking, "Okay, this is amazing. Just make sure this thing is recording."

Then they went to have coffee in a staff break room, down in the basement. It was such an amazing part of the White House that no one sees.

**Denis Jensen:** One of the most impressive things was how Obama really could hold his own comedically with Jerry.

**Josh Ricks:** It's one of my favorite stories. The president says, "Okay, everyone, let's go to the Map Room and we'll take a picture."

**Denis Jensen:** Jerry says, "Oh, that's okay. The crew sees me all the time."

**Josh Ricks:** The president didn't skip a beat. He goes, "Well, they don't want a picture with you, Jerry. They want a picture with the president of the United States of America." We all just started laughing. We were like, "Yes, we do! We want a picture!"

**Tammy Johnston:** It's a strong word to use, but I think Jerry was shocked. I think he was still in this moment that it was all so surreal on some level what we had just done—that we had, in fact, pulled this off.

**Ted Nelson:** He was on cloud nine. He couldn't believe how well it went. He said, "I can't think of a time that a sitting president ever did anything like that." We thought that we had broken new ground.

**Denis Jensen:** The only flak we got was over the title. I don't know if it was from the White House or Sony. We were going to title the episode "Don't Shoot Him"—referring to what Obama had said to the Secret Service before Jerry came to the window. But it sounded like we were talking about the president.

## IV. EDITING

**Tammy Johnston:** After we shot the first episode and started editing, we realized that idea [of a fixed length] just wasn't really a viable way to approach this. If the content keeps you interested and entertained for eight minutes, the episodes will be eight minutes. If there's only four minutes of good content, then the episode will be four minutes.

**Ted Sarandos:** What I'd come to love about the show—and we've kind of followed the platform—is that it doesn't really matter how long the episodes are. If you watch current Netflix episodes, we have some that are seventeen minutes. What is the exact running time for each episode? It depends on the person, depends on the topic, depends on the show. Don't be a slave to the story line if you don't have a linear schedule. Jerry was early on that: understanding that there was no linear schedule. There's no reason it had to be twenty-two minutes or thirty minutes.

**Ted Nelson:** On a guest day we had four handheld cameras plus the three in-car cameras. There's probably eighteen to twenty hours of material that had to be scrubbed through. Jerry would scrub through it all—every aspect of every shot from every episode.

**Peter Holmes:** People agree that he's a great comedy writer, but I think he's a fantastic editor. When he finds a good premise, he'll explode it into a field of variations or possibilities. Then he'll cull the best material and go to work on it, shaving it down until there's not a wasted syllable. Then he'll throw away the bottom third. Not because it's bad, but because it's not as good as the top two-thirds. At times he can be brutal with throwing away things in the edit, but I can't argue with the results. When you're onstage, you can't slow down or you'll lose the audience, and he brought that to the pacing of the show.

**Ted Sarandos:** I think he applies what he's learned about editing his act to editing the show. Jerry has very much squeezed every wasted word out of his act. Every syllable, every pause—they're all very intentional. There's not a lot of wasted anything in the show. It's very economical. It's very to the point. Just like Jerry himself. The show reflects Jerry's discipline. Because these episodes could have been two hours, three hours, five hours.

**Denis Jensen:** The Fred Armisen shoot was about five hours of footage. All five hours were entertaining.

**Tammy Johnston:** We start with watching every single piece of footage and slowly but surely begin to cull that down. Jerry really is like the master planner. He will look at a bit. He knows whether it will work or it won't on tape. He knows there are pieces you can lift from the story and still make the story work and still make the comedy work but keep the episode really tight and concise.

**Tom Keaney:** Having sat through several of the edits, I'd say Jerry is basically creating an orchestra in that room. He's not taking a sequential chronological story and unspooling it, chopping it down. He's creating something that is there but is not really what is there. That is a very different thing. That's the magic of the show.

**Yossi Kimberg** (editor): He was more concerned with the comedy and less concerned with the continuity. For instance, in the diner they would start by ordering coffee and something to eat. And Jerry would want to reorder the conversation so that something that came later would come earlier. If you're paying attention to the comedy and you're laughing along with Jerry and the guest, you don't pay attention to the fact that the food all of a sudden is disappearing or reappearing. Continuity becomes secondary.

**Denis Jensen:** It's not a mistake when you see something like that in the show. It's just that Jerry's first priority was the comedy.

**Peter Holmes:** We quickly discovered that close-up shots of laughter just didn't work. So the typical cadence would be to cut back and forth as the joke builds, be on a close-up of the speaker as they land the punch line, and then cut to the wide shot for the laughter to explode.

**Yossi Kimberg:** Jerry's memory is just amazing. It's stunning. He remembers every line that was said in the show. He actually remembers every line that was said ten episodes ago. There were times when we'd have a guest on more than once, like Bob Einstein, and Jerry would say, "On the first episode, I know I told Bob this, this, and that." Sure enough, he did.

**Tammy Johnston:** Music was a huge part of the show and gave each episode its own **personality**.

**Denis Jensen:** For the voice-over, we would give Jerry details about the car as provided by the owners—engine specs and other technical details. Other times it was something special that's specific to that exact car. Originally we would give the notes to Jerry in advance, and he would come back with a script. Eventually it evolved into him wanting to create something on the spot. He would look at this page full of car notes, maybe write down a couple things, and within a few minutes just read something into a microphone in the edit bay. It would be edited a tad. But he would come up with that on the spot, almost verbatim to what you see in the show, just him riffing from this page of notes.

After he was done, he would wad up that piece of paper and throw it in the trash. A couple of times, I took those out of the trash, thinking, "This is worth saving."

**Yossi Kimberg:** Jerry would nip and tuck the wording in an episode. Very often we would ADR [re-record] a word here and there to make it even funnier. He's a real wordsmith. And language for him is comedy. If you don't use the right word, it's not as funny. So you need to find the right word, the right space, the right trim. At the end of the punch line, at the end of the bit, if I came out a little too early, he'd say, "Can you find me ten more frames at the end of this?" Sure enough, those ten frames made a difference.

**Peter Holmes:** Jerry is like a jeweler when it comes to the editing process. Nothing escapes his eye. He'll find micro trims in places that I didn't think were possible. Over time we built up a shorthand with each other. He'd say "razor in"—meaning remove everything starting from here until he says "razor out."

**Yossi Kimberg:** We all sit in the room—Jerry, Tammy, Denis, and I—and we view the entire show. Could be two, four hours, five hours. And then we listen to Jerry's cues as far as what he likes and what he doesn't like. He'll say, "That's not funny" or "Oh, that's funny."

**Denis Jensen:** He generally knows what he likes and what he doesn't like immediately. Which makes our jobs much easier than dealing with someone who doesn't know what they want.

**Yossi Kimberg:** Most producers have no idea what the hell they want. But here is the main man sitting next to us and he's telling us, "I like this. I don't like this. Let's change this. Let's change that." And that's the end of it.

**Gio Lima:** Jerry was always really, really communicative about what he wanted.

**Denis Jensen:** He'll never say "no" to anything. He'll just say "eh." Then you'd know, "Okay, he didn't like that."

**Ted Sarandos:** Because of the pacing of the show, how propulsive each episode is, when you're finished with one you want to watch another one. The average view time, if you push play on an episode, is well over an hour and a half. People just seamlessly go into it, from episode to episode.

I would share little tidbits of information with him. Jerry was hungry for every detail of everything. It's like why he loves performing onstage so much: that instant feedback loop. I'm sure what's frustrating in television is how long you have to wait to get a feedback loop. It's not very precise versus telling a joke and getting a laugh. And if his comedy brand is anything, it's precision.

## V. THE GUESTS

**Ted Sarandos:** I always asked Jerry who the dream guest was, and he always told me Eddie Murphy. He could never get him to do the show.

**Denis Jensen:** Eddie Murphy was one of those guests that we just wanted for years.

**Ted Sarandos:** I was on the set of *Dolemite Is My Name*. I called Jerry and said, "Do you still want to get Eddie?" He said, "Absolutely." And he told me the story real quick about how he remembered being a young stand-up at the same time as Eddie—they were both coming up—and Eddie pulled up in front of the Comedy Store with a new

> "Jerry is like a jeweler when it comes to the editing process. Nothing escapes his eye."

*Jerry: I don't like to bother people.*

car. Jerry said that was when he realized that you could make money being a comedian. *That guy—he can afford a car!* He was so amazed by that. In that way, Eddie was a huge inspiration for Jerry, on top of him being a fan.

So after I hung up with Jerry—I was literally on the set of *Dolemite* when he told me that story—I leaned in to Eddie and said, "Hey, do you watch *Comedians in Cars Getting Coffee*?"

He goes, "Absolutely. I've seen every single episode."

And I said, "Well, Jerry would love to have you on the show."

He goes, "Of course. Take this number down, give him this number, let's set it up."

Within forty-eight hours, it was all set up. I love that the connection between them was a car.

**Steve Mosko:** Michael Richards was just a very heartfelt, warm moment. You could tell Jerry was emotional. It was emotional on both sides. It gave Michael a chance to talk to somebody he trusted to explain what happened [Michael's 2006 performance controversy]. That Jerry hung in there as his friend and that Michael expressed appreciation for that speaks volumes of both of those guys. There was just something very human about that. Something very funny. Something very warm. To me, that was what the whole thing was meant to be. It felt like you were sitting in on this really personal conversation.

**Josh Ricks:** Julia Louis-Dreyfus was really special because it was like we weren't there. They were just two old friends. That was really special to watch.

**Peter Holmes:** I love the Miranda Sings episode. I love any episode where the guest isn't afraid to push Jerry's buttons, and I love watching her work Jerry like an accordion. We did a lot of fun things in the edit, like using all the outtakes of coffee pours that went wrong that we had accumulated over the years. It wasn't something that we planned. I just thought it would be fun to repurpose "bad" footage that you would normally throw out.

**Ted Sarandos:** The Mel Brooks and Carl Reiner episode. The Jerry Lewis episode. At that stage in their lives to be able to have that level of reflection on their body of work, and what it meant, and the people it inspired. And the fact that even at that later stage in life they could still be very, very funny. It just reminds you that at the core of it, they understood what made people laugh.

I really do think comedy is an important art form. I think what makes people laugh defines people. You learn a lot about yourself by figuring out what makes you laugh. It says a lot about who you are. And who we are as a culture. What made people laugh in the 1940s? What makes people laugh now? I know that it's an endless source of fascination for Jerry. It's his lifeblood. He was able to capture that in those episodes. I would say those are probably among the most valuable archived conversations with those artists about their contribution to film, television, and comedy that exist.

**George Shapiro:** I was really close friends with Garry Shandling. He and Jerry both did their first *Tonight Show* in 1981. They worked at the Comedy Store together, which they loved. They loved being together. And then they had both of their shows in the '90s—*The Larry Sanders Show* and *Seinfeld*—two of the greatest comedy shows ever produced. They used to go and visit each other on the set. What an amazing connection.

Garry sent me an email raving about *Comedians in Cars Getting Coffee* and he said he would love to do it. I forwarded his email to Jerry. Jerry called him immediately and he booked him immediately. Their conversation was gold. Gold, I tell you. Garry was so thrilled with that whole show.

**Steve Mosko:** It was beautiful. I mean, that opening where they said they loved each other . . . it gives me chills just saying it.

# VI. LEGACY

**Tom Keaney:** One time, a long time ago, Jerry said something to me about late-night talk shows and all the intrigue when a new host is taking over. He said, "There is no *Tonight Show*. There's Carson, there's Leno, there's Letterman, there's Fallon. No one cares about *The Tonight Show*. No one cares about these brands." But I don't think that's true with *Comedians in Cars Getting Coffee*. No one else can do it. It's really the alchemy between Jerry and the guest that makes the episodes really great.

**Ted Sarandos:** If you look back at how many shows have taken a run at comedians talking to each other about comedy, they haven't worked. They've been super inside, in a way that is not very inviting to a comedy fan.

**Tammy Johnston:** I got a text from Tom Keaney saying, "You guys have been nominated for an Emmy." The show was still done by Sony then, so I also heard from them. They were beyond thrilled about this whole thing. A lot of my back-and-forth with Jerry is text. So the first thing that I did was text him congratulations. Who would have thought that our little show—which is how he always referred to it—would be something?

**Ted Sarandos:** I'm really proud of the partnership. I'm proud of the affiliation with the show, and with Jerry.

**Peter Holmes:** Honestly, every day I came to work it felt like I was stealing money. It really was a dream job, and I'm proud of the way *Comedians in Cars Getting Coffee* was received by the rest of the world.

**Jill Penuel:** My favorite TV show I've ever worked on is *Comedians in Cars Getting Coffee*. And it is because you were constantly on your toes. I was always thinking about what was happening next. So it was hard to even be in the moment of what was happening at the times when it was happening. But everybody was like that. And it's such a small crew. So we really bonded.

> ## "We talked about a whole bunch of [international comedians]. We just never got to them. Yet."

**Denis Jensen:** The process of *Comedians in Cars Getting Coffee* really taught me quite a bit.

**Yossi Kimberg:** We all took away a lot of lessons from this experience.

**Peter Holmes:** Even today, when I'm working on other projects, I hear Jerry's voice in my head say, "Nah, you don't need that."

**John Taggart:** *Comedians in Cars Getting Coffee* has been the most creative job I've had in all my years of filming. I learned a ton from Jerry about just relating to people, just the way you approach a project. His work ethic is unbelievable and it really rubbed off on everybody else.

**Tammy Johnston:** Jerry's work ethic within his own world and the way he approached things really made you want to step up your game and keep up with him.

**Yossi Kimberg:** It was a fun journey, I got to tell you. I really do miss it. I miss the energy. I miss working with the team. I miss working with Jerry. When we were editing together, the first half hour, we'd just talk and chat. Jerry would tell us about his kids and family or whatever. He would soften up the room a little bit before we'd get seriously into the editing. I miss that. The way he approached the edit is the way I think he approaches his life. Just very generous with his time, very generous with his compliments. He was one of the few clients who would say, "Yossi, that's great. You saved that joke. Thank you so much." No one else does that anymore. He's just very generous with his feelings and certainly with his humor. I miss him, and I miss the show. Hopefully it will come back in some way.

**Ted Sarandos:** What we never got to that we talked a lot about were the international comedians—going abroad and doing some of the international comedians at home. We talked about a whole bunch of those. We just never got to them. Yet.

# GROWING UP

## BRIAN REGAN

**Brian:** My mom and dad have eight kids.

**Jerry:** Wow.

**Brian:** Four occupations. Two comedians, two firefighters, two schoolteachers, two salesmen. Everybody found a sibling and said, "I'm goin' with you."

**Jerry:** "You got an idea, that's good enough for me."

**Brian:** [laughs] That's right.

**Jerry:** One idea per two Regans, right?

**Brian:** Yeah. That's right.

**Jerry:** That is great. That is so bizarrely funny.

**Brian:** Let me ask you this. Sometimes I wonder, "What's the maximum fun a person can have?"

**Jerry:** I can tell you the happiest a person can possibly be. 'Cause I've taken note of it. The happiest you can be is to be from a Latin country and score a goal in soccer. It's probably four to eight seconds. But I don't think it's possible to be happier than that. I've never seen a greater happiness than that. Can you name me a happier person? Happier than that?

Happiest you can be. I don't think you can beat it. No sex stuff either. That's too easy.

**Brian:** I have my answer.

**Jerry:** All right. I'm excited.

**Brian:** It's not a funny answer. But when I was twelve, we were on vacation. We were up in the state of New York. We went to a lake with all of our cousins. Twelve years old, in the summertime, so there's no school. You know, you're not behind in any homework. The next school year hasn't started yet, so you're not behind on anything. You have no homework due, no papers due. You're not old enough to have a mortgage or any responsibilities whatsoever.

**Jerry:** That's a great answer. I love that. I'll give you mine. I got my first Schwinn Sting-ray. I had a stingray before that. But it wasn't a Schwinn. I wanted a Schwinn. And I got the Schwinn. And it was summer. And you know a new bike, how the spokes sparkle when it's new, just for a couple days before they get dirty? I remember just pedaling down the street. And I thought, "This is the greatest I've ever felt in my life."

**Brian:** We take the kids bike riding. And I think I'm guilty of not getting them out as often as I should.

**Jerry:** But your parents didn't get you out. You just went.

**Brian:** Now you plan it. "We're going bike riding tomorrow at 9:00 to 9:45. And I have a business call at 10:00. We're going to enjoy ourselves from 9:00 to 9:45. And then we go back, and Daddy goes to work, and you do your homework."

**Jerry:** "And we're all going to stop enjoying ourselves at 9:46."

**Brian:** Yeah. One time my mom made me—I ate a lot, you know, when I got to eighth grade—so I would get three sandwiches.

**Jerry:** Three?

**Brian:** Three sandwiches—all six pieces of bread were heels. How is that even possible? All six.

**Jerry:** One of my favorite [George] Carlin jokes of all time: "We say that we care about other people, but when we take bread out of the bag, we take the slices out of the middle."

**Brian:** Every time my dad came home from work, he was in a good mood. And I know that can't always be the case. He did it for us. I know that now, but as a kid, you just go, "Wow, my dad's a happy-go-lucky guy."

**Jerry:** My dad was similar. Never saw him in a bad mood. You think that's somewhat generational?

**Brian:** I don't know. But I wish I had more of that with my kids. Because I can wear my emotion on my sleeves. I just wish I had more of that ability to compartmentalize difficulties.

**Jerry:**    Yeah, well, your dad, God knows he tried to give it to you. But I guess it wasn't good enough. He did his best.

**Brian:**    "Where was I supposed to learn that from?" Right.

**Jerry:**    Yeah. "If only I could've learned that somewhere . . . "

**Brian:**    "Gee, I wonder where. If I had some kind of role model, some kind of father figure."

## SETH MEYERS

**Jerry:**    What about you and Adam Sandler and Sarah Silverman being from the same town?

**Seth:**    It is true. Sarah and I are technically from one town over called Bedford. But we all went to high school in Manchester [New Hampshire].

**Jerry:**    Seth, Sarah, and Sandler.

**Seth:**    Yeah. And when I was in high school, that was when Sandler first was sort of coming up, and I remember thinking, "I can't believe a guy from

my town is on *SNL*." And then when I was in college, Sarah was on, and I was like, "I can't believe two people from my . . ." At that point you start thinking, "Well, there's not going to be three. At some point they're going to have to say, 'We have to spread it out to other towns in America.'"

## JAY LENO

**Jay:** When I was a kid, I was very anti whatever people wanted you to do. I was just "contrarian," my mother would say. Because think about the time before you were officially a comedian, or you knew what a comedian was. You didn't quite fit in.

**Jerry:** No.

**Jay:** You didn't fit in. You kind of hung with the cool kids, but you weren't one of them, and you really weren't with the dorky kids. As a young comic, you don't really fit in anywhere.

**Jerry:** That is true. That's true.

> "As a young comic, you don't really fit in anywhere."

**Jay:** You're really just obnoxious. I remember being in the fourth grade, walking around going, "And, uh, as, uh, President Kennedy . . ." You know, just doing the Vaughn Meader. My mother going, "Stop doing that! Stop doing that voice!" I don't know why, I just found it fun to do. So when you're a kid, before you're officially a comedian, you're just an obnoxious person.

## HOWARD STERN

**Howard:** You know, my parents—and you probably had this too—if I told a story that went on too long, it was, "Hurry up, hurry up, tighten it up." I would sit there and entertain and do impressions of all the kids in the neighborhood and the parents in the neighborhood, and my father would go, "Hurry up, hurry up. When you tell a story, everyone is bored. Everyone. Everyone here is bored. You went on too long."

## SARAH JESSICA PARKER

**Jerry:** When I was a kid, I thought the world is great because it has bicycles, it has toys, and it has cute girls. And then I saw my first Tampax commercial and I thought, "There may be more to that thing than meets the eye."

**Sarah Jessica:** Right, you didn't see any weird bicycle commercials.

**Jerry:** I remember my mother in the car saying, "I'll turn around and slam you!" That's what she used to say.

**Sarah Jessica:** "You want something to cry about? I'll give you a reason to cry."

**Jerry:** My friend Mark Schiff says, "Mothers don't have headaches. They always have *splitting* headaches." You don't think it could be from screaming nine hours a day, do you?

## KEVIN HART

**Kevin:** This is probably in the top two best conversations I've ever had in my life. The first one would be my dad explaining to me why drugs were "in" back then. That's the first best conversation I've ever had in my life. My dad one time explained to me why he had to do drugs "I had to. Listen, everybody did it, okay? You think I was by myself? Your aunt, your uncle . . ." The best conversation I've ever had.

## FRED ARMISEN

**Fred:**    When I was born, I had a different name. I was named Fereydun. This is
no joke.

**Jerry:**    Wow.

**Fred:**    I was called Fred. And then when I was ten years old, my parents were
like, "Okay, you can change your name to whatever you want." And I was
like, "Okay, I want to keep Fred."

**Jerry:**    But the original name was Fereydun. How do you spell that?

**Fred:**    F-e-r-e-y-d-u-n. It was my dad's name too. But everyone called us Fred,
so we just changed it at the same time.

**Jerry:**    So he's Fred too.

**Fred:**    Yeah. He's Fred Armisen.

# TREVOR NOAH

**Jerry:** Your mother and your father, how did they spend time together?

**Trevor:** [My mom and I] lived in Soweto, which was the township that all black people basically lived in. Most black people lived in this area. And as a black person you could go into the city to work. You have your work permit, you go into the city, you work, you have to leave before the sun goes down. If you're in town when the sun is down, you get arrested. That's how it works. So you have your work permit with you. It's your information card. It was a pass. The South Africans called it a "dumbass," which literally translated means "stupid ID." That's what the locals called it, because they're like, "This is dumb." So, my mom would take that and go with me into the city. She would say that she was babysitting me for a friend of hers who was my skin color. So you have white, you have black. The problem is, every time people break the rules, which is very rare, this comes out. But in South Africa this is not black. They don't call me black.

**Jerry:** They don't?

**Trevor:** No. There's a term. They say, "You're colored." So, black is black, white is white, colored is colored. Then what happened was people would go, "How do you have a colored baby? Who helped you commit this crime?" My mom would go, "No, this is not my baby."

**Jerry:** Oh my God.

**Trevor:** "This is my colored friend's baby, and I'm just looking after him."

**Jerry:** And this is late '80s?

**Trevor:** This is late '80s to early '90s.

**Jerry:** You were five, six, seven years old?

**Trevor:** Yeah, yeah.

**Jerry:** It's like a ridiculous board game. It's like Risk, where all these different colored little cubes . . . "Gimme the green, I'll give you the yellow, but the brown is equal to two of these pink." You know, it's an absurd board game.

**Trevor:** But the whole system was absurd. Apartheid was an absurd system that was perfected. It doesn't make sense. Racism, all of these things, when you look at them they don't make sense. You know, Hitler—it doesn't make sense. When you look now, you go, "How did that craziness happen?" It doesn't make sense.

**Jerry:** Right. [*laughs*]

**Trevor:** But there's just a moment in time. If you find the right balance between desperation and fear, you can make people believe anything. When I grew up, I didn't know that my mom was black and my dad was white. I didn't know that. I literally thought it was a lottery. Your mom could be black, your mom could be white. Because I would see black moms, I'd see white moms, I'd see black dads, I'd see white dads. So I'd go, "This happens. It can happen to anybody."

## BARACK OBAMA

**Jerry:** When you were a kid, did you have a favorite president?

**Barack:** Teddy Roosevelt is a cool character. In fact, he may be the guy who would be the most fun to hang out with. He just does crazy stuff. Teddy Roosevelt would go up to Yellowstone Park for like a month. And nobody knew where he was. Nobody could get in touch with him. Can you imagine that?

**Jerry:** Wait a minute, in office?

**Barack:** In office. Sounds pretty good to me.

**Jerry:** Boy, that's a lot of messages when you get back.

*"Teddy Roosevelt is a cool character . . . he may be the guy who would be the most fun to hang out with."*

## KATHLEEN MADIGAN & CHUCK MARTIN

**Jerry:** I heard you have a farm or something.

**Kathleen:** Yeah, there's not animals and stuff. I call it a farm because I would really sound like a redneck if I called it the property. Whenever you refer to something as the property, you've just crossed the line of hillbilly.

**Jerry:** Or really rich. No, they say "land."

**Kathleen:** You're never going to hear some really rich person go, "I'm going to be heading to the property."

**Jerry:** No?

**Kathleen:** No. Well, at least in the Midwest every sign says "keep off the property." It's a lot of land. There's a bunch of four-wheelers. My dad and my uncles have built hunting cabins and it's the woods really.

**Jerry:** It was in *Napoleon Dynamite*. "Get off my property," right? We used to say it when we were kids. You would stand on the front lawn and you would tell other kids to get off my property. "Hey, get off my property."

**Chuck:** This is our property.

**Kathleen:** As if you had any ownership in it anyway.

# J.B. SMOOVE

**J.B.:**   You know, I was actually afraid to fail. Not just disappoint my parents, but I was afraid to fail. I did not want to walk home with a bad report card. I don't know how parents are now, but back then, if your parents had to come to school for you, you were in trouble, man. You know what I mean? If they had to show up to that school, [some kids might] say, "Oh man, my mom is here, or my dad is here. Oh, darn it." But for me, that's a lot. I had to change gears quick. See, I lost my father at fifteen.

**Jerry:**   Wow.

**J.B.:**   I had to really step up, 'cause I was the oldest. So I had a different motivation to success, to set an example for my brothers. I had a whole different world, when you take on responsibilities. Here's my first job I had. I had some funny jobs, man. Believe me. My first job was in a perfume company. And I remember, it was the same day I was trying out for the wrestling team. So I'm actually in my wrestling leotard.

**Jerry:**   Which is not flattering.

**J.B.:**   Yeah. It's not flattering at all.

**Jerry:**   No, no. It's embarrassing.

**J.B.:**   'Cause you really can't hide anything, man. It's the most embarrassing outfit ever. You know what I mean? It's really like a wedgie as soon as you put it on. Do wrestling teams have cheerleaders?

**Jerry:**   No.

**J.B.:**   No. See? There's nothing—you're not playing to anybody. You can't do anything about it. So I'm on the ground wrestling and my counselor comes in, and she's like, "Um, you applied for a part-time job?" I said, "Yeah." So I'm just sitting there like, "Damn. Do I take this part-time job? Or do I stay on the wrestling team?" My first day there, trying out for the team. So I say, you know what? I need the money. You know, lost my dad. I said I need to get me a car. I need certain things. So I ended up taking the job. I worked at this perfume company after school for a few years. I mean, when I tell you this guy taught me how to mix perfumes . . . I knew everything. I knew the ingredients. Lavenders and rosemarys and all these ingredients. A certain amount of alcohol that goes in it. I was a chemist at fifteen years old, baby. He taught me how to weigh it and everything, man. Isn't that crazy?

**Jerry:**   Yeah.

**J.B.:**   I could have been a perfumer. You know? Very easily. That's how much I knew about it.

## JUDD APATOW

**Judd :**  I said to my mom once—she was having financial problems, and she needed to buy a car, and a little money came in and she got a Mercedes. And I said, "Mom, why didn't you buy a Camry so that you had money to spend on things like food?" And she said, "Because I'm not an animal."

## NORM MACDONALD

**Norm:**  Oh my God, my father didn't like anything fantastical. One time, me and my brother watched *The Twilight Zone*. Never forget. My dad came in disgusted, and he pointed at one of the characters on the TV, and he said, "I suppose that one's a goddamn ghost."

**Jerry:**  [*laughs*]

**Norm:**   Didn't have time for that. They didn't have time in the old days for imagination and stuff, you know?

# JERRY LEWIS

**Jerry S.:**   What were you like as a little kid? Did your parents think you were crazy? They did? Did you drive them crazy? What did you do?

**Jerry L.:**   Everything I do now.

**Jerry S.:**   Did you have brothers and sisters? No brothers and sisters?

**Jerry L.:**   My dad was lazy.

**Jerry S.:**   Right. That is lazy.

**Jerry L.:**   I said, "Dad, you know how you got me?" He said, "Yeah." I said, "You got to do it again."

# KATE McKINNON

**Kate:**   We had the most old-fashioned mischief, my friends and I. We were going to buy a rowboat to go from one end of Oyster Bay Harbor [Long Island] to the other. For lunch. That was our big mischievous activity. And so we bought a rowboat one summer. Never went on it, but we sure saved up. We had a coffee can with change in it to buy a rowboat. It was so innocent.

**Jerry:**   Could you have done it? Would you have made it?

**Kate:**   No, we wouldn't have made it. It was too far.

**Jerry:**   Oh, that's funny. I saw it on a map. It does look like that's a big body of water there.

**Kate:**   Yeah. But we knew it at the time. We had pizza parties and we played little games and we saved up for a rowboat and that was our mischief. And you don't do that now. No one's doing that.

**Jerry:**   It sounds so wholesome.

# EDDIE MURPHY

**Eddie:**   See, that's a big difference in growing up in America. Blacks and whites. You've never punched anyone in the face. I've punched a lot of people.

**Jerry:**   Really?

**Eddie:** And been punched in the face. That's part of growing up.

**Jerry:** In Roosevelt [New York].

**Eddie:** Just, you know, being black. There will be punches in the face.

**Jerry:** Really?

**Eddie:** Absolutely.

**Jerry:** Because of racial things.

**Eddie:** No, no, no. You'd be getting punched in the face. Usually it's someone of your own ethnicity that's punching you in the face. And who you're punching in the face.

**Jerry:** And were you a good fighter?

**Eddie:** Oh yeah, man.

**Jerry:** Really?

**Eddie:** Yeah. I could scrap back in the day. I still got a good one if it came to that.

# GETTING STARTED

## *BRIAN REGAN*

**Brian:** When I was in college, one of the reasons I got into comedy was because of the hours. I had a 7 a.m. class that I couldn't wake up for. My nickname in college was Rip, for Rip Van Winkle, 'cause I didn't know how to wake up . . . 7 a.m. It was dark, you know? You'd wake up and it was dark out. And you'd go, "Why are people up?" You're allowed three cuts. I took all of them the first week. Monday, Wednesday, Friday—they were gone.

**Jerry:** I never heard of that—that you're allowed cuts.

**Brian:** Yeah, you're allowed three misses. So I used those up. And I remember thinking, "If this is what the world is, where you got to get up and go to a job, I don't know what to do." Then a comedian performed at our college and his show started at 8 p.m. And I remember sitting in the audience going, "I can get up by eight at night. If I just have to get up before eight . . ."

**Jerry:** In comedy, you don't have to work. But when you're working, you're really working.

# COLIN QUINN

**Colin:** I told you the first time I went to Pips [in Brooklyn], right? Doing comedy, like, three times. I go onstage on open mic night. And about six guys come in, telling people, "Show's over." Start throwing tables. Big Italian dudes. "Everybody, show's outside. This place stinks." They go outside. I'm standin' with the owner, like, ready to fight.

**Jerry:** Marty.

**Colin:** I'm squaring off with Marty and them on their side 'cause I want to be in the club. That's how bad the addiction of comedy is. I'm like, "Yeah, I want to work this club, man. I'll stay with this guy. I'll get my ass kicked." 'Cause you wanted to get in the club. I had no gigs.

**Jerry:** I'm not clear on what's happening here.

**Colin:** Some guys come in in the middle of the show and start throwin' tables, and they chase the customers out, and the customers leave. This is when I should've left the comedy business. Their friend Joey, the week before he hadn't passed [his audition], so they were protesting him as if it was a job site. They have a flatbed truck outside. He's up there: "Hey, folks. You ever notice you're smokin' a joint . . ."

**Jerry:** So this kid is standing on the truck doing stuff? Oh my God.

**Colin:** He didn't pass the week before, so he's out there on a truck doing his act right in front of the club. About three or four of the customers are sitting there watching, laughing at the jokes that he's telling on the truck. I'm standing there with the owners, ready to fight.

**Jerry:** They must've been impressed with your sudden allegiance.

**Colin:** No, I didn't pass. I went that Friday and didn't pass.

> "In comedy, you don't have to work. But when you're working, you're really working."

# DAVID LETTERMAN

**David:** I had to go to a place in Denver called the Turn of the Century. You ever hear of that place?

**Jerry:** No.

**David:** It was the Bicentennial week, and I was opening for Leslie Uggams.

**Jerry:** Wow.

**David:** There's a bill. And you're supposed to do forty-five minutes.

**Jerry:** Forty-five?

**David:** Forty-five.

**Jerry:** To open?

**David:** To open. And the guarantee is they were going to turn the house. Well I had about thirty-five, and they didn't turn the house. So the second show, it's just, "Hi, where are you from?" And the guy says, "I'm from Denver."

> "As Colin Quinn says, 'Comedy is the closest thing to justice.' You're funny, you survive. If you're not, you don't."

And I said, "Oh, great. Where are *you* from?" "Denver." And the guy says, "Look. We're all from Denver. You're in Denver." "Thank you. Good night. And now, Leslie Uggams."

**Jerry:** Do you remember in the Comedy Store in the '70s, [Richard] Pryor would come in and he would try to break all new stuff. That was really impressive, wasn't it?

**David:** It was very impressive. I had the great fun to follow him one night, and it really was a movie scene, because the Comedy Store after Richard did everything but explode. Honestly. Everything but explode. People are laughing so hard. And then, "And now, ladies and gentlemen, Dave Letterman . . ." So of course, I have to fight people who are leaving to get to the stage. I kind of got friendly with Richard and really thought he was a dear guy. He was always very nice to me. And that night—he was writing onstage—he closed with a bit about having sex with a dog. And I just thought, "Well, okay. There are many facets of genius." Which room did you like better, the big room or the original room?

**Jerry:** Well, I'll tell you, David, Mitzi Shore was not a fan of mine, and I could not get spots. This was 1979, and I asked her if I could talk with her. She said sure, and I went to her office and she sat me down and she looked me in the eye and she says, "I don't like you. Too many people like you, and that's not good for you. And you need someone to step on you, and I'm going to be that person." I remember every word that she said. She said, "If I had four spots in a week and Mike Binder was available and you're available, I would give all four to Mike Binder."

**David:** Did you talk to her subsequent to that?

**Jerry:** No.

**David:** Or was that it with you and Mitzi?

**Jerry:** Well, don't you think that would be it, at the end of that conversation?

**David:** Yeah. Except that now you come back in a year, you come back in six months, and the landscape is completely different. You'd think maybe she would be contrite. You'd think maybe she would say, "Oh, Jerry, I'm so sorry . . ."

**Jerry:** No, David. I'm very sensitive. You know what the funny ironic thing was? In a way, it did happen. I was so resentful of her and of that, that I did start to work a lot harder. And it really ended up being one of the things I think I'm grateful for, is that she did try to step on me, and I resented it so much.

**David:** Did Johnny [Carson] talk to you during commercials?

**Jerry:** Yeah.

**David:** And what kind of things would he say?

**Jerry:** He had the new Corvette. Remember when the new Corvette came out in '85?

**David:** Yeah.

| | |
|---|---|
| **Jerry:** | And he had that white one. And I thought, "Oh, Johnny's got the new 'Vette. I'll talk to him about that in the commercial." I sit down, we're going to the commercial, and I go, "How's that new 'Vette?" And he goes, "Hot car." That's it. |
| **David:** | When in your timeline did you start guesting on that show? |
| **Jerry:** | I was on May 7, 1981. It was my first shot. I was twenty-six years old. |
| **David:** | And this is long before your TV show. |
| **Jerry:** | Nine years before. |
| **David:** | So the pressure of "Maybe I'm never coming back." |
| **Jerry:** | Yeah. Either I have a career or I don't. |
| **David:** | That's right. That's exactly right. |
| **Jerry:** | I never have to wonder what those skiers feel like at the top [of the mountain] in the Olympics. I know what that feels like. "I either make it or break it right here—right now in the next five minutes." |
| **David:** | That's right. The guy pulls the curtain open and the rest of your life is right there. |
| **Jerry:** | Yeah, it's kind of sad that there's no such thing [today], right? |
| **David:** | I think so. I think absolutely. |
| **Jerry:** | As Colin Quinn says, "Comedy is the closest thing to justice." You're funny, you survive. If you're not, you don't. The words do not make people think, "That guy was great." |
| **David:** | It's a different world now. |
| **Jerry:** | Not long term. Not long view. Comedy's not an eight-year thing. You're not a pop act. This is a fifty-year gig. |

# DON RICKLES

| | |
|---|---|
| **Jerry:** | Take me back to 1958. Could you afford a car like this in '58? |
| **Don:** | My mother, rest her soul, she had her friend drive me to jobs. That's the truth. And they used to sit in the kitchen and wait for the boss to come out and say, "We don't want this man here. He's ruining our business." So my mother said, "What'd he say?" "He said, 'The man's wearing a stupid shirt. We don't need that.'" And in those days I was just starting out doing what I do. |
| **Jerry:** | In '58? |
| **Don:** | I don't know, when did I start? |
| **Jerry:** | I don't know. |
| **Don:** | You tell me. Way back? Well, my best recollection is I started out in New York. I went to the American Academy of Dramatic Arts first. |
| **Jerry:** | Right, that's not comedy. |
| **Don:** | So I come out as an actor— |

| | |
|---|---|
| **Jerry:** | This is a show about comedy. |
| **Don:** | Really? |
| **Jerry:** | In Vegas, you were doing shows, like, twelve and— |
| **Don:** | Back a hundred years ago, yeah. At twelve, two, and five in the morning, over a bar. |
| **Jerry:** | Five? |
| **Don:** | Two and five in the morning. Twelve, two, and five in the morning. |
| **Jerry:** | So three shows a night? |
| **Don:** | Three shows a night. Over a bar. With guys like this: "What is this guy, funny?" That was fun. It was tough. Tough. Oh jeez. I'd say, "Sir, when you get a minute, can you look up?" They didn't even look up sometimes. Like we're sitting here, they just kept eating. They'd say, "There's somebody up there yelling at everybody." Then I started something that nobody ever did in Vegas, to this day. They talk about it too. It was packed. I was doing so good in the lounge they charged a five-dollar cover, which they never did in the lounge, ever, in Vegas, you understand? Louis Prima almost |

had a nervous breakdown, 'cause he was the star in those days. And I loved Louis. He was great. Personally, you know—anyway, that's another story.

So I'm onstage and it's packed, the lounge. And the casino's packed. And it's noisy as hell. There's no way to stop it. And I go into the casino, just one night, by accident, and get on the side of the craps table and yell, "All right, that's it! I'm on a goddamn stage and this noise has got stop, you understand me! It stops!" I swear on my father's grave, guys were like this [*mimes astonishment*]—they couldn't move. "Shhh. You're offending me! You should have some class when I'm out there killing myself!" And then they'd applaud in the craps tables. I did that.

When I did it the first night, the dealers went, "Oh, Jesus!" They didn't know what the hell happened. It's a true story. I never told that to anybody. Yeah. It took a lot of, you know . . . Boss could've said, "Get rid of him." Milton Prell, rest his soul, was the owner then. Guy goes up to his office there: "Rickles is running into the lounge, to the craps tables,

## "There was a lot of heartache. It was hard work . . . You worry every night, three a night."

and making everybody stop gambling!" He said, "He's doing what?" He came down and went by a craps table, unbeknownst to me, and he said, "That's funny."

**Jerry:** Would you say those were the most fun days of your early—

**Don:** Everything is relative. It was fun and it wasn't. 'Cause there was a lot of heartache. It was hard work, you know. You worry every night, three a night. God! And the money in those days was great, but it was three, four weeks at a time. And then we used to go early in the morning—I got pictures of it—out to Lake Mead. Me! I learned how to water-ski, and I got pictures of me on the one ski, two skis. Six in the morning on Lake Mead.

**Jerry:** After you finished staying up all night?

**Don:** Yeah. The water-skiing. And then we'd get back to the room and I had the sunburn and everything. It was like I was paralyzed. . . . Milton Berle, I loved him when I was a kid. He was my idol. Then when I grew up, I knew I was wrong. You know what he did—I'll tell you. When you did a Milton Berle or a Bob Hope special—a Bob Hope special in particular: "Okay, Don, here's the scene. Now you come in. Okay." "Hi, Bob." "Is that the way you're going to do it?" I know you can appreciate that. And I go, "Well, what's wrong, Bob?" "You don't know? You don't know." I said, "No." "Go up on the steps here, try it again." Three times: "Hi, Bob." "It's wrong." Then you go with Harry Crane, those old writers who would just sit up there with the hats and the cigars: "It's wrong, kid." I never got past "Hiya, Bob."

**Jerry:** With Hope or with Berle?

**Don:** Both. We did the sketch, but they were so busy showing who they were, you know what I'm saying? And in those days, God, when you did sketches—when I got off the cards [cue cards], I got screams.

**Jerry:** Right.

**Don:** As soon as I stayed with the cards, I was right in the toilet. It just happened with the show—I don't want to say that either.

**Jerry:** Okay.

**Don:** [whispers] Betty White. You know, I did her show [Hot in Cleveland]. I got off the cards—laughs. And then I see the show, right back to their shit. You know? The old days you could change. Dean [Martin] was great. Dean would say, "Don, do that. That's funny." We had fun. Frank [Sinatra] too.

**Jerry:** That's what we're selling, is fun.

**Don:** Yeah, that's right.

**Jerry:** That's why I struggled until I got control of my own material.

# SETH MEYERS

**Seth:** Right out of college—well, even during college—I started going into Chicago and taking improv classes and joined an improv troupe at this place called ImprovOlympic. Then only about eight months out of college, I auditioned for this comedy theater in Amsterdam—like a Second City–type theater over there.

**Jerry:** Amsterdam, Europe?

**Seth:** Amsterdam, the Netherlands, yeah. I moved there basically a year out of college and lived in Amsterdam for two years doing comedy.

**Jerry:** But what are you doing there? How can you be funny to those people?

**Seth:** I thought it was great because if you can make a Dutch person laugh, it's like swinging a bat with a doughnut on it. Also, I feel like young comedians sometimes get caught up in reference comedy, like pop culture comedy. So if you go someplace where you don't share the same references or pop culture, it kind of forces you to find more universal ins.

I moved out to LA after I got back from Amsterdam and was trying to be an actor and going out on sitcom auditions. But *SNL* had seen me in Chicago doing a two-person show. A girl I'd worked with in Amsterdam and I came back to Chicago. We started doing this two-person sketch improv show based on relationships. It was just a little quiet success in Chicago—"Pickups and Hiccups." And we would play eighty-seat theaters, but we could sell it out. So I hadn't really thought about who I wanted to be by the time I started on *SNL*, which is kind of the craziest part. I was still figuring out who I was when I started there.

**Jerry:** It's a tough thing to figure out.

**Seth:** It's impossible.

**Jerry:** Well, it's not impossible, but it's tough.

**Seth:** Right. It is tough. And I've completely benefited from Lorne [Michaels]'s patience with me. Because I think he hired me to be a cast member, and then I think he liked my writing probably more than me as a sketch performer. Kept me around, and as things opened up, he found a home for me that allowed me to play to my strengths.

**Jerry:** And then you figure out you're funny when you're you.

**Seth:** Which is the greatest gift on earth.

**Jerry:** It's not bad. So you've been doing shows of some kind, because I follow you on Twitter.

**Seth:** Yes, I've been doing stand-up.

**Jerry:** Really? Just straight-up stand-up?

**Seth:** Straight-up stand-up.

**Jerry:** And when did you start doing that? When I told you to, right?

**Seth:** Well, yeah. For real. This is very important. I'm glad we're getting this out here, so you can get the credit you so justly deserve.

| **Jerry:** | That's really the craziest part of your life. |
| **Seth:** | Is that I do it? |
| **Jerry:** | Yeah, that you just up and did that. |
| **Seth:** | The control freak part of me was like, "Oh, this is where it's at." If it goes bad, there's no one to blame but yourself. Also, if it's going bad, you could adjust and fix it. It's in your hands, as opposed to the hive mind of a good improv show. |

## LOUIS C.K.

| **Louis:** | I desperately wanted to go to New York University Film School like Spike Lee and Martin Scorsese and be a filmmaker. I wanted that desperately. But I couldn't fill out the form at my high school. I would go to the guidance counselor's office where you get all the college stuff and I would get sleepy. She would give me this stuff and I would start falling asleep and I |

would get some food on it or something. And then I just would never do it. That's why I didn't go to college.

**Jerry:** And then stand-up seems like a good—

**Louis:** It's just walking in, yeah.

**Jerry:** It's a good life if you can do it.

**Louis:** I started doing it in Boston and there was this community of comedians who would play softball at noon every Monday, Wednesday, and Friday. And I went to one softball game. I was working as a car mechanic. I didn't even care about being a nationally known comedian. I just wanted to be a Boston comedian and play softball with other Boston comedians. That's all I wanted.

**Jerry:** Right, that's a good plan.

**Louis:** Do stand-up at night, sleep a lot during the day, and see shows. I loved being at shows. When I was a kid starting in Boston, it was all about jokes. All the comedians wrote really good, 'cause Steven [Wright] had gotten famous doing that—just crystal jokes laid end to end. He kind of left a wake of a bunch of guys doing that in Boston. And I wanted to do that. I failed at it. But then when I saw you—'cause I opened for you. You let me open for you at a few shows and I got to see you. The great thing about it wasn't my performance, it was standing in the wings and watching you run a stand-up show for an hour and a half, or an hour, on a theater stage. That's when I learned this thing of staying on a subject for a while and hitting it from all these different angles, and how to not do anything in between. This is the biggest advice you ever gave me and I've carried it my whole—I don't know if I ever told you this. People used to applaud after jokes—more in the '80s, I feel like. Those comedy applause breaks were big in the '80s.

**Jerry:** Yeah, yeah. Right.

**Louis:** And I never encountered them. I just did shitty clubs and Mexican restaurants and stuff. And then you took me to these big theaters. I was, like, nineteen, twenty years old. And when they liked a joke, [it'd be] a theater of, you know, twenty-five hundred people applauding. And I didn't know what to do. So I asked you, "What should I do? Like, do I take a bow? Do I say thank you?" I actually thought you should say thank you. And you said, "No, just stay in the bit. Just stay in the moment that they're applauding for. If you're angry and that's funny to them and it makes them applaud, just stay with it." That was a massive revelation to me.

**Jerry:** That's funny.

**Louis:** And it works on the other side too. If they boo or if they're quiet, rather than letting it break you out and going, "What happened?" you just stay with it. It guided me through a lot of figuring stuff out.

**Jerry:** Yeah, because, first of all, the bit is where you're supposed to be. That's what they're enjoying. They don't want you enjoying the show.

> *"If you're angry and that's funny to them and it makes them applaud, just stay with it."*

| | |
|---|---|
| **Louis:** | No. Not at all. |
| **Jerry:** | No, the show's for them. The bits are for you. |
| **Louis:** | That's like if you're watching a guy running on a football field and the crowd starts roaring and he stops and goes, "Right? Is this good? You like this?" Actually, Jackie Gleason's a great example of that. He said that about doing sitcoms. The crowd will tell you how long the bit's funny for. So if people were going crazy, he really stayed in the bit. |
| **Jerry:** | Yeah, you don't want a dog that takes both ends of the leash. |
| **Louis:** | There was a moment in my life when I was doing comedy clubs in New York. I had a motorcycle. I lived on Bleecker Street. On Saturday nights you'd get $50 to $75 a show. And because of the motorcycle I could get to shows quicker. So I would do the Cellar, bomb up to the Comic Strip, catch Midtown and do the Improv. That's when everything was open then. The Village Gate, Comedy Cellar. And I would do shows from 7 p.m. through to 3 a.m. I would do, like, nine shows in a night. They'd just hand you cash. And then I'd come home and put my motorcycle in the garage. I remember one night, I've got bills just crammed in my pocket, and I'm walking in my apartment and I thought, "I have life by the balls. There's nothing above this. I don't need anything else." I'm young. I had a full head of thick hair. I was kind of in good shape. |
| **Jerry:** | What year was this? |
| **Louis:** | Maybe '90? And I went to sleep feeling this contentment. The next day I'm going down Second Avenue on my motorcycle and a guy just creams into me. I went to the hospital. I didn't break anything, but I had bruises all over my body. They didn't admit me, 'cause I didn't break anything. But the doctor said, "You're going to be in really bad shape for a while." And I went home and I just felt weak and unable to do anything, and I slept for, like, two days. And then I wake up, I look in the mirror, and I see that I'm balding, and my motorcycle is in pieces. Three days later the Improv closes. Catch a Rising Star within a year after that. And it just— |
| **Jerry:** | So you were correct. |
| **Louis:** | I was. I was at the pinnacle. Yes. That's what I told myself. That's the top. And I really believed over the next two years that everything declined. Every month got worse than the last. My life is only going to get worse. That's the best it ever got. And I was bald within—like, so fast. And I had no income. It was so hard. This was '90 to '93. |

## PATTON OSWALT

| | |
|---|---|
| **Patton:** | I realized really early on, "I'm going to have to have a day job for a while. There's just no money if I want to go on every night." That was another interview of yours that I remember I read, I think it was in *Rolling Stone*, |

about how you would always pick the shittiest day jobs so that it was never anything that you could go, "Oh, you know, I could just fall back." It was like, "No, this job is so horrible that it just makes me work twice as hard at stand-up."

I grew up in Virginia, moved to San Francisco in '92. So that's where I learned to be a comedian. I did stand-up for four years on the East Coast, and I met you very briefly. There's no way you remember it. You were doing a theater, and some guy that booked a club was like, "I know people who know Jerry. You can come and see him." You were offstage and—this was actually a big moment for me—I just said, "Hey, I think you're really funny." They were literally saying your name, and you were like, "Yeah, cool, I'll talk to you in a second." And you just walked onstage and went into it, and I was like, "Oh, *that's* where I have to be as a comedian." There's no "I need an hour to get in my space." It's like the way I'm talking to you now—I'm just going to walk right up there. I was doing the "I need, like, ten minutes. They're about to call me. I need ten minutes." No, no, it all needs to be the same thing.

| | |
|---|---|
| **Jerry:** | If you want to be a warrior you must sleep with your sword. |
| **Patton:** | It wasn't until I actually got to do [*Seinfeld*] that I saw how it was. I would start watching just 'cause I'd seen the other side of it and I wanted to see, "How does this work?" |
| **Jerry:** | So you had not seen the show when you did it? |
| **Patton:** | Nope. |
| **Jerry:** | Come on. That's so funny. |
| **Patton:** | I had never seen it at that point. 'Cause I was always onstage. I didn't have a VCR. There was no internet, there was no DVR. |

# JAY LENO

| | |
|---|---|
| **Jay:** | If you watch my very first *Tonight Show*, you hear, "Ha-ha!" You hear Robin Williams laughing off to the side. |
| **Jerry:** | Really? Wow. |
| **Jay:** | And all the other comics, and that's what we did because— |
| **Jerry:** | Because it was such a big deal. |
| **Jay:** | It was a huge deal back then. |
| **Jerry:** | Yeah, it was a huge deal. |
| **Jay:** | And it wasn't like it is now. Comics could go and hang around backstage and stuff. |
| **Jerry:** | Jay, you know why we became friends? It's because we shared this basic outlook on our profession, which is there's no awful gigs. |
| **Jay:** | Yeah. |
| **Jerry:** | That all gigs are great. Because they're paying you to do something that |

you love to do, and you think, not only do you love to do it, there's a value in it that's even beyond you.

**Jay:** There are awful gigs. I remember I used to do the Playboy Clubs. The Playboy Clubs had a room director, and at the end of the day he would take out a card and he'd go, "Okay, I'm going to grade you on your act, and this card goes right to Mr. Hefner. You have to sign it." So one day I'm at the Playboy Club in New York and I go onstage. Not a laugh. Nothing! I mean, I'm sweating. I go, "What's going on?" I come offstage, the guy goes, "Hey, come here. You get an F. You got to sign." I said, "What is this crowd?" He goes, "They're from Portugal. It's a bus tour." "From Portugal? You didn't tell me they're from Portugal!" He goes, "So you just make your act Portuguese." I go, "I can't make my act Portuguese. I don't speak Portuguese! They don't even speak English! You can't give me an F." He's going, "No, you got to sign it." "No, no, I'm not signing that!" "Well, you'll never work here again." So I had to sign the card that goes to Mr. Hefner, and I got an F. That was a bad gig.

**Jerry:** You got paid, didn't you?

**Jay:** I did get paid.

**Jerry:** All right.

**Jay:** But it was a bad gig. It wasn't fun.

**Jerry:** So what! It's a funny story. Now it's a funny story.

**Jay:** That's right, but—

**Jerry:** The Portuguese gig. I'll take that gig tomorrow.

**Jay:** Wouldn't you, if you got the choice between getting half the money and killing and getting your full check and just doing okay, I think you would take the half the check. I would.

**Jerry:** Yes, I would.

**Jay:** Yeah. That's a real comic.

**Jerry:** I'd try to get both gigs. You know, Jay, when I met you in the '70s, I used to come to your house every night. We'd always hang out in LA. I was twenty-three or -four when I met you. And it was just the way you're talking about comedy now, you formed my whole professional attitude as a young man. I'm always grateful to you for that.

**Jay:** Oh, well, thank you.

**Jerry:** I always tell people that. "I learned comedy from Jay." I learned that this is a thing of value that you take care of, that you work on, that you appreciate, and you don't ever trash it or give it short shrift.

**Jay:** Most comedians tend—it's like water going downhill. They go where their audience is. "I didn't like that crowd. I like this crowd." No, no, you got this crowd. Work to get that crowd.

**Jerry:** Right.

**Jay:** So when I would follow Richie [Pryor], I really tightened everything up. And, yes, did I bomb? Most of the time. People were getting up and leaving, or laughed out. But the few that stayed, I would hear those. So it just made me a stronger comic. How many times you hear comics go, "I just do colleges." You know, "I just do this hip little club on the East Side."

**Jerry:** Yeah, yeah, the Largo.

**Jay:** "I only go here. Because those people are idiots." No, they're not. They're not idiots. You know? They want to laugh. You're just not doing your job.

**Jerry:** Right. Well, that's definitely a change in the comedy culture. I remember coming to see you, thinking, "That was the greatest thing I ever saw. This guy's so strong, he can get up in front of this crowd, my parents' age, and get laughs." That was something I admired. I don't think comedians today admire that. They don't look to say, "How can I broaden this so that everyone gets it?"

# TODD BARRY

**Jerry:** Here's what I'll tell you: Getting a hundred friends together so you guys can put on a show, you're better off standing in front of one guy who paid to get in. And we did that a lot. A lot of 3 a.m., standing in front of two, three people.

**Todd:** I feel like that's the difference between whether you can really do it or you're the funny guy at the office.

**Jerry:** Right.

# TINA FEY

**Tina:** When I first moved [to New York City], my mom would say to me, "Why don't you just get a job being one of the girls who gives out fragrance in, like, Bloomingdale's? Your cousin has a job handing out—" and I had to be like, "Mom, are you going to make me explain to you that I'm not pretty enough to get that job at Bloomingdale's? You're going to make me say out loud that I'm not pretty enough to hand out fragrance cards at Bloomingdale's? Don't make me say it." I still couldn't get that job.

**Jerry:** You're pretty enough to do that job.

**Tina:** Thank you. No, not then. Not without the help of professionals. My cousin was tall and she had blond hair and she was good at makeup. You have to be good at doing your own makeup and be personable. I'm none of those things.

**Jerry:** Yeah, that doesn't come in the comedy kit. Tall, personable, and good at makeup.

**Tina:** No.

## GEORGE WALLACE

**George:** What was your first paying gig? How much money did you make?

**Jerry:** The Good Times. Third and Thirty-Third. Two shows, $35. And I still have the money.

**George:** I think I drove you to that show. I think we left your house for Thanksgiving. You know how you took me to your house for Thanksgiving and I didn't want to go?

**Jerry:** Yeah.

**George:** Because I didn't know what Jewish people ate for Thanksgiving. And it bothered me. I was so disturbed about going to your house. It was the first time I had been to any other ethnicity—

**Jerry:** It wasn't ethnic, okay? We're Americans. Thanksgiving in a Jewish home is normal.

**George:** It was a bunch of Jews, as far as I'm concerned.

**Jerry:** It was, but there was normal food.

**George:** And your people were nice. I didn't know what to do. I didn't know what to expect. And your daddy was crazy. Your daddy kept saying, "Take another piece of cake. Take another piece of cake. Eat another piece." And he says, "They're going to say you ate it anyways, so . . ." Your dad was a funny guy.

**Jerry:** That's funny. It's so hard to remember sometimes. But you did that line perfect. That is just the way he did it. He could hit a line, my dad.

**George:** And the next week, I had a paying gig. I went up to the Nevele Hotel [in Wawarsing, New York], and bombed for forty-five minutes. Didn't get one laugh.

**Jerry:** You walked outta there, they said, "Here's your ass. You may want to take this with you."

**George:** I mean, I don't know whether you ever been to a funeral or not, but . . . I was dejected and rejected every way.

**Jerry:** The same thing happened to me when I first went to the Catskills. They handed me my ass on a platter. That's the toughest audience in the world.

**George:** I wanted to drive off the Tappan Zee Bridge. I'm serious.

**Jerry:** I called George Schultz at Pips and I said, "I think I'm going to quit. I don't think I can do this." And you know what he said to me? He said, "If you do well up there, you have no career. If you can make those people laugh, you'll never get anywhere."

## ROBERT KLEIN

**Jerry:** Robert, what year was it when you first stepped onstage as a stand-up comedian?

**Robert:** Officially, or as an amateur trying to?

**Jerry:** Officially. The Improv on West Forty-Fourth Street. Wouldn't you say that was your official—

**Robert:** Absolutely. I would say so. Yes, I would.

**Jerry:** What year was that?

**Robert:** That was in the fall of '66.

**Jerry:** Wow, look at you.

**Robert:** Of 1866. Lincoln had just been shot, the country hadn't gotten over it. It was a sad time—people needed laughs, Jerry.

## AZIZ ANSARI

**Aziz:** Comedians are so lazy about weird things. Being a comedian is very hard.

**Jerry:** It's very hard. I always remember being a teenager and watching comedians on TV. I had no idea what they were doing. I thought they just talked

> *"When I first went to the Catskills, they handed me my ass on a platter. That's the toughest audience in the world."*

like that. You know what I mean? I didn't even know that those were bits. I thought, "Well, that's just the way they talk."

**Aziz:** Yeah. I used to think that too. Like, "Oh man, he just started talking about the way he felt about things. Good thing they captured that." I remember one of my first bits I wrote that I really liked was—it was when there was a big gay marriage debate going on, and this one senator, John Cornyn, he had some amazing quote where he said something like, "If your neighbor marries a box turtle, that doesn't affect your everyday life. But that doesn't mean it's right." I heard that and I started doing jokes about, why would he pick box turtle? Of all things, that seems like such a specific reference. So I thought, "All right, this guy's definitely thought about fuckin' a box turtle."

## JON STEWART

**Jon:** Did you ever work? Did you start working as a comic almost immediately?

**Jerry:** Almost immediately. I had a couple little jobs. I started in September, by January I was making a living.

**Jon:** That's amazing.

**Jerry:** I was emceeing three nights at the Comic Strip. I got one night, then I got two nights, and when I got the third night I was able to quit my waiter job during the day at Brew Burger on Forty-Seventh and Third. And I was making $115 a week. I was golden. That was the biggest moment in my career, when I handed that guy the apron. And I knew that was it. I did a *Nightline* with Ted Koppel back in, like, the 2004 presidential election. And he said to me, "When did you know you had made it?" And I was like, "The moment I moved to New York." 'Cause making it was getting onstage.

**Jon:** That was going to be my life, whether or not I was successful. That was not the issue. I was doing stand-up. I was in a club onstage in the Village. First night was on Bleecker Street at the Bitter End. And I was terrible. But to me, I had already made it because I had broken away from what my life was going to be. I was living in Jersey. I was bartending. I was out of school. I had no idea what I was going to do. And I'd always wanted to try it.

**Jerry:** I think you see these horrible shows, *American Idol* and *The Voice* and everything, and they tease these people with, "Hey, you're really good. You're going to do this for a living. This is going to be your life." And it's not.

**Jon:** No.

**Jerry:** But for us, it was more real than that. Because there was no joke. There was no tease. It was like, you're standing up and it's one in the morning.

> ## "I was living in Jersey. I was bartending. I was out of school. I had no idea what I was going to do."

|        | You're in front of fifteen people. And they're laughing at this nonsense that you think. |
|--------|---|
| **Jon:** | That is correct. I always view stand-up in some ways like I view bartending: if I learn how to do this, I'll never starve. Somebody's always going to want to laugh . . . And you would get your forty-five [minutes] and then someone would pull you aside and go, "You ready for the check spot?" "Check spot? What are you talking about? No, I got my forty-five." "You got your forty-five, but at thirty-five they're going to drop the check. You got to cover that, get them back and continue." "What?" The whole thing got way more complicated. |
| **Jerry:** | For people at home who don't know what the check spot is: you're doing your set, and then all the waitresses give the entire audience their check at the same moment. |
| **Jon:** | The exact same time. |
| **Jerry:** | In the middle of your set. And all of a sudden everyone who was listening and enjoying whatever you were doing, the heads go down. Arguments. |
| **Jon:** | The arguments were the best. You'd hear some stuff. "Miss, miss, these are not daiquiris. We didn't order daiquiris." People go crazy. |
| **Jerry:** | It's like you're flying and they just cut the engines for a minute and then you're plummeting to earth. |
| **Jon:** | But I remember walking home from the Comedy Cellar at three in the morning through Bleecker Street, just walking through it and being like, "I cannot believe I'm doing this." I was the day bartender at Panchito's right up the block, and I just loved everything about it. I was like, "This is so much better than what I was doing." |
| **Jerry:** | Okay, so not to belabor it. Given that sense of who you are, that you know that in that moment in your life—that's what makes it such a Technicolor moment. You find out who you are in a couple of months. |
| **Jon:** | We came out. We came out as comics. |
| **Jerry:** | Yeah. [*laughs*] |
| **Jon:** | That's what we did. |
| **Jerry:** | It's true. It felt just like that. I was so embarrassed to admit it. To my friends, to my parents. |
| **Jon:** | Were you still living there? |
| **Jerry:** | Yeah, still living at home. And I was never funny in front of them. |
| **Jon:** | By choice? How did you control it? |
| **Jerry:** | I didn't think they would think what I thought was funny. "They're not going to think this is funny. My friends will think it's funny, but *they're* not going to get my sense of humor." I think I was correct also. [*laughs*] |
| **Jon:** | When you did that, they must have been like, "You're doing what now?" |
| **Jerry:** | It was very tough to admit it to my friends. Because I felt like I was saying, "I think I'm funnier than you. And I think I'm funny enough that total strangers would pay me." The ego with that—I wasn't comfortable with it. That's very egotistical. Did you feel egotistical? |

**Jon:**      No, because I was much more solitary. I was not in my environment. When I moved to New York, I was alone. There was no one around.

## JIMMY FALLON

**Jimmy:**    I used to wear Nikes because that's what you used to wear. You made me wear Nikes.

**Jerry:**    And I used to wear Adidas 'cause that's what [Bill] Cosby used to wear.

**Jimmy:**    I started wearing Adidas 'cause that's what Letterman used to wear. He used to wear those kind of wrestling shoes.

**Jerry:**    Yeah, I love those.

**Jimmy:**    When did he stop wearing those?

**Jerry:**    A few years into *Late Night*, he stopped. But I always thought it was cool. Wrestling shoes.

**Jimmy:**    That was the coolest. Comedians used to have outfits, right? Kind of costumes, at one point. Rolled-up blazers. Sneakers with suits. That was kind of a thing. And then it just sort of went away. But that was a style at one point.

**Jerry:** These young guys dress too down for me. What do you think?

**Jimmy:** Too down. But I think in the middle somewhere. I'd never want to ever say, "Oh, you shouldn't do that."

**Jerry:** Why not?

**Jimmy:** [*laughs*] I don't know. You mean, you go suits all the way?

**Jerry:** No, you can let 'em wear what they want, but you could also say, "I don't like that." You could have your opinion.

**Jimmy:** But then, if someone's great, you go, "Well, it doesn't really matter." It's weird, 'cause if you wear that outfit and you get used to being funny in that outfit, then you go on a show and you wear a suit, doesn't it throw your game off?

**Jerry:** It does. When I first started going on *The Tonight Show* in a suit, I didn't know how to work the suit. It wasn't until I learned how to get a suit fitted right, so you feel comfortable in it, that I could perform. But the first time you get a suit, you don't know what it is.

You know what I miss? I miss being an opening act. I'd go out in front of Frankie Valli, and people go, "Who the hell is this guy? We don't want to see him. We want to see Frankie Valli." And then you would just go, "What about this? What about this junk? Why are they putting pictures of the criminals on the walls of the post office? Why don't they hang on to this guy when they're taking his picture?" And then they go, "Hey, that's funny. That's pretty funny. That's really funny." So that's that feeling. You'll never have that feeling again of "Who the hell is Jimmy Fallon? Why is Jimmy Fallon here?"

**Jimmy:** Yeah.

# *JIM CARREY*

**Jerry:** What was it like when you were really in stand-up days? What was it like for you?

**Jim:** I was doing fifteen minutes as a cockroach trying to avoid the vacuum cleaner. He knows that there's a couple spots in the living room he can go. You know, there's the baseboard over there.

**Jerry:** I like that bit. That's funny.

**Jim:** [My manager] would preface the gig by saying, "A lot of people are going to leave the club. But they're going to come back, because they won't believe what they saw." And that's how we sold it. And it was true. One of the first headlining gigs I did was the Comedy and Magic Club down at Hermosa Beach [in LA]. Steve Oedekerk, who wrote many, many things

## "[There is] a thin line between revulsion and love."

with me, was part of the reason why I am where I am. He's an incredible writer. He was opening for me, and I did the first couple of nights. People were leaving. And the club owner told Jimmy Miller, who was booking the club at that time—he was the booker for that club before he was my manager—and he told Jimmy Miller to talk to me.

**Jerry:** Mike Lacey?

**Jim:** Mike Lacey. Yes, thank you. Mike Lacey asked Jimmy Miller to talk to me and asked me to do my old act.

**Jerry:** The impressions?

**Jim:** Yeah, the impressions. The crowd-pleasers. Standing-ovation act. Understandable. He called me up, and Jimmy said, "I know what you're doing, and what you're experimenting with. Could you just for this gig, since you're headlining, could you do some of the old act?" And I said, "No, fire me."

**Jerry:** Wow.

**Jim:** And he said, "I don't want to fire ya. It's just, Jim, you know, just do a little bit, maybe just a coupla little bits. You can put a couple bits in there just to spice it up." I go, "No. Fire me." And he said, "Would you mind if Steve headlines?"

**Jerry:** Really?

**Jim:** "He could do the headline. You could open with the stuff you're doing." I said, "No. Fire me." He said, "Ah, I don't want to fire you, Jim. Jesus Christ." I made a couple of adjustments, but I didn't go back to the impressions. And by Thursday night the same people who had left were bringing people back to see the car wreck that was now more fully formed. And by Friday, Saturday, Sunday, I was getting standing ovations again.

**Jerry:** Wow.

**Jim:** I remember being in the dressing room, and Mike Lacey and Jimmy Miller coming back and sitting in the dressing room with me, just sitting there befuddled, completely befuddled, and going like, "I mean, it's . . . the same people. A thin line between revulsion and love, I guess. How do ya quantify that?" Jimmy was just going on and on. Lacey, the same thing—kind of red-faced and saying anything. But they're sorry: "Hey, do this anytime you want to do it here." And from there Jimmy started booking me, and I continued to do clubs all around the country. I had twenty minutes that I stretched to an hour and fifteen probably, maybe thirty. And I just played and had fun. Judd Apatow was my opening act.

**Jerry:** Oh my God.

**Jim:** How crazy is that?

**Jerry:** That's so crazy.

# BILL MAHER

**Bill:**   I think you were good from the beginning.

**Jerry:**  I was good enough to feel encouraged and to go, "I can't believe I'm even doing this." I found that exhilarating.

**Bill:**   I experienced that, but not right away. I could tell you the date, the exact date of the first time I felt that, 'cause I remember it.

**Jerry:**  Wow.

**Bill:**   It was a red-letter date in my life.

**Jerry:**  Give me the date.

**Bill:**   June 20, 1979. It's the first time I went onstage, did fifteen minutes, got laughs all the way through, and felt like, "Oh my God, I'm really going to be a comedian."

**Jerry:**  And how many sets had you done at that point?

**Bill:**   I don't know. A hundred.

**Jerry:**  Oh yeah, I'm way better than you. Way better. [*laughs*]

**Bill:**   Well, you were. I think that to be good right away in stand-up comedy is rare to the point of maybe being unique.

**Jerry:**  What does "good" mean?

**Bill:**   I can get laughs. It's not something that most people . . . I don't know anybody who has your story. Goes up there for the first time, and the first ten times, the first fifty times, and really knows what they're doing. You have to find your voice. And you have to get used to the fact that this is very different from what you thought it would be, which would be just like the way you make your friends laugh. But an audience of strangers is not your friends.

**Jerry:**  That's correct.


# TREVOR NOAH

**Trevor:**  I went to the UK, did my first gig, got booed. It was the first time. I didn't know that happened. Because South Africa's similar to America: heckling is not allowed. In the UK it's a very real part of comedy. You don't say, "Don't heckle the comedians." You'd rather say to the comedians, "Don't get heckled."

**Jerry:**  Right. [*laughs*]

**Trevor:**  I didn't even say a joke. I just said, "Hi, I'm Trevor Noah, I'm from South Africa." And some guy just went, "Boo, get off the stage." And I panicked. I didn't know what to do. And then I had to sit down the whole week. Instead of writing a set, I had to plan in case of any eventuality. "If someone says this, what do I reply? If someone says that, what do I reply?"

**Jerry:** What could you reply to that? "Boo, get off the stage."

**Trevor:** So at one of the shows, a guy did the exact same thing. I had prepared for it now. I got onstage. I said, "I'm from South Africa." Somebody: "Boo! Get off the stage, get off the stage." And then I kept quiet. The audience went quiet. And then I said, "Are you done? Is that it?" I said, "Forgive me, where I'm from, normally when white people come at you, they come with dogs and tear gas. Is that all you have?"

**Jerry:** Oh my God, that's funny.

**Trevor:** And the whole crowd turned on him, 'cause he was heckling the whole night. So it was like, "Yeahhh!" If you beat a heckler in the UK, you become the champion. The heckler is not part of the audience—he's like the villain. If you beat him, everyone cheers for you. But if he beats you, they're going to cheer for him.

> **"I know a guy who once got airlifted off a cruise ship because they disliked him so much."**

## STEVE MARTIN

**Steve:** I remember when I was doing my stand-up act, if I got stuck I would make a total left turn. And it seemed to work for me. You know, into something else, or look like I'd lost my mind for a moment. And sometimes I would just stand there like this [*puts hands on waist*], and then laugh.

**Jerry:** But isn't that the form that you worked in? It's a series of left turns, isn't it?

**Steve:** Yeah, I think so. But that was because my act started as a variety show. There was this moment, before the act got really big but I had it in place, so whenever I worked somewhere, most people had never seen it. That's when I'd say it was the funniest I ever was. When you're doing material that is totally surprising them, and you also feel in your head really funny. You feel it.

**Jerry:** Right.

**Steve:** It's the perfect combination of material and a sense of freedom and fun. I remember some nights I would sort of stop and I'd look out at the audience like this. [*sneers*] And we'd all just think it was funny. You know, sort of arrogantly look out there. Saying nothing.

I have a love of comedians. In fact, when I did [the film] *Roxanne*, we hired all comedians to play the firemen. And we're all sitting around telling our worst comedy stories, our worst stand-up stories. And one guy, I can't remember who it was, topped us all. He was playing a 5 p.m. show at I believe it was the Hyatt Hotel in Boston. In the atrium. So already it's bad.

**Jerry:** [*laughs*] Right.

**Steve:** And there was a huge window that looked out onto the bay and a pier. The day before, a person had committed suicide by rolling off the pier in a wheelchair. And in the middle of the act there was a crane going into the water and—

| **Jerry:** | Pulling the guy out? [*laughs*] |
|---|---|
| **Steve:** | Yeah. I wish I could remember whose story that was. |
| **Jerry:** | Well, after that show you go back to the room, and you think, "Well, it wasn't that bad. I wasn't in the wheelchair." I know a guy who once got airlifted off a cruise ship because they disliked him so much. They didn't even want him on the boat. So they brought a helicopter. |
| **Steve:** | You mean, his act bombed so much— |
| **Jerry:** | So bad that they didn't want to wait for the boat to get into port, so they choppered him off. |
| **Steve:** | Well, I remember once when I was starting out—I wrote about this in the book [*Born Standing Up*], actually—I was playing a club called the Ice House. |
| **Jerry:** | I played the Ice House many times. |
| **Steve:** | And I realized about halfway through my twenty-five-minute show that I had not gotten one laugh. I thought, "Why not go for the record?" |
| **Jerry:** | Twenty-five clean? [*laughs*] |

| | |
|---|---|
| **Steve:** | The twenty-five with no laughs, which is very hard to do. |
| **Jerry:** | Silence. It is kind of hard, yeah. Because people start to laugh when you struggle, when you're suffering. They laugh when you're suffering. What kind of cars do you like? |
| **Steve:** | I had a 1967 Jaguar XKE. |
| **Jerry:** | Wow. |
| **Steve:** | It was painted yellow. It was beautiful. So, so beautiful. And then I had a car that's not really known much anymore: an MGB GT. |
| **Jerry:** | When did you have that? |
| **Steve:** | I had that about early '70s. Maybe even late '60s. It was gray, red interior. It was beautiful. Drove it around LA. That's when I was writing on television shows and I had a little money. |
| **Jerry:** | Man, what a moment. What a moment. That car. You're writing on *The Smothers Brothers*. And you've got a stand-up act that you're doing on the side? |
| **Steve:** | Yep. In fact, I remember Bob Einstein said to me once—remember I started on these shows when I was twenty-one. And the act was very unformed. He said, "You know what'll help you?" And I said, "What?" He said, "Age." And he was right. Get a little older. |
| **Jerry:** | That's funny, yeah. |
| **Steve:** | Now the people like really young comedians. But I didn't really have any success till I was about thirty. |
| **Jerry:** | Right. And that's when your hair turned gray too, right? |
| **Steve:** | It did. Well, it was turning gray from day one, really. |
| **Jerry:** | It was such a cool look. |
| **Steve:** | I never thought to dye it. Can you imagine if I had to dye my hair every week? For *The Smothers Brothers*—actually *The Glen Campbell Goodtime Hour*—I don't know how I got hired. I was a local stand-up comedian, and they wanted young people. It was all that mantra, "Don't trust anyone over thirty." I was under thirty, so I got hired. I didn't know what I was doing. I didn't know how to write a joke at all. I'd maybe written two jokes in my life. And here I was. Because you're working with a partner, you can kind of suss it out. But I feel now I've really learned how to let my imagination go to come up with a joke. You can't really know how to write a joke, but to use your imagination. At age twenty-one, I would've been panicked. Now I feel, "Oh, you need something for this? Okay." |
| **Jerry:** | Yeah. [*laughs*] |
| **Steve:** | I remember one of my first hot gigs at the Boarding House in San Francisco. And I was so broke. I had just played the Playboy Club for $1,500. And I had borrowed $5,000 to live on. I was going to earn $1,500 and I couldn't finish the week because it was so awful. And I quit. And then about a month later, I went to the Boarding House, and things started |

to break. And they gave me $4,000 in cash. And I, stupidly—there's no bad ending to this—walked home to the hotel with it. At midnight in San Francisco.

# GARRY SHANDLING

**Jerry:** When's the last time you were here, by the way?

**Garry:** It's always tough for me at the Comedy Store. There's a vibe that never changes here.

**Jerry:** Never. It's horrible. But let's deal with it. Come on.

**Garry:** Oh, this is a little uncomfortable for me. The Comedy Store. But they're great now.

**Jerry:** But, Garry, you came out from Tucson, I came out from New York, and this was the kingdom and the power. This was the place that we had heard about, that we had to come to.

**Garry:** You know there's a guy who jumped from the top of that [the building next door], right?

**Jerry:** Steve Lubetkin.

**Garry:** Yeah.

**Jerry:** Jumped from up there.

**Garry:** Yeah. Let's go up there. So, yes, I came from Tucson, Arizona. You came from New York.

**Jerry:** Yeah. And I started to work really hard. So when you look back on your life—and I say this to young people—when you look back on your life and you look at the bad things, those are the last things you trade away.

**Garry:** So I'm onstage once, I'm up at the microphone and I'm working the Comedy and Magic Club in Hermosa Beach where we go. And I'm talking and I'm working on stuff and it's going fine. And I see movement out of the corner of my eye. I see movement right over here. You know what that's like—you can sense everything.

**Jerry:** Oh, sure.

**Garry:** It's like having that radar, right?

**Jerry:** Yeah, right.

**Garry:** And I look down and a new waitress has got her tray and she's come up this way onto the stage to serve these two tables, and I'm actually standing there like this. [*arms crossed in disbelief*] I'm not mad. I just can't believe what I'm seeing. And the audience is laughing. She doesn't know what they're laughing at and she's on the stage serving. So people say, "Wow, do you get nervous when you go on TV?" They don't understand the shit we've seen.

> "When you look back on your life and you look at the bad things, those are the last things you trade away."

# SEBASTIAN MANISCALCO

**Sebastian:** You know, I waited on you at the Four Seasons Hotel [in Beverly Hills]. I was not like, "Good evening, mister." I wasn't that guy. I'm like, "What's going on? What do you need?" And you said, "Where are you from?" I said, "Chicago." And that was basically the end of our interaction, 'cause you moved out of my section and somebody else took over. But I remember that. God, it must have been about 1999, maybe 2000.

**Jerry:** Wow, that's so funny. And now here we are.

**Sebastian:** Here we are. That's crazy.

**Jerry:** Now, what were you doing at that time, stand-up-wise?

**Sebastian:** I was doing open mic nights. I used to work at the Four Seasons, and then during my break I'd go into the Comedy Store, do a set, run back.

**Jerry:** Did you have any other abilities that you could have done or might have done?

**Sebastian:** Ah, man, I don't know.

**Jerry:** What would you be doing in life?

**Sebastian:** I would like to think I would be in the hospitality business, although I had a problem with people.

**Jerry:** Yeah, that's going to be a bit of a stumbling block in the hospitality field.


# JOHN OLIVER

**John:** Jon Stewart offered me the job [on *The Daily Show*] in 2006. I came over [from England] in 2006. Pretty much straightaway I thought, "Okay, I'll do some stand-up on the weekends. I've got nothing to do. Let me fill the void." So I went to [the] Hartford, Connecticut, Funny Bone [and then the] West Virginia Funny Bone, where they're smoking inside. Two really bad strip-mall gigs. Really bad. And I loved it. So then I just started bouncing around all over the place. Just insane. There were some really nice rooms as well, like Denver Comedy Works. Great.

**Jerry:** Uh-huh. Sure.

**John:** Those are great, those are lay-ups. So I started bouncing around. I loved it. I loved doing gigs in the South just because there's so much friction in the room when you open your mouth. One of the hardest I ever bombed was there—this guy had a Speak and Spell. And he made it swear. He typed swearwords. This was his closer. Brings it onstage.

**Jerry:** There has always seemed to be a bi-level culture [in the UK] of this incredibly low-minded moronic crap and then Python, the most sophisticated.

**John:** Exactly. The greatest.

**Jerry:** The greatest.

| | |
|---|---|
| **John:** | That's why I loved Edinburgh. I used to go to the Edinburgh Festival every year because then you got an hour on your own. You live and die on your own show. You have a sitting audience, and you do it thirty times over thirty days, and you just can't help but get better at the end of that. Even if you're bad, you can't help but get better. God, that's a furnace, doing thirty days in a row. Doing an hour in front of what could be six people. |
| **Jerry:** | Six people? |
| **John:** | Yeah, I mean there's so many shows up there. I had a 100 percent walk-out in Edinburgh. Started with six people. Two leave by ten minutes in. Twenty minutes in, another two leave. I'm down to two, a couple. The guy says, "I'm going to the bathroom." All right, that's terrible boyfriend behavior on his part. So now I'm just left with the woman. She's there with her bag and I see her hand reach down into her bag [at] about twenty-five minutes. I said, "Are you leaving?" She said, "Yeah." Picks up the bag, walks out. I remember the sound of the door closing behind her. Now I'm in an empty room with a sound technician saying, "Do you want to carry on?" "No. It's over. The gig's over. Thanks so much." |

## MARGARET CHO

| | |
|---|---|
| **Margaret:** | Joan Rivers. When she was on *SNL* in 1981, that changed my life. She was hosting and she also did a set in the middle of the show. And she killed. And it was like, I knew I was going to be that. |
| **Jerry:** | So, '81, you would have been thirteen or twelve. |
| **Margaret:** | Yeah, twelve. And then two years later I started doing comedy at the Other Café with Sam Rockwell. |
| **Jerry:** | The actor? |
| **Margaret:** | Yeah. He and I would do comedy. We were like a really young Stiller and Meara. Like, I'd mix drinks standing there and we would do little comedy sketches. I don't even remember what we did. . . . I lied my way into a college comedy competition. There were winners from each region. So it's John DiMaggio, who's a very funny comic actor. He does a lot of voice-over stuff now. Jon Glaser, who's on *Delocated*—it's a TV show. He's a really funny guy. He's a writer on [*Inside*] *Amy Schumer* now. So the three of us won, and the chance was to open for you. We were sent to Daytona Beach, Florida, where you and Mario Joyner were doing a show. And then you guys both did sets. I think we went after you—or before you. I can't remember. |
| **Jerry:** | I think it was after. I remember it so well. |
| **Margaret:** | Yes. The three of us performed five-minute sets, and you guys picked John DiMaggio. And then you took me aside and you said that I had a very unique point of view and that if I chose to continue in this profession, that I would be very successful. And that was all I needed. I want to cry. |

[*laughs*] That was all I needed. But we all lied. None of us were in school. We all lied to get in. We all got to be in front of you, and I remember your set was so tremendous and so exciting. Just being there in the room with you and Mario was a dream come true. And for you to say that to me just made everything possible. And then my father went to a fortune-teller in Korea who told my parents that I would be an international star in two years. So then they forgave me. And then I was on TV. So it was all very fast, but it was all you.

**Jerry:** That's great. You know, the same thing happened to me, actually. I was doing comedy at a place called the Golden Lion Pub on Forty-Fourth and Broadway. Like, eight or ten people in the room. And Jackie Mason came over to me afterwards. I was maybe performing three months. And he said the same thing. He said, "You have a great point of view. I think you're going to be a giant star." And, you know, you're a kid. I'm twenty-one. I don't even know what I'm doing. That's very powerful when something like that happens to you.

**Margaret:** It's powerful.

## KRISTEN WIIG

**"I went to get paid and the owner said, 'I didn't even know you were on.'"**

| | |
|---|---|
| **Jerry:** | It took a while with that character? The Target lady? |
| **Kristen:** | No, no, no. That one didn't. I actually did that one at the Groundlings [in LA]. And then I did it in my [*SNL*] audition. I did two auditions. I did my audition, and then two or three months later, they asked me to come back, and I was like, "Um, I did everything I could ever do in that first one. I don't have anything else." So I came up with some impressions and just wrote stuff. And then, you know that show. You don't hear for a while. It's very ambiguous. I didn't know what was going on. I [had] met with Lorne, and everyone's like, "Oh, well, you met with Lorne. You've got the job." I was like, "Oh my gosh, this is amazing." Never heard anything in the summer, and then the season started and I was like, "Well, I'm not there." |
| **Jerry:** | What were you doing? |
| **Kristen:** | I was living here [in LA] and doing the Groundlings. |
| **Jerry:** | But there's no money. |
| **Kristen:** | I was waiting tables and things like that. I actually waited tables at Universal Studios in the executive dining room. So I see people now and I'm like, "I used to give you the . . ." It's very weird. I waited on Don Langley and all those people. I had the tie. And then it was about four shows in, and [*SNL*] called me and they were like, "Can you come next week?" I'm like, "Yes." [*laughs*] I'd never spent any time in New York. I went once when I was in eighth grade for the day. And then for the audition is the only time I'd ever been there. So I didn't know where to live. I called—I'm like, "What are the good neighborhoods?" I didn't know anything. I got there and moved my stuff out and found an apartment. I don't think I told anyone I was joining the cast. |
| **Jerry:** | Really? |
| **Kristen:** | Yeah. I came in and I was like, "Hi. This is so awkward." It was so uncomfortable. |
| **Jerry:** | When I had to do *The Tonight Show* in 1981, I'd never even worn a jacket. I'm in comedy clubs. I had never been in front of an audience of more than a hundred people. And now I'm going to be on the Johnny Carson show on national television, when everybody watched *The Tonight Show*. I'd never even worn a jacket, and now I have to walk out there like an adult. I'm twenty-six. I mean, they do these things to performers. They just throw you in. |
| **Kristen:** | Yeah, you wonder if that's even the best way to do it. |
| **Jerry:** | It is the best way. |
| **Kristen:** | Well, I didn't get *SNL* until I was thirty. |
| **Jerry:** | Really? So, wait a minute. You never had a job? Did you get any acting parts or anything? |

| Kristen: | I did pilots. I did commercials. |
|---|---|
| Jerry: | Were you making enough money to live? |
| Kristen: | Yeah, and I was waiting tables and doing a lot of odd jobs. |

## NORM MACDONALD

| Norm: | I started stand-up in Canada. [I] got to go right away with experienced co-medians across the country and do stand-up. So we all thought that's all we'd ever do. And that's all we did do. And then when I came to America, I remember the first thing, I was stunned when I went to the Improv how handsome everybody was. |
|---|---|
| Jerry: | Really? What year would that be? |
| Norm: | I think it was the year that Johnny Carson retired. |
| Jerry: | That would be '94. |
| Norm: | So my plan was to become the last comedian that Johnny Carson anointed. That was my plan. |
| Jerry: | That's a good plan. |
| Norm: | I said, "I'll go there and I'll be the last comedian to ever be anointed by Johnny." I mean, I started in the last comedy boom before this, and it was just basically [doing] stand-up at any venue. Go to a disco and do it there, you know? One time I went on and it was a dance floor, and they didn't advertise me, and they gave me a Mr. Mic. Do you know what a Mr. Mic is? |
| Jerry: | Of course. |
| Norm: | So I'm holding the speaker and the mic and talking. And then a guy comes in from the street, you know? And there's no sign they're advertising for me. So he thinks I'm a psychotic person, and he starts approaching me like, "Give me the gun." And I'm like, "No, no. I'm the performer. I'm the entertainer." When you have to tell them that you're the entertainer, that's not good. |
| Jerry: | Oh my God. I did a similar gig at a disco in Queens. |
| Norm: | At a disco, wouldn't you agree, would be the worst place, 'cause here's guys trying to get girls. Do you think they want another guy to be the center of attention? |
| Jerry: | No. |
| Norm: | No. And what happened in Queens at the disco? |
| Jerry: | Oh, I died a miserable death. I went to get paid and the owner said, "I didn't even know you were on." I said, "Nobody did." |

## CEDRIC THE ENTERTAINER

**Jerry:** Where were you in the '80s? Still in Saint Louis?

**Cedric:** Saint Louis. I graduated from high school in '82, and then I went to college at Southeast Missouri. I got out in '87. Then I worked for State Farm. I was a claims adjuster. I could've insured this car. [*laughs*] I was the worst at claims adjustment though, man, 'cause I started doing comedy at the same time I got the job. Like, literally three days after I got the job, I discovered I could do comedy. This guy, this comedian, he was working, and he would ask to borrow things I would say. He was like, "Can I say that?" I was like, "Dang, I don't know. I got a job, you know, so . . ." Then he entered my name in a comedy competition, and I went and I did it, and I won $500 the first time I did it.

**Jerry:** Wow. Well, that had to blow your mind.

**Cedric:** Yeah, he helped me shape what I should say. Which was cool. So I would do comedy at night, and I was the worst [claims adjuster], man. People would have rental cars for two, three years. People would be mad. They would want their car back. I wrote in a book that I was bilingual, 'cause I spoke regular English and angry Negro. 'Cause black people would always come in and threaten, you know? "I'll blow this building up." I'm like, "Damn black people can't get dynamite. Don't have that kind of credit. Don't worry about that guy—that is an idle threat for sure. Let me go talk to him." "What's the problem, brother?" The comedy club circuits were really big at the time, right?

**Jerry:** They were really big then, yeah.

**Cedric:** I was known. I finally decided to step down, and I took a leave of absence. Even to this day, I never really quit my job at State Farm, 'cause I wasn't sure.

**Jerry:** You're still on leave from State Farm.

**Cedric:** Yeah, I can go back at any minute.

## JERRY LEWIS

**Jerry S.:** What do you think you would have done if there was no entertainment industry available?

**Jerry L.:** I'd have held up banks.

**Jerry S.:** You played baseball in school? What position?

**Jerry L.:** First.

**Jerry S.:** Did you hit?

**Jerry L.:** Mm-hmm.

**Jerry S.:** If you could have done that as a career, do you think you would have pursued it?

| Jerry L.: | I had an impeccable eye for the ball. I could swing at it and hit it, and not have even seen it. I had that kind of timing. I was swinging when he was letting it go. |
|---|---|
| Jerry S.: | And what happened ultimately? |
| Jerry L.: | I slid into second and there was nobody there. So I ran into the bag, broke my right leg. That was that. Burt Newsome was one of the Dodgers' scouts. He got me all set up for a tryout with the Dodgers. That was over. |
| Jerry S.: | I have a great curiosity about New York in the early days, before you even met Dean [Martin]. Hanson's. What was the other place? Lindy's. Can you tell me what it was like in those places? |
| Jerry L.: | It was crowded. Everybody was thrilled to see everybody. |
| Jerry S.: | So it was just like a coffee shop but a lot of acts would hang around. |
| Jerry L.: | Yeah. And telling the other acts they got work and where and so on. It was very cannibalistic. |
| Jerry S.: | I love how comedians talk in minutes. Very few people talk in minutes, because to survive in comedy, ten minutes is very different from fifteen minutes versus five minutes. Right? |
| Jerry L.: | Of course. |
| Jerry S.: | It's all about minutes. Nobody else talks about, "How long do they want you to do? How much do you have?" |
| Jerry L.: | Exactly. "Well, you don't want what I got." "Well, what do you got?" "Three hours." "No, no, no. We need twelve minutes." |

# ALEC BALDWIN

| Alec: | You ever give any thought to what you would have done if you didn't make it? |
|---|---|
| Jerry: | It took me many, many years to figure out when you go to LA, they don't go, "This is a very interesting talent you have. We're going to devise something that fits into and produce it, and then we'll call you. We'll place you inside that machine." Or as you have often called it, "We're going to strap you into the rocket." When you were doing *The Hunt for Red October*, right? That was fascinating, the way you described it. That doesn't exist in comedy. In comedy, you want to get to the next level, you have to build the rocket. There is no rocket unless you build one. You don't understand. Stand-up comedy is an island off the coast of show business. It happens to be paradise, but you don't know that when you're young. You don't know that. You want to be on the mainland. And it ruins a lot of careers trying to get there. . . .

I'm at Catch a Rising Star in New York and I'm talking with Larry David. I say, "Hey, I had a meeting at NBC the other day about doing a TV series." He says, "What's it about?" I go, "I didn't have any ideas, but it was |

really fun. I got to go to NBC." So we go across the street to Mr. Lee's Deli, a Korean deli. And we're making fun of the products at the cash register. He goes, "This is what the show should be. Just two comedians making fun of stuff." I go, "That's a pretty good idea." So then we get together a couple more times and start figuring this out.

**Alec:** His idea was two comedians doing it.

**Jerry:** Right. George [Costanza] was a comedian in the beginning. And then we abandoned the idea. We thought, "Well, you got two acts that you want to see." How a comedian gets his material—that was the idea. Essentially that was what I went in and pitched, and they bought it, made the pilot.

**Alec:** How many years [before it took off]?

**Jerry:** Four and a half years.

**Alec:** You were waiting for David Hasselhoff to die.

**Jerry:** We were waiting for Ted Danson.

**Alec:** Waiting for Ted Danson to go.

**Jerry:** To go, "I can't do this anymore," yeah.

**Alec:** Amazing. Waiting for Ted Danson to say, "I've had enough."

**Jerry:** Yeah. And so it was dying on Wednesday nights after *Unsolved Mysteries*.

**Alec:** Robert Stack. [*laughs*]

**Jerry:** Getting my ass kicked by *Jake and the Fatman*.


# ELLEN DeGENERES

**Ellen:** I grew up listening to Steve Martin's albums and Woody Allen, and reading Woody Allen's books and Steve Martin's. I mean, I was obsessed with comedians, but I never thought I was going to be a comedian. I just appreciated them. It's such a fluke that any of this happened.

**Jerry:** So what was the hinge that it happened?

**Ellen:** Someone asked me to do something to help raise money. There was some legal thing. Some friends had to raise some money. Someone played guitar, and we were charging $15 a person to try to raise money. And someone said, "You get up onstage and be funny." I guess I was funny around people, enough that they thought I would do that.

**Jerry:** This is in Louisiana.

**Ellen:** Yeah, this is in New Orleans. And I just didn't have anything. 'Cause I'd never written. So I got up onstage, and I brought a bag of Burger King—a Whopper and fries and a shake. I started a sentence. I said, "I'm so sorry, but this is the first time I've ever been onstage, and I'm so nervous that I didn't eat all day and I realized that on the way over, so I stopped to get this. I hope you don't mind." And then I started a sentence, saying, "I don't know if you've ever noticed, but when people . . ." Then I took a bite and put my finger up. You know how people do that? Like, why start a sentence and then, you know . . . So I started the same sentence over and over, and finished the entire Whopper and fries, and then said, "Oh, I'm so sorry. That's my time."

**Jerry:** That is a funny bit.

**Ellen:** That's what I did for the first time. Someone saw me there and asked me to perform at a college. And I played, like, four chords on a piano and I said, "I wrote a song when I was in the hospital." It was just me screaming. Literally chords and me screaming. And then I had to start writing material, come up with ideas. And then the thing that changed my life, of course, is my girlfriend was killed in a car accident, and I had to move out of the place we were living together. I was sleeping on a mattress on the floor. It was a basement apartment where you couldn't even stand up, and there were fleas everywhere. And I kept thinking, "Why is this twenty-three-year-old girl that I loved just [*snap*] gone? Dead." And I just thought, "What if we could just pick up the phone and call up God and ask these questions and have a conversation?" People pray all the time, but really, wouldn't it be amazing if you could have a connection? So I literally started writing. I didn't mean for it to be funny. I just thought it would ring a long time. [Heaven is] a big place. And then finally when God answers, I'd be put on hold. And it's "Onward, Christian Soldiers." But it's not a tape. It's live.

**Jerry:** Right.

**Ellen:** And then he makes fun of my name, DeGeneres, and then he asks if I'm still doing comedy. I literally wrote it without putting my pen down. I finished it, and I was like, "Oh my God, I'm going to do this on Johnny Carson, and I'm going to be the first woman in the history of the show to be called over to sit down with Johnny Carson." And five years later, I was the first woman in the history of the show to sit down with Johnny Carson. Because of the phone call to God.

**Jerry:** Wow.

**Ellen:** I know. Crazy.

# ZACH GALIFIANAKIS

**Jerry:** Where did you do all your early work?

**Zach:** In Times Square, there was a place, I think it might still be there. It was an open mic in the back of a hamburger joint called Hamburger Harry's, where Jim Gaffigan would be.

**Jerry:** So how were you getting by money-wise?

**Zach:** When I first started out, I was a house cleaner and a nanny in New York. I would clean houses, and then three or four days of the week I would go pick up a kid at the Dalton School in the Upper East Side. And so I was a

nanny for these two boys and I was a house cleaner. I picked those because I knew I had my nights free to go bomb and do stand-up. My first paid gig was in Maysville, Kentucky. It was $100 plus driving. I remember calling my parents and [they] couldn't believe that I was getting paid. My dad still asks me if I'm getting paid for stuff.

## JOHN MULANEY

**John:**    I was so amazed to be able to write for the people on *Saturday Night Live*. And at the same time I'm doing stand-up every week and every night when I could. Then people would ask, "Don't you want to be on the show?" I was like, "Uh, no, they're better at that." Bill Hader, Fred Armisen . . . it's like I'm writing for Jimi Hendrix. I don't think I can do that at all. And I get to do what I'm good at on my own time and my own terms.

**Jerry:**    Right, right.

**John:** So it was the perfect situation. For someone who performs, I guess you could be there and be envious or want more or something. But I got to do my thing when I was onstage and I got to write for the funniest people in the world at once.

# DAVE CHAPPELLE

**Jerry:** What was your style?
**Dave:** Really laid-back. I was cutesy. I was a kid. I was probably fourteen, so I was vulnerable.
**Jerry:** Fourteen?
**Dave:** Yeah, I caught the train up to New York, tried to get the Improv. I didn't realize I was overstepping an entire comedy circuit. I just knew, "Oh, the Improv. I've seen it on television. I'll just go there."
**Jerry:** Now, what about school?

**Dave:** I used to go after school. It's funny. I went to an art school not far from here [*Washington, D.C.*] for high school. So if I had a gig—by the time I was sixteen, I was gigging—it'd be an excused absence.

**Jerry:** Wow.

**Dave:** Yeah, you know, "Listen, I've got a gig. Got to go catch an Amtrak up to Mystic." Or wherever I had to go. I'd get work that way.

**Jerry:** That's amazing that you could navigate that, the grown-ups, at sixteen.

**Dave:** When I first got out of high school, I did a bunch of really shitty tours, and that stressed me out. That was my foray into, like, "Man, this is a really adult world." My first night on the road and I'm in one of those awful motels and I hear a trucker and a prostitute fighting in the room next door. And then it gets really quiet all of a sudden. That kind of shit used to stress me out. It was back in those days when there was long-distance phone calls. You remember that? I couldn't even call home. It was crazy.

**Jerry:** They would make you run to the phone. "Come on, it's long-distance." You had to run across the living room to get on the phone.

**Dave:** Yeah. "Mom's on the phone, hurry." Every second.

# SETH ROGEN

**Jerry:** So how far down the road in stand-up did you go? Did you have a good twenty?

**Seth:** Yeah, I would headline. I would do an hour. In Vancouver, I did it from when I was thirteen to eighteen.

**Jerry:** Which is so crazy.

**Seth:** Five years, and I would perform three or four nights a week sometimes.

**Jerry:** While you're going to school.

**Seth:** Yeah, I was in high school.

**Jerry:** How could you do that? Isn't it exhausting?

**Seth:** I did not go to class that much. And I didn't graduate from high school. My mother would let me cut school if I had a show on a Tuesday night.

**Jerry:** She was encouraging.

**Seth:** A hundred percent. She came to every show I did. 'Cause I couldn't drive, so she would drive me to the shows . . . I had a joke about Krazy Glue. This stupid joke. "What's so crazy about it?" It was like that.

**Jerry:** That's funny.

**Seth:** I channeled you.

**Jerry:** Why is it so crazy?

**Seth:** It sticks to stuff really well. It's what it should do. It's the most sane glue there is.

# EDDIE MURPHY

**Jerry:** So the way I prepare for this show, I don't really do anything. I usually read the Wikipedia page---the first page. So I read yours this morning. And, you know, you don't know what's true on there. It said that you mark the beginning of your comedy career July 9, 1976.

**Eddie:** Yes.

**Jerry:** Is that true?

**Eddie:** Yes. That's the first time I got onstage.

**Jerry:** I mark mine July 4, 1976.

**Eddie:** Oh. So you've been doing it longer.

**Jerry:** [*laughs*]

**Eddie:** You've been at it longer.

**Jerry:** But obviously you were a kid.

**Eddie:** I was fifteen. The first time I heard a group of people laughing, I might have been eight or nine. We were on the bus coming from McCarren Pool in Brooklyn. And everybody that got off the bus, I was kind of doing what they sound like. And everybody on the bus was kind of laughing. And then they realized that each time they got off the bus, I was going to be doing it about them. I realized the whole bus was laughing. That's the first time it was a group. And when I got off the bus, they clapped. [*laughs*]

**Jerry:** Right. And that's a big thing when you're a kid.

**Eddie:** But I still wasn't going, "I'm going to be a comedian." I just was like, I knew I could make a group of people laugh.

**Jerry:** Did you ever do long sets at the small clubs? Or you do like just twenty or thirty?

**Eddie:** Yeah, I would do long sets. The long sets where all the new young comics get mad. "I got bumped." Have you ever been bumped?

**Jerry:** Have I? Sure.

**Eddie:** Who bumped you?

**Jerry:** Belzer.

**Eddie:** [Richard] Belzer bumped you. I got bumped by Freddie Roman.

**Jerry:** [*laughs*] Oh my God, that's funny.

**Eddie:** Freddie Roman bumped me. And Rodney [Dangerfield] bumped me. I was cool with Rodney bumping me. I was really pissed off that Freddie Roman bumped me. Motherfucking Freddie Roman.

**Jerry:** And where's the first place you remember standing onstage?

**Eddie:** At the youth center. They had a comedy show. They had a talent contest. The guy that ran the youth center, he was like, "Hey, you guys should emcee the youth center." [Me and] this other guy I used to hang out with. He said, "You guys should emcee this show. We get a lot of hecklers and stuff, and you'd be able to keep them in their place." Originally it was

> *"You get up on the stage and make people that don't even know who you are laugh. That's the moment."*

almost like a weapon. I was really good at ranking people out. Talking shit about people.

**Jerry:** That's really Long Island talk.

**Eddie:** Yeah, that's how it started out. Somebody heckles, you could rank them out. In between that, we had little impressions that we did.

**Jerry:** That was a big thing. I have not heard that phrase, I swear to God, since '68.

**Eddie:** Ranking someone out? Yeah [*laughs*]. You got ranked out.

**Jerry:** "He really ranked me out." [*laughs*] You realize your memory is amazing.

**Eddie:** You have a good memory.

**Jerry:** That's little details. You remember the name of the Chinese restaurant gig we did in Jersey.

**Eddie:** The Jade Fountain.

**Jerry:** That's crazy.

**Eddie:** The Jade Fountain. You don't remember that place? The owner would say, "Hey, let me put your picture up here. Give you exposure. Let me get all your pictures, you get exposure."

**Jerry:**   You get up on the stage and make people that don't even know who you are laugh. That's the moment. . . . Catch—that was the place. And I have talked about this—I imagine you have also—what that place seemed to be to us when we're kids.

**Eddie:**   Oh yeah.

**Jerry:**   That place had glamour. It had show-business twinkle.

**Eddie:**   Freddie Prinze and all those guys that came out of that club, so it kind of felt like . . .

**Jerry:**   Yeah, yeah. Rodney and [David] Brenner, that's where they went.

**Eddie:**   Yeah. You really felt like you could get discovered there.

**Jerry:**   It really had that.

**Eddie:**   But what is it you said? [Comic Strip Live founder Richie] Tienken said, "You guys are worthless," or some shit? 'Cause he said a similar thing to me.

**Jerry:**   Really?

**Eddie:**   Yeah.

| | |
|---|---|
| **Jerry:** | Here's the verbatim. I said, "All we're asking for is five dollars." We wanted five dollars a set. We were getting nothing. |
| **Eddie:** | Nothing. |
| **Jerry:** | It was a little bar-restaurant place. And I said, "All we're asking for is five dollars." And Tienken said to my face [*laughs*], "You're not worth five dollars." |
| **Eddie:** | "You're not worth five dollars." |
| **Jerry:** | I could've tattooed that on my eyelids, that's how mad I was. But those things, don't you agree, Eddie, and answer me this: those little things that people did to us in the day. That pushes you. |
| **Eddie:** | Yeah. What'd he say to me? He was managing me at the time, and I was like, "You guys have to take a cut in your percentages. You have to go from fifteen to ten." And it was like, "The way I see it, I got fifteen percent of nothing." That's what he said. |
| **Jerry:** | You were crazy, by the way, to work with them. But what did you know? |
| **Eddie:** | What did I know? *Saturday Night Live* makes so many funny people. So many funny people come off that show because the environment is . . . You hosted this show, right? |
| **Jerry:** | Yeah. |
| **Eddie:** | It's not a fun environment. |
| **Jerry:** | Right. |
| **Eddie:** | It's a high-pressure environment. And that makes . . . |
| **Jerry:** | Competitive. |
| **Eddie:** | Super competitive. Just knowing that you can get fired at any moment, and there's a line of people that are qualified to do what you're doing. That pressure makes you better. Just imagine every day you went to the job, you could get fired any second if you don't fucking live up. You're going to fucking do it the best you can every day. . . . I did a jazz club—the worst I ever did, ever—out in Queens. Gerald's. There was no dressing room. So I bombed, then afterwards had to go sit in the room with the people I just bombed with. [*laughs*] You sitting there, people were walking by going, "Oh, shit." I'm, like, seventeen. |
| **Jerry:** | [*laughs*] |
| **Eddie:** | So the band plays, and then they said, "Okay, we're going to bring that comedian back." And you would literally hear people go, "Oh, shit." So I go back up, and that was the worst ever. And I actually started doing everybody's bits, all the comics. I was like, "They're never going to see this. Who had some bit about Carvel?" I did one of Bob Woods's bits. All the stuff that didn't work. And then afterwards I go up to Gerald—he's a grown man too, was really mean to be like this to me—I was like, "Yeah, I was supposed to get, uh, fifty dollars for tonight." And he turned around and said, "You better get the fuck out of here." |
| **Jerry:** | [*laughs*] |

**Eddie:** Then my father had to drive out to Queens at two in the morning and drive me back. "Oh, you a comedian, huh? You going to get you a job and you going to get out at nine in the morning and you come back after five. Comedian, my ass. Don't you say a fucking word." [*laughs*]

# JAMIE FOXX

**Jerry:** You only hang out with funny people.

**Jamie:** Yeah, yeah, yeah.

**Jerry:** If someone doesn't have anything, I'm not hanging with you.

**Jamie:** Right, right. [*laughs*]

**Jerry:** But you don't know that you have this other thing. The other thing is the gunfighter thing.

**Jamie:** What is that?

**Jerry:** Well, look. You know, a lot of guys and women when you were a kid, they were all funny. They're all good. But when you put that big, hot light on it . . .

**Jamie:** Oh, that thing goes away.

**Jerry:** Something changes. Now, you don't know if you have that when you're a kid. Until you step up there, right?

**Jamie:** Right, right.

**Jerry:** When you can stand there and stare into that blackness and not shrivel and go, "I got something for you." I didn't know if I could do that. I didn't know until I stood up there.

**Jamie:** When did you know? When was that?

**Jerry:** First time I got up there.

**Jamie:** First time.

**Jerry:** First time.

**Jamie:** That's when you know. So when you get up there the first time, what was the angst?

**Jerry:** Terrible. Terrified. Terror. It was just terror. Absolute terror. I think, "These people, they're not my friends. They don't even know me."

**Jamie:** "How could I make them laugh?" Making someone laugh when you're young, it's based on how you know that person.

**Jerry:** That's how you made them laugh. "I know what makes this guy laugh." And you play to that thing, right? You learn your audience. But now, here's thirty total strangers and they're older than you. They're grown-ups. I'm twenty. How old were you when you stepped up there?

**Jamie:** I had to be eighteen. The Comedy Store in San Diego. I went to college [on a classical piano scholarship] at California International University. I went and got a little job playing at the Elephant Bar for maybe one or two nights. And then right across the way was the Comedy Store. I said,

"Well, I need to get at it." 'Cause there's girls in there. [*laughs*] . . . I had to maneuver away from [Chris] Rock. I had to maneuver from those types of guys to get into the "How y'all feel out there tonight?" I'm in the hood. I'm feeding off the energy. And that bothers me. Even to this day. 'Cause I'm getting ready to do my new stand-up . . . and I've done the showy, the energy. Now I got to stand flat-footed and now box southpaw. Because people are watching and listening for the content. And so that's when I look at Rock, I look at you. . . .

**Jerry:** What's that got to do with anything?

**Jamie:** Because it's going to be the difference. It's going to be the difference in people watching what I do and saying, "There's been growth." Or watching and saying, "Oh, he relied on . . ."

**Jerry:** Eh, I'm not for that. Whatever you feel, that's what I want to see. If you like it, I like it. And if you love it, I love it. I'm with you.

**Jamie:** Yeah. But do you understand what I mean?

**Jerry:** Of course I understand. Every word. So I'm twenty-two years old. I'm walking on the west side of Columbus Circle. I'm doing comedy. For real. Every night about a year. This black dude stops me. Columbus Circle. "Saw your set the other night." I'm going on 2 a.m. to 4 a.m. That's the only time I can get on.

**Jamie:** Wow.

**Jerry:** Right? Black dude stops me. He starts talking to me: "I saw this bit. I like what you were doing." "Oh, thank you very . . ." You know, at that age you remember every person who responds to you. Twenty-five years later. I'm in LA. I get invited to this restaurant. Private thing. Denzel [Washington]'s there and he's like, "Oh, I love this guy." I meet him, shake his hand. I go, "Thrilled to meet you. I'm a huge fan of your stuff." He goes, "We've met." I go, "Where?" He goes, "Columbus Circle. You remember?" I go, "Oh my God, that was you?"

**Jamie:** What? How great is that, man?

**Jerry:** Isn't that great?

**Jamie:** That's incredible.

# RELATIONSHIPS

## LARRY DAVID

**Jerry:**  How's the social life? Good? Very good? Excellent? Average?

**Larry:**  I'm still seeing—

**Jerry:**  Still with?

**Larry:**  Yes, still with.

**Jerry:**  Wow, nice. And what's the frequency?

**Larry:**  Twice a week.

**Jerry:**  God bless that. I know I don't have to tell you anything, 'cause I know you know everything there is to know. But God bless the twice-a-week man. [*laughs*]

**Larry:**  Twice a week. But text daily.

**Jerry:**  And now you're like a guy trying to hold smoke in your hands—trying to keep the smoke from filling the room.

**Larry:**  Well put. [*laughs*]

## SARAH SILVERMAN

**Jerry:**   A lot of times in marriage, people think they have to do what's right. And that's wrong. You don't do what's right. You do what makes the other person feel good.

**Sarah:**   You be each other's cheerleaders.

**Jerry:**   Yes. And the first step to that is lying.

## DON RICKLES

**Don:**   We have such a good time, and it's the wives. If you like the guy and she don't like the woman, it's over. Am I right?

**Jerry:**   That's it.

**Don:**   I can say, "This guy's great, Barbara." Barbara will say, "You're not going to see him again." I exaggerate Barbara. You know how she talks. "Just don't get excited, you're not going to see him."

**Jerry:**   You do her like a gay man. She never said to you, "Why you got to say these things about me for?"

**Don:**   No, because I never say anything mean or hurtful. Never. I exaggerate. It's an exaggeration. Like in Europe, and this is the truth. In those days we used to go all the time. We used to go into Harrods and she'd say, "I'll get these gloves. And listen, I'll have that skirt. Oh yeah, and that jacket. Oh yes, and give me that scarf." And I'd say, "Oh boy, this is a beautiful tie." "You don't need that."

**Jerry:**   I picked my wife up in front of a department store one time and she had four shopping bags. The first thing she said is, "You're not going to believe how much money I just saved."

**Don:**   Oh, Jesus Christ, that's funny.

## CHRIS ROCK

**Chris:**   You can only have one girlfriend. It's like, "Ooh, I'm dating Beyoncé and Alicia Keys." No, you're not. You're going to date one of them or you're going to lose both of them. Or they're going to kick you out. As my brother would say, "Pick a bitch." I remember years ago, I was hanging out with Prince in Minneapolis. He was like, "Ah man, I got to go make that call." [*laughs*] Prince, calling his wife. "Yeah, okay. Yeah, yeah . . ." He made the most routine call to his wife you could ever think. I was right there.

> "You don't do what's right. You do what makes the other person feel good."

> ## "Soon as you get married, top goes up, windows go up, the air conditioning comes on, motorcyle is sold."

## JAY LENO

**Jay:** I always meet guys who when they're single, the wife loves riding on the motorcycle and loves the sports car. Oh, she loves having the wind through her hair. Soon as you get married, top goes up, windows go up, the air conditioning comes on, motorcycle is sold. That does it.

My trainer, the guy I work out with, said, "I'm getting married." I go, "Oh, really?" He'd bought this black couch and black leather chair. I said, "Does your wife like that black couch and black leather chair?" "She loves it. She comes to my apartment, she thinks it's so masculine. She loves it." Gets married. Month later I get a phone call: "Jay, you want the couch?" "Why you getting rid of it? I thought your wife liked it?" "Nah, she doesn't like the black leather couch with the black leather chair in her living room." "I'm stunned!"

**Jerry:** That's funny.

## GAD ELMALEH

**Gad:** I met your wife, and you never met my girlfriend. She's very supportive. And she wants to meet you.

**Jerry:** I'm looking forward to meeting her.

**Gad:** This is something I'm a little bit afraid of.

**Jerry:** Why? What could go wrong?

**Gad:** Because . . .

**Jerry:** Because you're afraid I'll say something nice and then—

**Gad:** [*laughs*] "Hey, you look beautiful. But what's with the shoes?"

**Jerry:** No, I won't do that. I won't.

## HOWARD STERN

**Howard:** Today's my anniversary. We went out for dinner last night.

**Jerry:** Oh, really?

**Howard:** Yes, five years.

**Jerry:** Happy anniversary. I always say that a wedding anniversary should be for just the man. Because if the relationship works, the man did the work. The cake should say "Happy Anniversary, Howard."

## BILL BURR

**Jerry:** If I could give you three words of marriage advice? I'm married fourteen years.

**Bill:** All right.

**Jerry:** Never stop apologizing.

## ALI WENTWORTH

**Jerry:** I'll tell you what, your husband [George Stephanopoulos] has got one of the greatest husband lines I've ever heard, and I'm going to do it for you now. I said to him, "So you've moved into this place now on Seventy-Second. Are you happy there?" And he says, "I hope we are." [*laughs*]

**Ali:** [*laughs*] I love that.

**Jerry:** Of course, the point being he has no idea. He'll be informed if he's happy or not.

Here's the level I'm on, okay. And please don't take this as bragging in any way. I have absolutely no interest in being right. Zero. I used to care. I used to have feelings. Those feelings got in my way. I got rid of those feelings. I don't need them. I know I'm a little android. I know that. That's one of my gifts. I'm now using it for the forces of good, not evil.

## JULIA LOUIS-DREYFUS

**Jerry:** Marriage just cracks me up. It just cracks me up.

**Julia:** You had always said you would never get married.

**Jerry:** I still feel that way. [*laughs*]

**Julia:** How long have you been married now?

**Jerry:** Fifteen years.

| **Julia:** | Really? |
|---|---|
| **Jerry:** | Together seventeen years. |
| **Julia:** | Very good. |
| **Jerry:** | Thank you. I grew up. And she really did the work, unfortunately. That was a grimy job. |
| **Julia:** | Yeah, somebody had to do it, I guess. |
| **Jerry:** | That was a Roto-Rooter job. Thigh-high boots, a lot of long tools, a lot of messy gloves, and a lot of lye. |
| **Julia:** | Disinfectant. |
| **Jerry:** | Yeah. A lot of hazmat bags. "Just take this outta here. This has all got to go." |

# SEBASTIAN MANISCALCO

| **Jerry:** | How do you do socially when your wife says, "We're going to go out with this couple?" Break that down for me. This is my favorite thing: comedians attempting to function as normal people. Disguised as a normal person. |
|---|---|

**Sebastian:** I have problems with it. I have problems connecting sometimes with people I don't know. I don't know if it's because, like you say, what we do is a lot of one-sidedness. I mean, we're talking to people for an hour and a half or an hour and fifteen minutes a night. It's a one-sided deal. No one's talking back to us. When we sit down and start having a conversation with people, I, for whatever the reason, tend to retreat. I'm not saying every experience is like this. I'm just saying that some of the times when I have to go and be around a lot of people, that's not my most comfortable place to be.

**Jerry:** Did she know before you got married that this is what she was signing up for?

**Sebastian:** She did, but I don't know if she knew the extent.

**Jerry:** Well, women do this for men in general. Women socialize men. We're kind of beastly. We're just about work, survive, earn, survive, eat, survive, some sports, eat, work.

## WILL FERRELL

**Jerry:** Your wife is Swedish.

**Will:** Right. So that's kind of the big thing.

**Jerry:** Do you remember that I am the one who told you to just get married?

**Will:** Just get married, yeah. I followed your advice.

**Jerry:** And we didn't even know each other.

**Will:** No. And you just said it. You could've ruined my life.

**Jerry:** Yeah. I could've said, "Just go to a whorehouse."

**Will:** But it's been the best decision.

**Jerry:** I was right.

**Will:** What if one of my kids goes on to win the Nobel Peace Prize? He'll have to thank Jerry Seinfeld in his speech, because he wouldn't have been there without you.

## JIM GAFFIGAN

**Jim:** Whenever a comedian, male or female, is getting married, every other comedian is like, "Really?" It could be a thirty-year-old guy or fifty-year-old woman. We're just like, "Really? So you got one of those mortals tricked?"

**Jerry:** That a comedian can spend ten minutes with anyone in a relationship is a miracle. I also have many friends who have never married or had kids. And it's like watching one of those trees that grows back into the cement.

**Jim:**     [*laughs*]

**Jerry:**   It's still growing, but it's a horrible thing to watch.


## JOHN OLIVER

**John:**    There's nothing that makes me happier than this. Nothing.

**Jerry:**   Isn't it weird?

**John:**    I'm telling you, I'm at a ten. This is as comfortable as I get. You've seen me in ways that my loved ones don't see me.


## NORM MACDONALD

**Jerry:**   You've got kind of a jaunty Bob Hope walk there.

**Norm:**    I remember Barbara Walters's [interview with him]. You know, Baba. And Barbara Walters says, "I did research on you. You grew up in England. You had ten siblings and three of them died before they were ten years old. And you were dead broke. You had a cold-water flat and you had to go to work when you were a child to support your family." He goes, "Isn't that wild?" He had, like, no emotions. And then she goes, "You had one of the longest marriages in Hollywood with Dolores." And he's getting nervous. Now he's got the golf club, just hitting it against the floor, you know?

**Jerry:**   [*laughs*] Yeah.

**Norm:**    She goes, "What's the secret to your marriage?" And he goes, "Well, you know, we've got the dogs."

**Jerry:**   [*laughs*] Oh my God. That's hilarious. "We've got the dogs."


## LEWIS BLACK

**Lewis:**   We're sitting around, maybe seven years ago or something. We're at breakfast at the Mirage sitting around a big round table. I turn to my mother and I asked the question I never really asked. I said, "Whose idea was it to have children?" And my mother points to my father sitting next to her and goes, "It was his idea. If it was up to me, there wouldn't have been any children." And then she goes, "You know, maybe that's not something you should say to your son." [*laughs*]


> "Whenever a comedian, male or female, is getting married, every other comedian is like, 'Really?'"

## BARRY MARDER

**Jerry:**    At some point in the relationship you have to reveal to the person, "By the way . . ." Showering, swimming—at some point, the truth about a toupee comes out, no?

**Barry:**    Well, *she* may have to reveal something to you. When I was married to Laura, my fourth wife and finally some happiness, I pulled out a clump of her hair. She was a gorgeous girl. She still is. And I thought, "What is this?" Wondering what the heck's going on here.

**Jerry:**    Your hand was in her hair. Perhaps you were having an intimate moment. And a clump of hair came out of her head.


## SETH ROGEN

**Seth:**    Do you like your kids?

**Jerry:**    What?

**Seth:**    I'm always looking for someone to admit they regret having children. I'm married. I'm married forever. I mean, I've been with my wife for thirteen years.

**Jerry:**    Okay. So . . .

**Seth:**    We don't have kids.

**Jerry:**    You are in the parking lot at Disneyland.

# TV & MOVIES

## "The BBC just sounds more intellectual."

### LARRY DAVID

**Larry:** I go to these premieres and I love the movie and I think it's wonderful. The audience loves it. And then I read the reviews and they're terrible. The movie does no business. And it's gone in two weeks. There's something going on at that premiere. And that's affecting the way you view the movie.

**Jerry:** Right. You think you feel people's desire for it to be good.

**Larry:** I think so. Yeah.

### RICKY GERVAIS

**Jerry:** The BBC just sounds more intellectual.

**Ricky:** There was a guy that took over in the '30s in the BBC, and there was a press conference. And when journalists said, "So you're going to give the people what they want?" he said, "Lord, no, I'm going to give them something much better." Isn't that wonderful?

**Jerry:** [*laughs*] That's great.

## ALEC BALDWIN

**Alec:** My favorite Burt Lancaster story. When they went to Burt Lancaster's trailer on the movie *Tough Guys* with Kirk Douglas, and they had a stack of glossies of the two of them to sign. The kid knocks on the door and Burt says, "Come in." And they come in with a big marker, and Lancaster's going to sign it, but he goes, "Never mind. I've got my own pen." He takes out a big thick Sharpie and signs "Burt Lancaster" on the picture. He signs a stack of 'em, and they leave. They go to Kirk Douglas's trailer. They knock on the door. He says, "Come in." They open the door and come in with a stack, they hand him the marker, and he goes, "Can't you give me the pen that he had?" And they go back to Burt Lancaster's trailer and knock on the door, and Burt comes with the pen and goes, "I suppose you're looking for this."

**Jerry:** [*laughs*] Rip Torn did a part in *Bee Movie* with me. I love that guy.

**Alec:** I can't believe you just said that, 'cause he's doing [*30 Rock*] with me and I go, "Where do you live?" And he goes, "I live up there in Salisbury." I said, "What's it like up there where you live?" And he said, "Oh, I've got my house, I've been up there for a lot of years with Aimee, and we've got a little theater, a little children's theater. In the summer, we do readings and things." I said, "What's the town like? What are the people like?" And he literally said to me, "Well, some of the people up there are a little strange. One time I was in a bar up there and these two guys at the bar gave me the eye, see? And I knew something was going to go down. I start to go out the door, go to the car, and the one guy makes a move on me, so I crack him in the jaw, then that guy smashed me with a bottle in the face. I kicked the other guy in the balls, I stick a fork in . . ."

**Jerry:** [*laughs*]

**Alec:** You know, he's describing this sleepy little bar, a little shop in Salisbury, Connecticut. And these three guys are pounding the shit out of each other at, like, six o'clock in the afternoon somewhere with children around flying kites and feeding the ducks down the park, and they are hammering each other like it's a Tarantino movie. And I look at him and I go, "When did this happen?" He went, "Last summer."

**Jerry:** [*laughs*]

**Alec:** He's, like, seventy-four.

## "When I was a kid, I really just thought God made the movies."

## JOEL HODGSON

**Jerry:** Yeah. Why are movies so much more fun to make fun of than television? Is it because the moviemakers are so self-important? They're fun to poke at?

**Joel:** They're trying so hard to blow your mind. TV is a lot different. It's a lot more subdued, and weekly. You know, we need to keep the ball in the air for twenty minutes.

**Jerry:** It's like a newspaper. It's not going to be perfect, but you'll get it every day.

**Joel:** Yeah. When I was a kid, I really just thought God made the movies. Like, that's how you got them. Who makes them? What is it? Why is this happening? And I really think that for a time in our history, people really behaved like that. Like, *It's a Mad, Mad, Mad, Mad World.* Who else could make that?

## CARL REINER AND MEL BROOKS

**Jerry:** Can we go back to *Get Smart*? Because that was another show that changed my life.

**Carl:** He just played it here last night. Because he did a thing about *Get Smart*.

**Mel:** Oh, I'm doing a box set of it.

**Jerry:** Oh, really?

**Carl:** We played a piece of it yesterday. The pilot we played yesterday for—

**Mel:** I got Buck Henry to come over.

**Carl:** Buck Henry was here yesterday sitting there.

**Mel:** And he's such a sweet guy. And he had problems. He doesn't get around. But now he's okay. So we watched the pilot. I said, "Buck, just for my box set, do me a favor. Let's watch the pilot again, see what we can remember and talk about it." But he was better than I was. Because I don't remember. I ascribed some jokes to him, some to me. And I was all wrong. He knew exactly. He said, "I came up with the Cone of Silence."

**Jerry:** Really?

**Mel:** "You came up with a shoe phone." "Oh, all right."

**Carl:** I remember so well when he started that, Buck Henry. They were trying to figure out what kind of credits they're going to get. Mel Brooks created it, right? Written by Mel Brooks. And they couldn't figure out how to—could have been just the two names.

**Mel:** My agent really screwed it up. They did the credits. And I said, "I'll leave it to you." And they did a terrible thing. They said, "Written by Mel Brooks," because I was more famous. They came up with this foolish "with Buck Henry."

| | |
|---|---|
| **Jerry:** | But what does that mean? |
| **Mel:** | I don't know. You tell me what it means. If they put the two names together, it'd be equal. "Mel Brooks and Buck Henry." Equal. "Mel Brooks with Buck Henry . . ." Okay. He said, "I was very angry till you came in the room one day and you said, 'I think the billing should really be '"Mel Brooks or Buck Henry."'" [*laughs*] He said, "That 'or' . . . I loved you again." |
| **Jerry:** | Mel, what happened when *The Producers* was first released? Because I saw it in the theater. I loved it. That was '67? |
| **Mel:** | Actually, it did open in one theater, I think in Philadelphia, in '67. It was a disaster. It wasn't reviewed or anything. |
| **Jerry:** | Nobody cared? |
| **Mel:** | But it really opened in '68. At the Fine Arts Theatre on Fifty-Eighth Street. And there were lines. I don't know how there were no reviews. There were no pre-talk or pre-sales. Somehow there was word of mouth. And maybe two people have seen the picture and they liked it. And Peter Sellers nearly ruined me, but he wrote a review of it, something about— |
| **Jerry:** | The actor? |
| **Mel:** | Yeah, the actor. He said, "This is the greatest comedy ever made." And the critics said, "Well, we'll be the judge of that." But he didn't really help me. |
| **Jerry:** | Why not? What do you want him to say? |
| **Mel:** | I didn't want him to say anything. I wanted him to be quiet, you know? And don't make trouble for me with the critics. Don't say anything. So anyway, it opened in '68. And Renata Adler of the *New York Times* didn't like it. She didn't like it at all. So I was crushed. I thought, "I got a hit show with *Get Smart*. I'll go back to television," you know? And then Gene Shalit, a week later, in *Look* magazine: "No one will be seated for the last eighty-eight minutes of the running of *The Producers*. They'll all be on the floor laughing their heads off." He made it a hit. |
| **Carl:** | Golly, I remember that. |
| **Mel:** | Gene Wilder was brave. |
| **Jerry:** | They were an amazing chemistry [Wilder and Zero Mostel]. I mean, did you have them audition together? Did you see what they were like together? |
| **Mel:** | No audition. I knew. |
| **Jerry:** | You knew? |
| **Mel:** | I'm telling you something nobody knows. Dustin Hoffman was going to play Franz Liebkind, the German playwright. Signed, going to do it. We lived on Eleventh Street, Anne [Bancroft] and I. Dustin lived up the block. And he said to me, "Mike Nichols called me." He had worked for Mike on an Off-Broadway play. He said, "Mike wants me to audition opposite Anne." I knew the script, you know, for *The Graduate*. "I don't know. I'm signed with you to do—" I said, "Go. Go on the audition. You're a mutt. |

Movies? You're one of the weirdest-looking creatures." I said that to him. [*laughs*] I said, "I'm not worried. You're Franz Liebkind." He was a great Franz Liebkind. He had a German accent and the helmet was a little big, you know? He just was wonderful. But I took a good bounce. I mean, he got the job. He called me. And he said, "They want me to—" I couldn't believe it.

**Jerry:** The thing I read that you said—and don't get the impression that I prepared for any of this. This is really just stuff that I know. I think this must have been around the time when *The Producers* came out, the play [in 2001], is that you thought that there was a profound revenge for Hitler's crimes in making fun of him, that in a way surpasses everything. Because there's no revenge.

**Mel:** There's no revenge.

**Jerry:** There's no revenge, but if there is any satisfaction . . . I thought about that. And I think it's a brilliant thought.

**Carl:** Absolutely. Because if Hitler knew he was being laughed at, he would have died. He would have died.

**Mel:** There's no way to match him tirade for tirade. He's going to beat you. You've got to find another way to defeat him. . . . The movies were most fun till I got back to Broadway. And Broadway was absolutely—I can't say fun. It's absolutely thrilling. It's absolutely thrilling.

**Jerry:** Because of the live audience?

**Mel:** Because of the live. There's really nothing like that. You take a big chance. And when you're rewarded with a big response, things are emotionally, mathematically balanced and you're in heaven.

**Jerry:** Well, I would say this, though. To me, when you take a big chance is when you bring a posse of cowboys onto a soundstage, where a huge orchestra is getting ready to play [in *Blazing Saddles*]. And that set—I saw that a few weeks ago. And then I thought, "The balls on this guy. That was some balls to put all that together." And I'm just imagining all the people around. "Are you sure he knows what he's doing?" "He thinks it's funny. Let's do it." And it was funny. When I think of taking a chance, that to me is really risky.

**Mel:** Billy Wilder said, "The reason I'm having lunch with you now is because you had a hundred cowboys break through a set at Warner Brothers, where gay dancers—I've been around. I've never seen anything like that."

**Jerry:** Were you absolutely sure that this was going to work?

**Mel:** No.

**Jerry:** No?

**Mel:** Whenever I lecture or teach, I say, "It's got to please you. You're the only audience. If it pleases you, it will please them. If you don't laugh, they're not going to laugh. If you don't cry, they're not going to cry." I knew it tickled. I even wrote a line where one of the gay dancers says to a rough

> "If it pleases you, it will please them. If you don't laugh, they're not going to laugh."

cowboy after he fights with him, he cries and the cowboy pets him. And the cowboy takes him and they're walking. And the guy was just, "I'm parked just behind the commissary." I mean, I even memorialize it in a line, you know?

# SARAH SILVERMAN

**Jerry:**    Here's another one of my theories of television, sitcoms, or even this show, is you have to give the audience a vision of utopia. My TV series was a kind of utopia, right? Nobody had to be at work. They always had time for sexual adventures. You hang out with your friends. There's always something interesting going on. Don't you think every successful sitcom presents a kind of utopia, right? Give me—what's your favorite sitcom?

**Sarah:**    God, *Taxi* maybe? *Mary Tyler Moore*?

**Jerry:**    Okay, you've got a shitty job, but there are all these people, they all hang out.

**Sarah:**    Yeah, you're with your friends all day.

**Jerry:**    It's fun. My favorite is probably *Mary Tyler Moore*.

**Sarah:**    Yeah, I love *Mary Tyler Moore*.

**Jerry:**    No show ever had two equally funny universes: home and work. Whichever place you were at, you knew this was going to be great.

        Here's what *Real Housewives* is. Allow me. Have you noticed—I'm sure you haven't because there'd be no reason for this ever to cross your mind—the popularity of mixed martial arts fighting, ultimate fighting, and the *Real Housewives*: these two things are two weights on the same barbell. What it is, I think, is the worst aspects of my gender exaggerated to the maximum.

**Sarah:**    Amazing.

**Jerry:**    We want a hideous spectacle you can't look away from.

**Sarah:**    Well, they're just willing to—I feel like there should be a warning in front of it. Like there's a warning in front of *Walking Dead*. There should be a warning in front of *Real Housewives* that says, "This is not acceptable behavior." Young girls watch this, and these are—I've been working on a thing in my act that's like, "Dear women of a certain age: Your drastic and heartbreaking attempts to look younger are the reason your daughter doesn't dream about her future."

        You did do a guest thing on a sitcom in that prime—*Golden Girls* or . . .

**Jerry:**    I did *Benson*.

**Sarah:**    You were in *Benson*.

**Jerry:**    I was in *Benson* three times, as a joke writer. And then they fired me. And that made my career.

| Sarah: | Really? |
|---|---|
| Jerry: | Because that was when I realized, "These people have power over me." But if I really get my act together and really become a strong stand-up, then they wouldn't have power over me. And after that happened, that's when I got down to business. |

## DON RICKLES

| Jerry: | What was it like playing the Copacabana in those days? Tell me what the best part was. |
|---|---|
| Don: | Well, the tables were right on top of you. While you talk, the guy's steak juice was getting on your tuxedo. That's how close the tables were. But it was exciting. Everybody that was important came. Really. Good guys. And some pains too. And a lot of the wiseguys in those days. But they were great. They really were. Jesus, they really were. |
| Jerry: | Do you think that Scorsese captured it well in *Goodfellas*? |
| Don: | Well, you know, I thought that was tremendous, tremendous. When I was in *Casino*, I said, "Gee, Marty, why am I in this?" He said, "I wrote you in." I said, "Why?" He said, "Because your image, believe me, Don, even when you're standing next to Bob [De Niro], your image is there, helps the scene of those days." That's what he said. You know what I did, my opening line, this is God's truth, Jerry. With the lights and Scorsese and everything, and the first thing is walking down the hall in the Riviera, and they go, "Rolling!" and I'm supposed to be his bodyguard, whatever the hell I was, and he goes, "[*mumbles*] and Charlie will take [*mumbles*]" and I say, "Hold it! Hold it!" And I said, "Marty, I can't work with this man. No, no. Man's mumbling and spitting up all over, I don't need this, Marty. I can get some money here in Vegas. I'm walking." The crew was on the floor because they said, "Don't say nothing. Bob don't like to be kidded." But by the second day we're having vodka in the dressing room every night. "To It'ly," boom, you know. |

## JAY LENO

| Jerry: | Did you see *Gravity*? |
|---|---|
| Jay: | I did see *Gravity*. I thought it was fantastic. I thought it was great. And I love the people nitpicking it. "Well, you know, the debris is coming the wrong direction." Hey, how 'bout this: the astronauts are Sandra Bullock and George Clooney! How 'bout that, huh? How 'bout that for phony? You ever think about that? I mean, it's so stupid. Really, you're upset because the debris is coming the other way? |
| Jerry: | They're not astronauts! They live in Beverly Hills! They're pretending! |

## EDDIE MURPHY

**Eddie:**  Did you like *Titanic*?

**Jerry:**  Yeah, sure.

**Eddie:**  That's *Gravity*. It's the same movie.

**Jerry:**  It is the same movie.

**Eddie:**  It's the same movie. Like *Planet of the Apes*. Did you like *The Wizard of Oz*?

**Jerry:**  Oh, love *The Wizard of Oz*.

**Eddie:**  *Planet of the Apes* is *The Wizard of Oz*.

**Jerry:**  It is?

**Eddie:**  Think about it. The movie starts off, she wants to go over the rainbow.

**Jerry:**  Right.

**Eddie:**  And Charlton Heston: "There's got to be something better than man." She gets hit on the head and goes to sleep. He takes his shot, he goes to sleep. They wake up in this strange place. She meets Munchkins, he meets monkeys. And at the end, you were home all the time. "God damn you all to hell!" "There's no place like home. There's no place like home." Same movie.

**Jerry:**  Wow.

**Eddie:**  And I was such an *Ape* maniac that I remember when the last whipping I got was, they had "Go Ape for a Day" in Hempstead, Long Island. They're going to show all five *Ape* movies back-to-back. I went by myself in the morning, and I watched all those movies twice.

**Jerry:**  [*laughs*] Wow.

**Eddie:**  Twice. I sat there for ten *Ape* movies, and when I got out, it was dark. And I went home, and my mother gave me my last whipping because I went on some *Ape* movie marathon.

**Jerry:**  "Go Ape for a Day." Is that what they called it?

**Eddie:**  "Go Ape for a Day." I remember riding out to Roosevelt Field.

**Jerry:**  So there was *Escape*, there was *Beneath*—

**Eddie:**  *Beneath* was first.

**Jerry:**  *Beneath* was the second one?

**Eddie:**  *Beneath* is before *Escape*. The first is *Planet of the Apes*. Then it's *Beneath*.

**Jerry:**  Right. *Planet*. *Beneath*. Then it's *Escape*.

**Eddie:**  Then it's *Escape*. Then it's *Conquest*. Then it's *Battle*.

**Jerry:**  Then it's what?

**Eddie:**  *Battle for the Planet*.

**Jerry:**  But you know, chimps have done such horrible stuff since then. I'm sure they were doing it back then also, but we didn't know about—

**Eddie:**  Chimps?

**Jerry:**  Chimps ripping people's faces off.

| | |
|---|---|
| **Eddie:** | Oh yeah, yeah. |
| **Jerry:** | I think when we were kids, apes were so cool, because they looked like us but they had these other, you know— |
| **Eddie:** | We didn't know they was ripping people's faces. |
| **Jerry:** | No, we didn't know about that. |
| **Eddie:** | Curious George. |
| **Jerry:** | Right. |
| **Eddie:** | Get Curious George attacking somebody. |
| **Jerry:** | Yeah, we didn't know he was curious about what your head looked like without a face. |
| **Eddie:** | [*laughs*] |
| **Jerry:** | "I'm just curious." "Ah!" |

# TODD BARRY

| | |
|---|---|
| **Jerry:** | Did you see *Captain Phillips*? |
| **Todd:** | No, I didn't. |
| **Jerry:** | It's good. The best part about *Captain Phillips* is he goes through this Somali hijacking, this very bad experience. And they beat him up and it's just the worst possible experience you can have. And then he's saved in the end, and a year later he's back out doing the same thing. |
| **Todd:** | Did you just ruin the movie for me basically? |
| **Jerry:** | Yeah. |
| **Todd:** | You did? You just ruined a movie that I had no intention of seeing, that's terrible. But you did ruin it. |
| **Jerry:** | I did. But that's what I got out of the movie, is that people do what they do and they're going to do it. I mean, if you got kidnapped by a Somali pirate in the middle of a stand-up set and they hauled you off and kept you in a dressing room and just beat you in the dressing room, and eventually you were saved at gunpoint and there was bloodshed and they took you to the emergency room and you started crying in front of the nurse, you are not going to say, "I am finished doing comedy, I hate it! These Somali pirates have ruined it." |
| **Todd:** | Yeah, I'd probably say that was a fluke thing. I won't work that club again, I think. |
| **Jerry:** | Right. But you'll be back. That's what *Captain Phillips* was about. |
| **Todd:** | I would tell the club, "You've got to hire at least two more bouncers." |
| **Jerry:** | Do you go to a lot of movies? |
| **Todd:** | I can't remember the last movie I saw at the movies. |
| **Jerry:** | I guess *Captain Phillips* is out. |
| **Todd:** | Yeah, you killed that one for me. I shouldn't ask you what else you've seen because you'll just ruin those for me. |

**Jerry:** I've seen everything.

**Todd:** Have you?

**Jerry:** Yeah. Sandra Bullock gets home fine in *Gravity*.

**Todd:** Oh, don't ruin that one. I do want to see that one.

**Jerry:** She has a lot of difficulties. But thanks to her resourcefulness and George Clooney, it all works out.

## *SARAH JESSICA PARKER*

**Jerry:** Do you remember *Then Came Bronson*?

**Sarah Jessica:** No, not at all.

**Jerry:** With Michael Parks.

**Sarah Jessica:** Wow.

**Jerry:** It was a great antihero TV show in the '70s, and I'm going to do the opening for you now word for word.

**Sarah Jessica:** Wow. Yeah. Okay.

**Jerry:** The opening is a guy working with [another] guy. Construction. The [first] guy commits suicide, and in the suicide note, he leaves [the second guy] his Harley chopper. He decides to get on the chopper and just drive across America and discover America and himself. Why just work? "I'm sick of working for the man." So he gets on the chopper and he's driving cross-country. He's got a little pack on the handlebar and on the back. That's all he's going to live on. And he pulls up to a light. This is the opening of the show. A guy in this car pulls up next to him. He's got the Don Draper little hat on and he's got the suit. He's got a wife and kids and a job. He's trapped, right?

**Sarah Jessica:** Right. Yes.

**Jerry:** It's the '60s, he's trapped. And he looks over at him. The window's down. He looks over at this cool Michael Parks in a leather jacket on his Harley, right?

**Sarah Jessica:** Free.

**Jerry:** Free. Right. He's trapped. He says—and this is word for word, okay?—he says, "Where you going?" Michael Parks was like TV Steve McQueen. Well, [the husband guy] says, "Where you going?" [Michael Parks] says, "Oh, I don't know. Wherever I end up, I guess."

**Sarah Jessica:** Wow. The hatted fellow.

**Jerry:** The husband guy says, "Wow, sure wish I was you." And Michael Parks goes, "Yeah, well, hang in there." And he roars off. That was the coolest thing I ever saw in my life! Every week started with that scene.

> *"That was the coolest thing I ever saw in my life! Every week started with that scene."*

## AZIZ ANSARI

**Aziz:** I watched [Eddie Murphy's] *Delirious* the other day and it was totally different because now I perform in that same venue . . . Constitution Hall.

**Jerry:** Can you explain to me how is it that Eddie Murphy in *Beverly Hills Cop*, one of the most famous little moments, as he's walking in Beverly Hills, right? And he sees the two guys in the crazy leather outfits go by him, and he laughs. Remember? In his gray Mumford T-shirt. He's walking through Beverly Hills and then these two guys in outlandish leather outfits walk by him, and he just stops and laughs on the street, to himself. And then, in his comedy special, he's wearing that outfit.

## KEVIN HART

**Jerry:** I don't have on demand. We have a Jewish on demand.

**Kevin:** What is that?

**Jerry:** It's when you get a chance. Whenever you get a chance.

**Kevin:** Why don't you have on demand?

**Jerry:** It's a joke.

## ALI WENTWORTH

**Jerry:** The Pop-Tart and the Schwinn Sting-ray. That's my whole childhood right there. Those two events. Maybe *Get Smart*.

**Ali:** It was *Charlie's Angels* for me. I used to play it with my friends and nobody wanted to be the Kate Jackson one, the smart one.

**Jerry:** [*laughs*] Right.

**Ali:** Everyone wanted to be Jaclyn Smith or Farrah Fawcett. That was the fight. And then finally you'd go like, "Leslie, so you're Kate Jackson." "All right. I'll be the smart one." I actually got in trouble because I had a problem that my parents were concerned about, when I played house or stuff I got so immersed you couldn't get me out of it. So I would have friends come over and play *Charlie's Angels*. Most people would stay in the basement and play *Charlie's Angels*. But I would take it outside. And I went to a real strip bar in DC with a fake picture of my sister, and I walked in saying, "Have you seen this girl?" I got a little bit too close to the fire.

**Jerry:** [*laughs*] Oh my God.

## NORM MACDONALD

**Jerry:** I tried to make a *Get Smart* joke the other day on a text. Someone said to me on text, "What is your ETA?" And I said, "When I arrive." [*laughter*]

**Norm:** Yeah. That's a *Get Smart* joke. "Don't tell me you're the head of the syndicate." "I'm not in the syndicate." "I told you not to tell me that."

When I first came to Hollywood, I wrote for *Roseanne*. And I wrote the first script, you know? When you come at it from a stand-up perspective and you read these jokes, it was a bomb. And I remember telling everybody, "People are going to be booing." And everybody said, "No, no. It's fine." Because I didn't know how it worked. I didn't know that the audience was complicit in the whole affair.

**Jerry:** That's funny.

**Norm:** If they don't laugh, the warm-up guy stops the show and says, "Whenever the guy stops talking, laugh." You know what I mean?

**Jerry:** Right.

**Norm:** But how insulting is it when you're watching TV and every joke kills? Every single joke. I mean, isn't that a little insulting?

**Jerry:** I'm comforted by the fact that most of these shows tank. Here's a company, okay? A television network. "We're going to make a piece of entertainment. We're going to bring it to your living room, give it to you for free." And the public says, "We don't want it." How bad is that show? That's the balance of that scale. You brought it to my house. For free. And people saying, "I'll pass." That, my friend, is what we call justice.

**Norm:** You want to hear my favorite joke from any sitcom? It was the pilot of *The Beverly Hillbillies*. Mr. Brewster shows up from OK Oil and he tells Jed how rich he is. "Mr. Clampett, you have to move out of this one shack." And Jed goes, "Well, what could I afford?" He goes, "Why, Mr. Clampett, with your money you can afford the Taj Mahal." He goes, "I'll take it." He goes, "Oh, no, no, Mr. Clampett, the Taj Mahal is not for sale. I was just making a little joke." Jed goes, "Oh, go ahead. I like a good joke." Mr. Brewster, he goes, "Uh, well, Mr. Clampett, why, the Taj Mahal is in India." And then Jed puts his arm around Mr. Brewster and says, "Mr. Brewster, you're a nice fella, but I've heard better jokes."

**Jerry:** I cannot believe you can remember that entire sequence. I find that mind-boggling.

## CHRIS ROCK

**Chris:** Every year they have the Academy Awards, and they honor the best movies in the world. What is a movie? *Batman* cost $200 million. It kept everybody's attention for an hour and a half, hour and forty minutes. I do that for a living! You do that! And guess what? Most nights you're better than Batman. You're better than the fucking Dark Knight!

**Jerry:** Really? That's exciting to think about. Yeah, the Dark Knight. Maybe I should start billing myself like that.

## DAVE CHAPPELLE

**Jerry:** Did you ever see the movie *Lenny* with Dustin Hoffman and Valerie Perrine?

**Dave:** I love that movie. Bob Fosse. I love that movie.

> *"What is a movie? Batman cost $200 million. It kept everybody's attention for an hour and a half, hour and forty minutes. I do that for a living!"*

**Jerry:**    Love that movie. When he meets her in the cafeteria at midnight and he's in the tux with the tie down and he's moving the tray along.

**Dave:**    Oh, yeah-yeah-yeah-yeah.

**Jerry:**    That's where they met. I thought, "That's the life I want." The tie, it's midnight, and you're first having dinner.

## BARRY MARDER

**Jerry:**    What shows will you watch tonight?

**Barry:**    Well, I've got my half hours. I like *Ray Donovan*.

**Jerry:**    Is that a revenge show?

**Barry:**    In a way.

**Jerry:**    He's a fixer, right?

**Barry:**    He's a fixer. Just an interesting show. Jon Voight's good in it. I'm trying to watch that *Making a Murderer*, the second season.

**Jerry:**    I heard it's good.

**Barry:**    I've watched about an episode and a half. It's just all talking now. It's too much forensic, you know?

**Jerry:**    Oh, you want more murdering?

**Barry:**    Why not? That's why I'm tuning in. For murder.

**Jerry:**    Yeah. Why do people love murder so much?

**Barry:**    Gives them something to do, you know.

**Jerry:**    Wow.

## HOWARD STERN

**Howard:**    What is this show, honestly? What am I doing? I feel this is the most unimportant show in show business that I'm on right now.

**Jerry:**    Great. Then that's another win for me. I got you on the most unimportant show in show business.

# OTHER COMEDIANS

## SARAH SILVERMAN

**Jerry:**    I'm going to see Don Rickles tomorrow.

**Sarah:**    Oh! I love him so much.

**Jerry:**    Me too. So much. I got on the phone with him last week. I've talked with him a couple times recently. He doesn't say hello. "What is this, Jerry? What do you need? You haven't got enough money? What's the problem?"

**Sarah:**    He's so funny. He does that, and the reason is because he's so warm. And somehow it transcends even if it's not in anything he says.

**Jerry:**    That's interesting.

**Sarah:**    Because he's so mean. You want him to be mean to you.

**Jerry:**    I have to disagree with you. I think it works, and this is simplistic, but he's just so funny. He's just that funny. There's a guy, no one has ever said, "You ever heard the Don Rickles thing about this or that?" Never had a bit where it's, "Don Rickles looks at this thing this way"—doesn't have that.

He's still this indelible character of legend of this profession. Why do you think he's great?

**Sarah:** It's not what he's saying. It's just the cadence and the energy and the fact that he's hilarious. But I do think he's just the nicest man.

**Jerry:** He is the nicest man.

**Sarah:** And I think that when you're in the business of comedy, where you're on the offensive and it's about, you know, saying brutal things . . . There are people who do that and it's a turnoff, it's ugly. But I think that there's something that has to transcend. An intention.

**Jerry:** Okay, let me offer this theory. Tell me if you accept this. He's having fun doing it.

**Sarah:** One hundred percent.

**Jerry:** He's seen something, he's going to hit it, but with fun. It's not the warmth particularly, but he's going to make it so much fun for everybody.

**Sarah:** Yeah, there's joy in it.

**Jerry:** Yes!

**Sarah:** It's just like, you know how audiences can smell if a comic isn't confident? Even if your character is a nervous, unconfident person, they have to feel that you know what you're doing.

**Jerry:** Yeah.

> *"You know how audiences can smell if a comic isn't confident?"*

## SETH MEYERS

**Jerry:** I'm sure you remember the [ad sales] upfronts before Jay Leno's 10 p.m. show. Were you there that day?

**Seth:** Yes, remember that was the first time [Amy] Poehler and I did a *Weekend Update* and you sent me a note. That's the first time we ever had any interaction. And I will tell you something else: the next day, I ordered stationery. I was like, "This is the classiest shit on earth." I still have [the note].

**Jerry:** What did it say?

**Seth:** We had some good jokes, and you were really complimentary. And I was like, "This is the greatest thing ever."

**Jerry:** Why hunt somebody down or call them? It's like, if you want to give them a present, give them a present.

**Seth:** I met Rickles for the first time at the *Vanity Fair* Oscar party. He was sitting at a table alone and I was like, "I love him. I've got to say hi." So I knelt down and I was like, "Mr. Rickles, my name is Seth Meyers. I just want to say I'm a huge fan." He was drinking coffee. He looked at me, rolled his eyes, took a sip of his coffee, and then said, "I'm sorry to hear *Saturday Night Live* got canceled." I go, "It didn't get canceled." And he goes, "A guy can dream."

## JAY LENO

**Jerry:** At some point in the '60s, comedy changed from kind of a hacky thing. From schpritzy, hacky "joke" jokes stuff to . . .

**Jay:** The guy that changed it for me was Robert Klein.

**Jerry:** Yeah. I would agree with that.

**Jay:** Robert Klein was my guy. Because when I was a kid, comedians were older Jewish men who grew up in the Lower East Side of New York, like Alan King. Alan King was the best. And I used to say to myself, "Well, I'm not Jewish, and my dad's middle class, and we live in Andover, Massachusetts—little house in a rural area. I don't relate to any of this." And then Robert Klein came along, and he would talk about watching TV with his dad or trying to explain what the Beatles were, or whatever it might be, and I went, "Oh, here's a guy close to my age."

**Jerry:** Yeah, it was Klein and Carlin, I think.

**Jay:** I'm old enough to remember Carlin as the hippy dippy weatherman. I remember when it was Burns and Carlin. Remember when he was part of a comedy team?

**Jerry:** Sure. Jack Burns. I don't know if you ever saw, the *New York Times* asked me to write an op-ed about George after he passed away. And I really took it very seriously, and I worked really hard on it. But one of the things that I said in it was that the AM and FM didn't matter to me. He was just as funny doing the AM stuff as the FM stuff. I didn't care about the seven dirty words. That bit was never funny to me.

**Jay:** It wasn't my thing.

**Jerry:** He's a funny guy. And if the bit's funny, it's funny.

## HOWARD STERN

**Howard:** The best talk show guest ever was Don Rickles, in the history of talk shows.

**Jerry:** I'll agree with that. Maybe one of the best comedians ever.

**Howard:** I think so. I was at a dinner party with him in LA, at [producer and film executive] Brad Grey's house. There were a lot of famous people there: Jack Nicholson, Harrison Ford. It was an unbelievable table to be sitting at. The whole time he's eating and eating and you think he's not even paying attention. And he got up and blasted everyone. Everyone. It was insane.

**Jerry:** Yeah. He's got an incredible eye. You think he's not watching. He's watching everything.

**Howard:** And you think he's not with it and he's totally with it. Do you think he is

"The comedian wants to be himself. The actor wants to be anyone but themselves."

**Jerry:** prepared at all? Like, he couldn't have prepared to go to a dinner party. But are there stock things he does and then just substitutes the names? Or is he that quick?

**Jerry:** He's that quick. And there's certain attitudes that he knows, once he gets into that attitude or that angle, then it's going to go somewhere. But that's a lifetime. A lifetime. The comedian studies himself. The actor studies other people. The comedian wants to be himself. The actor wants to be anyone but themselves.

**Howard:** You're so true. Because I think being funny for a living, you've got to be so aware, hyperaware. I feel tortured. I'm so self-conscious, so self-aware. But you're not tortured.

**Jerry:** Right. Well, that would be something I'd like to see you make some progress with.

**Howard:** Well, I'm working on it.

**Jerry:** As you and I go into our sixties, let's make that a priority.

**Howard:** But you don't experience that. But you aren't—

**Jerry:** It's not about your looks, Howard. Don't you get that by now? Nobody cares what your hair looks like. Nobody cares about your face.

**Howard:** I care about it all.

**Jerry:** When you're twenty-five, yeah, it's fine for you to care. But they don't care if we care.

**Howard:** Right. You shouldn't care. Well, listen, that's exactly why I go to therapy.

# JON STEWART

**Jon:** What I respected so much about Rickles is what was so rough for me early on: meeting some of these comedy guys, these legends, and finding them to be so angry. Because I looked at them and thought, "That's the pinnacle."

**Jerry:** Yeah, these are the kings of the world.

**Jon:** You can't do better than those guys. And to meet them and to see them feeling as though they haven't achieved anything.

**Jerry:** I know—but, Jon, you cannot be unfamiliar with the stand-up comedian's self-negation of "I'm not in real show business."

**Jon:** Right.

**Jerry:** Because there's no craft service table.

**Jon:** Right.

**Jerry:** And there's no producer.

**Jon:** Right.

**Jerry:** And there's no script pages. That's real show business.

**Jon:** But that always struck me as so odd, because to me, what's better than nobody telling you what to do? Nobody. No network, no sponsor.

| **Jerry:** | I know. |
| **Jon:** | You write it. You get to say it. |
| **Jerry:** | Because you've been there. You've been there. When you haven't been there, it's just not the same. |
| **Jon:** | But I mean, you'd meet these older comics and they're so mad. |
| **Jerry:** | I know, because they felt like they were kept out of the kingdom. But they don't know that there's nothing in there. |
| **Jon:** | Or that other comics—I learned early on that success is not finite, and if somebody else gets something, that doesn't pick your pocket. |
| **Jerry:** | That's right. |
| **Jon:** | That's got nothing to do with you. And you can be happy for them because if they're funny and they're smart, well, maybe you'll get good at it and you'll have the same chances. And Rickles, I feel like, is that way. And [Bob] Newhart is that way. |
| **Jerry:** | Yes. |
| **Jon:** | But you'd meet a guy like Buddy Hackett and you'd be like, "Wow, you're hilarious, you've done movies, you've done television. What are you pissed off about?" |
| **Jerry:** | But that's just people. Isn't it? |
| **Jon:** | Yep. But didn't you always used to think doing what you wanted in life cured people? |
| **Jerry:** | Doing what you wanted in life? |
| **Jon:** | Yeah, I never thought that . . . success doesn't cure that. |
| **Jerry:** | No, it does not. |

## *DON RICKLES*

| **Jerry:** | Who were your friends? Who were the guys? Everybody knows that you and Newhart were good friends. Took a lot of trips together. |
| **Don:** | That was later. A guy called Herkie Styles, who's gone. |
| **Jerry:** | Herkie Styles. That's a good name for a comic. |
| **Don:** | Yeah, he was a wonderful comedian. Oh, he was wonderful. You know, when you think about back then, Jerry, it's hard to think of guys that I . . . I wasn't much of a hang-around guy. You know, some guys like to go to the coffee shop or they like to go down the street. Like Shecky Greene, God bless him, he used to hang out in the horse room or something. I never did that. |
| **Jerry:** | Where? The horse room? |
| **Don:** | You know, in Vegas. |
| **Jerry:** | Oh, you mean betting. |
| **Don:** | Betting, yeah. |

| | |
|---|---|
| **Jerry:** | So you didn't gamble? |
| **Don:** | No. And I opened at the Sahara and they said, "If you don't gamble, I'm telling you, Don, they're going to cancel you." I never bet a penny. And not because I'm cheap. I just . . . my father gambled, rest his soul. But in those days, five dollars, ten dollars, nothing. And when we buried him, we buried him facing the finish line at the racetrack at Belmont. We did. |
| **Jerry:** | That's great. |

## DAVID LETTERMAN

| | |
|---|---|
| **David:** | I remember there was nothing ever more exciting than being on *The Tonight Show* with Johnny. Nothing. |
| **Jerry:** | Nothing. |
| **David:** | And doing well. |
| **Jerry:** | Right. |
| **David:** | And that was it. And where does that happen anymore? It doesn't happen. |
| **Jerry:** | It doesn't happen. |
| **David:** | No. And the other thing was the Comedy Store. It was one after another of guys who were really funny and guys who had personality disorders. And it was a mural of wonderful behavior to observe. You know, Lenny Schultz comes to mind. |
| **Jerry:** | Really, you saw him? |
| **David:** | Oh my God, and we talk about Lenny Schultz once a week now. I mean, you saw him when he was big. |
| **Jerry:** | Sure, yeah. "More pigs, Lenny." Remember that? He would have the little toy pigs. |
| **David:** | Yeah. I remember one time Lenny's onstage, and in one of the Baby-Björn things he's got a plastic doll. And he's running around onstage with the plastic doll, and he has a little toy whip, and he's whipping the baby. You hear the sound effects of a crying baby, and Lenny is whipping the baby. "Be quiet. William Morris is here. Stop it. William Morris is looking at my act. Stop it, baby." And he's whipping the plastic doll, because William Morris is taking a look at him. It was delightful. You'd get to go to the Comedy Store every night, and there was never a dull night, you know? |
| **Jerry:** | No, there really wasn't. Do you subscribe to the [idea that] madness—or let's not say "madness," let's say some level of affliction, personality-wise, or socially—is what makes these people funny? Or do you think everyone's a little crazy? |
| **David:** | Well, that's an excellent question. I know in my own case, early on I realized I wasn't very good at anything, but I sometimes could make my |

"*There was nothing ever more exciting than being on* The Tonight Show *with Johnny. Nothing.*"

buddies laugh. And there was the reinforcement. And so you seek that. Now, I don't know what it was like for you, but—

**Jerry:** Yeah, but I didn't feel like I was an incompetent, other than that. I just felt like that was the most fun thing.

## JAMIE FOXX

**Jerry:** Man, what the hell is left for you?

**Jamie:** Stand-up. That's the thing about stand-up. It's vast.

**Jerry:** It's like an episode of *Star Trek*. There's always another planet.

**Jamie:** Always another planet. [*laughs*] Oh, that's right. How much do you like [Chris] Rock?

**Jerry:** Rock kills me.

**Jamie:** Rock kills you, right?

**Jerry:** He kills me. Very few guys that make you laugh so hard from the smartness. The smartness.

**Jamie:** Man, his take on everything. You know what else I like about Rock? His conflictedness of whatever is going on in the world. It's always, "You know . . ."

**Jerry:** He always has that other thing—the impending doom. He has a lot of impending doom. Leno's like that too. Always telling you some story about some security guard who used to have a series. You know, "He had his own series. Now he's security." You know those guys?

**Jamie:** "He was on top."

**Jerry:** All comes tumbling down.

**Jamie:** Leno's got some funny dirty jokes too.

**Jerry:** Yeah, I always say, "Where do you get these jokes?" He goes, "My limo drivers."

## CHRIS ROCK

**Jerry:** People don't understand that what makes a comedian funny is how serious he is.

**Chris:** That's a good one. That is absolutely [*laughs*] . . . No truer words have been said.

**Jerry:** No person in the audience ever would think that. Yeah, you want a guy who's not fooling around. [*laughs*] This guy's serious.

**Chris:** This guy's serious. Jay Leno.

**Jerry:** [*laughs*] Yes. Very serious.

**Chris:** Jay Leno is serious about some jokes. Dave Letterman, serious about some jokes.

| Jerry: | So how's that all going to end, Chris? Leno and Letterman? |
| Chris: | Leno and Letterman? That's ended. I mean, they had a little feud, which I still don't ever understand. Jay Leno's the only man in the world ever been punished for wanting to work. [*laughter*] How dare he want *The Tonight Show*! What? |
| Jerry: | Well, that was a funky thing there. |
| Chris: | It's funky, yes, but it's not wrong for him to want it. There's nothing wrong with wanting it. We've all had children. They should aspire to get to the top of whatever field they decide to get into. They should not go, "Ooh, this guy deserves it more than me." They should try to get the job. So I like them both. I want Jay to work out his contract and retire on the show. I do not want them to fire Jay Leno. But, go on. |
| Jerry: | I'm very interested in how people orchestrate their exits. Me and George Shapiro are always still upset about Michael Jordan playing for the Wizards those two years, that he didn't make that last shot his last shot. |
| Chris: | Here's the thing, Jerry. We're only good at one thing. We don't know what it feels like to be good physically. We suck. And when you suck, you hit |

> "The last
> joke is more
> important
> than every
> other joke."

the shot and you run home. But when you're great, you just keep beating people till you can't fucking win.

**Jerry:** The Washington Wizards?

**Chris:** It was the Washington Wizards. But you know what? Now he knows. And does the Washington Wizards take away from him? Not at all.

**Jerry:** I disagree.

**Chris:** Doesn't take one thing away. Yes, would it have been nice to hit that shot and leave? Yeah.

**Jerry:** It's a beautiful career.

**Chris:** It's still a beautiful career.

**Jerry:** The last joke, Chris. You're telling me the last joke is not more important than every other joke?

**Chris:** The last joke is more important than every other joke. It's very important. But you ever see *Richard Pryor: Live in Concert*? Arguably the greatest stand-up special of all time.

**Jerry:** Yes.

**Chris:** Last joke's not that good.

**Jerry:** There's no subject you cannot handle. And that's true of most comedians. Most comedians have given some thought to almost everything.

**Chris:** We're professional arguers. Not only can we argue about anything, we can argue either side.

**Jerry:** It's true. Okay, so here's what I want to ask you. So you're a comedian. And Letterman was somewhat of a comedian. Never did a gig—he had about twenty minutes.

**Chris:** But Letterman is one of these guys . . . Letterman, I'll even go, wasn't a good comedian.

**Jerry:** No, he wasn't, really.

**Chris:** But he's so funny.

**Jerry:** He's charming.

**Chris:** He's charming.

**Jerry:** Charming. Funny. Appealing.

**Chris:** Oh, he's funny!

**Jerry:** And really funny. Okay, so these guys, once they become comedians, well, then you've got to figure out what's the next place on the board I can get to. Right? Movies are very rare. Very few comedians do movies.

**Chris:** Very rare. I've struggled.

**Jerry:** Sitcoms, talk shows, that's about it.

**Chris:** Yup.

**Jerry:** So that's why these guys . . . I'm sure they don't want to work every day either, but that's the only option.

**Chris:** I guess in a weird way it's kind of like doing a sitcom for fifteen years.

**Jerry:** A talk show? No.

**Chris:** No? I guess not.

| Jerry: | No. |
| --- | --- |
| Chris: | A sitcom, you've got to work a lot too. But not, you know, multicamera? No. Not that much. |
| Jerry: | No, not if you have good writers, good cast. But I worked on my show every day. All day, every day. As you know. |
| Chris: | Well, if you're going to be great . . . |
| Jerry: | Yeah. Well, you got to be single for that. |
| Chris: | You can't be great on the side. Nothing great is done on the side. |
| Jerry: | Right. But you can't tell me there's another career move those guys could have made than this, than the one they made. |
| Chris: | Probably not. I mean, Conan was a big-time writer. One of the highest-paid punch-up guys— |
| Jerry: | There are no big-time writers, Chris. |
| Chris: | There are big, million-dollar writers, Jerry. |
| Jerry: | He was a *Simpsons* writer. That's not a big-time writer. |
| Chris: | Conan O'Brien would demand lots of money to punch up scripts. Like, the go-to guy. Will still occasionally pick up half a million, whatever, here and there. |
| Jerry: | Really? That's shocking news. |
| Chris: | When I was on *Saturday Night Live*, Conan O'Brien was a writer on the show. And he was one of the funniest guys on the show. And I'm talking about a show with [Adam] Sandler, [Chris] Farley, [Mike] Myers, [Dennis] Miller, Phil Hartman. Conan could crack up a room as hard as any guy. Squeaky-clean. Now, you're clean, but off camera you can go any way. This guy, even off camera, squeaky-clean. |
| Jerry: | Wow. |

# LOUIS C.K.

| Jerry: | Who was the first comedian that really lit you up? |
| --- | --- |
| Louis: | I loved Woody Allen. Woody Allen was the most surprising to me. Bill Cosby made me laugh really hard—he was just such a good comedian—but he didn't make me go, "Omigod, that guy's crazy." Carlin, the same thing—just a solidly great comedian. And then when I was a kid, my mom would show me Woody Allen movies. I don't know how. Now I can't picture—like, you didn't look at them on iTunes or anything, |
| Jerry: | So that must have been a giant charge to do the Woody movie [*Blue Jasmine*]. |
| Louis: | Yeah. I think Letterman said when he did *The Tonight Show* for the first time and he's shaking hands with Carson, it was like being on a five-dollar bill shaking hands with Lincoln. That always made an impression on me. |
| Jerry: | That's funny. |

| | |
|---|---|
| **Louis:** | So I've had a few moments in my life that have felt that way. One of them was shaking hands with Letterman on his own show the first time. And then meeting Woody was really out of reality. |
| **Jerry:** | I was walking behind him in Central Park the other day. |
| **Louis:** | Woody? |
| **Jerry:** | Yeah, but I didn't bother him. |
| **Louis:** | Nah, never do that anymore. I used to sometimes say hi to somebody if they were famous, but now I never do that. |

## *PATTON OSWALT*

| | |
|---|---|
| **Patton:** | I constantly read interviews with people that I admire. Just 'cause you get amazing insights into their processes. And Mel Brooks—he is a deep genius. |
| **Jerry:** | Yes. |
| **Patton:** | That's a guy that, if you look at all of his movies and everything he's done, that is such a tiny portion of what he's interested in. You only have so much time to do so many things, and he's an example of a guy that actually picked all the right things to pursue. It's just amazing. Today they would have *Blazing Saddles Again*, you know? I almost think he was making fun of that when he did *History of the World: Part 1*. 'Cause he covers everything in that one, so it's almost like a "fuck you" to the whole sequel thing. Like, "Why would I do a sequel?" |
| **Jerry:** | You think so? That's a good question. I would like to know the answer to that. 'Cause I always assumed there was going to be more. |
| **Patton:** | Yeah. But *History of the World: Part 1* did really well, I think. And he never bothered with a sequel. |
| **Jerry:** | That seems like the ultimate format, if you can make it work, right? |
| **Patton:** | Oh God, I would love to see an angry Mel Brooks take on, like, the 1940s America and McCarthy and the postwar, and show you that all this stuff you thought was amazing actually was kind of shitty. It wasn't really all that great. My favorite Mel Brooks story—now, I'm sure it's apocryphal, but a friend of mine said that he was at a funeral that Mel Brooks was at. It was somebody very famous, and they were standing at the casket and, you know, stuff was being read. And he couldn't help it. He kind of leaned forward and said, "Mr. Brooks, I just want to say that your movies—" And Mel's like, "You're at a funeral. This is a funeral!" He says, "Oh, I'm sorry, I'm sorry." And it got quiet. Then after a couple minutes Mel went, "What was your favorite one?" |

# JAY LENO

**Jay:** The reason you and I and maybe two or three other guys get all the corporate work is we work clean and it's broad-based. The idea of trying to make *everybody* laugh now is kind of . . . now everybody has a niche. And the idea of a Bob Hope or a Jack Benny appealing to the whole country doesn't really exist anymore.

**Jerry:** Does it not need to exist? Chris Rock would argue that those are the best comedians, because they can make anyone laugh.

**Jay:** That's what I think. That's always been my goal. I was never dirty enough to be a dirty comic. I had a couple of four-letter words in my act. I remember once, when Harrah's came in. Harrah's in Lake Tahoe, that was the place. Five-star hotel.

**Jerry:** Absolutely. That was the coolest gig.

**Jay:** They treated comics like kings. You got a suite with two bathrooms in it, this whole thing. So they came to the Comedy Store to see comics, and I was one of them. And just because something told me, I put on a jacket and tie. And I got hired. I remember the guy saying to me—I can't remember his name.

**Jerry:** Holmes Hendrickson?

**Jay:** No, it wasn't Holmes, it was the other guy. Very German guy, very frightening guy.

**Jerry:** Frightening. I know he didn't like me.

**Jay:** Well, he said to me, "You know why you got the job? 'Cause you're the only one that came dressed for the job. Who goes on a job interview with a T-shirt and jeans? When I see T-shirt and jeans—you're coming and auditioning for my club in a T-shirt and jeans? I'm not even listening to your act." He said, "You're the first one I listened to because you looked like you wanted to work at my club." So I got the job. And then people say, "Leno cheated. He wore . . ." No, I didn't cheat. I just did what's required of the job. I did what you're supposed to do.

**Jerry:** Right. But really, you think it was Pryor that made comedy have to speed up? I don't think so.

**Jay:** Well, to me, I think.

**Jerry:** Who was the first monologist who you would say is the forefather of our style of comedy?

**Jay:** I think certainly Cosby, somewhat.

**Jerry:** We're not like Cosby.

**Jay:** Well, don't forget, prior to Mort Sahl even, prior to the '60s, stand-up comedy was a combination of clown and comedy.

**Jerry:** Yes. And "joke" jokes.

**Jay:** Milton Berle with the big powder puff and the whole thing. I always liked comedians who looked like normal men or women until they opened their mouth.

| **Jerry:** | Such as? |
| --- | --- |
| **Jay:** | Like Benny, like Steve Allen. Steve Allen just looks like a guy. But then he sits and says something where he didn't have to pull a flower out and squirt water out of his lapel or do anything like that. He just spoke in a funny way. To me, comedy is like a concealed weapon. You carry it around and no one knows you have it until you take it out, and then suddenly . . . When you walk in wearing a striped suit and straw hat: "Oh, that guy's a gunslinger." But when you have it hidden, it's a concealed weapon. You have it and you're sitting there and then you say something and people laugh. You go, "Oh, wow, I've leveled the room here." |
| **Jerry:** | So who would be your favorite comic right now to watch do twenty minutes? |
| **Jay:** | Louis C.K. is great. |
| **Jerry:** | Yeah, he's great. I love Brian Regan. |
| **Jay:** | I don't really know Brian Regan. He's a Letterman guy, so he doesn't do us. I would love to have him on. But I love Louis C.K. I love the way he |

thinks. I love his bit on cell phones. You know you're a comic when you kick yourself you didn't think of that. He says, "Everybody goes, 'I hate my cell phone. It sucks.' Really? You connect within seconds to anyone in the world, and you hate it because, oh, it didn't connect you to China in, like, two seconds?" I mean, hilarious. Very funny.

**Jerry:** Regan has a funny bit about the walkie-talkie, what a funny name that is. He says it's like, it's such a kid's name for something. It's like calling a hand grenade a wammie-kablammie.

**Jay:** That's funny. I love Louis' bit about, "Why do women go out with men? We pick you up, it's dark, you get in the car with a guy you don't know and he takes you somewhere, you don't know where you're going. Why would you do that?" Yeah, Louis is really funny. I did his show [*Louie*]. I enjoyed it. We kind of ad-libbed it. It was fun. What we ad-libbed was, "You know, I used to be you, Louis. I used to be the hip guy. Then I was on TV every day. I was on every day. I didn't have that little tidbit every now and then, you know?" Taste is what's left after appetite is satisfied, and that's the way comedy works. When you're on every six weeks, oh, any taste is good. But then when you're on every day, they're full, so their taste level goes up.

**Jerry:** Taste is what's left after your appetite has been satisfied?

**Jay:** Yes. Does that make sense to you?

**Jerry:** No.

**Jay:** Well, think about it. If you're hungry, you eat.

**Jerry:** If you're hungry, everything tastes good.

**Jay:** Right, right. And then as soon as you're full, "Um, I don't want that. Give me that one over there."

**Jerry:** Ah, I see. That's funny.

**Jay:** You know what I mean? And it's true. It's like that with comedy too. When you're hot, whatever you do: "Oh, ho, ho." People laugh at everything you do. Then after they've seen you a few times, it gets a little trickier. Taste is what's left.

## BILL BURR

**Bill:** One of my favorite things to see is a comic who works clean and still be able to see that same sort of rage. Like Brian Regan. You watch Brian Regan, and people think it's goofy. No, this is an angry dude. The way he's telling this story is not the way he reacted when this shit happened to him, I'm telling you right now. This guy absolutely lost it. You're just watching this man's style.

**Jerry:** Do you think that there's any good, accomplished stand-up comedian who doesn't have a wellspring of anger to fuel it?

> *"Comedy is like a concealed weapon."*

| | |
|---|---|
| **Bill:** | Or frustration? |
| **Jerry:** | I think "anger" is the right word. |
| **Bill:** | There's got to be. I would say Andy Kaufman and some of those guys who did that—I don't know if avant-garde is the right thing, but what they did. I don't even know what the process of that is, so it's hard for me to try to break down something I can't see—like, how he went from point A to point Z. Or point B—however the hell you're supposed to say it. But I have tremendous respect for that guy, because to me, he is sort of like the Columbus of comics. |
| **Jerry:** | I grew up in Long Island in the '60s and '70s, and he was the guy that we heard about in Long Island: there's this guy that goes onstage at this club in New York, and he plays the bongos, and then starts crying as he's playing them. And we go, "Where is this going on?" |
| **Bill:** | Yeah, how is that funny? |
| **Jerry:** | And that's when we started going into the city and that's when I found out there's this other stand-up that's not the ruffled-tuxedo-shirt stuff that I'd seen on *Ed Sullivan*. So it was Andy Kaufman who made all of us . . . Everybody in Long Island is kind of funny, you know, or wants to be funny. |
| **Bill:** | I think everybody in that whole Northeast area, they're just funny. And a lot of them aren't even trying to be funny. I don't know if it's because I grew up there, so I relate to everybody, but I find people from New England all the way down to right through Jersey and into Philly—somewhere around Philly it starts slowing down. |
| **Jerry:** | There are places that are definitely not funny. I don't think anybody funny ever came out of San Diego. |
| **Bill:** | San Diego? It's just too nice. |

## *BRIAN REGAN*

| | |
|---|---|
| **Jerry:** | I idolize Jerry Lewis. I think if you can be funny, just be funny. There's not a lot of funny. We need funny. |
| **Brian:** | I like Jerry Lewis too. The French think he's a genius. I loved watching *The Bellboy* and *The Nutty Professor* and— |
| **Jerry:** | Oh my God, yeah. Great stuff. |
| **Brian:** | Silliness gets belittled. But silliness done well . . . You have to be smart to pull off silliness and make it be funny. |
| **Jerry:** | Extremely. |
| **Brian:** | Steve Martin. Some of his stuff can seem silly and dumb. No, no, then you don't get it. It's very smart. |

## MATTHEW BRODERICK

**Jerry:** You know who grew up on Rivington Street [in New York]? George Burns.

**Matthew:** Really? Boy, this street has changed, I'll bet. I don't think there was a crêperie when George Burns . . .

**Jerry:** No. [*laughs*] Did you like him?

**Matthew:** Yeah, I love him.

**Jerry:** Yeah, me too.

**Matthew:** Though I remember once when they were talking about him celebrating his hundredth birthday, they were going to make a big thing of it. And my mom, who was always nice, she said, "Do you think George Burns has overstayed his welcome?"

**Jerry:** [*laughs*] And your mom was Irish?

**Matthew:** No.

**Jerry:** Your dad was Irish?

**Matthew:** My dad was Irish, my mom was—

**Jerry:** See, that sounds very Irish to me.

**Matthew:** Yeah, she was Jewish, but every now and then quite biting.

**Jerry:** The day he died, I was in LA, and I knew where he lived. He lived on Maple Drive, in the Flats of Beverly Hills. There were no gates or anything like that. You could just walk right up to anybody's house. And I went and sat on the stoop of his house and smoked a cigar. The day he died.

**Matthew:** Wow. What a good idea.

# MICHAEL RICHARDS

**Michael:** Did you know that Red Skelton was my mentor?

**Jerry:** I knew you were a great fan of his.

**Michael:** You came into the office when he passed way, and I was crying. I was watching one of his old specials and I had tears in my eyes. He was a sweet man. He hurt his knees. He had done so many pratfalls that he was confined to a wheelchair when he was eighty-one. I was in Lake Tahoe, and I brought him up [onstage]. I said, "Ladies and gentlemen, Red Skelton." Red gets outta the wheelchair. Doesn't come up to the dais where I was standing. Goes out on a little ramp. He's got his hat with him. I thought he was going to say a few words. He does an hour of stand-up, all the characters, everything. The whole house comes up. There's about fifteen hundred people. They're on their feet applauding. Walks back and sits down in his wheelchair. I went, "That's showmanship."

**Jerry:** Wow. He stood up out of a wheelchair.

**Michael:** Did an hour. Killing. Doin' all the characters, all the routines, everything. It was beautiful. Except he didn't take a fall. He always took a fall. He didn't take any falls. Pouring sweat. Shirt's open, everything. He goes, "I want to thank you for coming and watching my show. God bless." He's walkin' back to the wheelchair. I'm watchin' him. He's all sweaty, you know. He sits down. Now, what demon is at work in this man's being? The body's breakin' down, but somethin' inside's comin' through that carried him along all those years. What a profound performer. And at the end, coming out and being so personal. So present with his audience and thanking them like that. And it was genuine. He loved to perform. You know those performers who just love it? There's always a struggle with me. I don't know if I'm going to get it right.

## TINA FEY

**Tina:** I used to love to go watch Colin Quinn, when we worked at *SNL* together. I remember feeling so dumb one time, because I watched a set of his and he was really funny, and he dealt with someone in the audience in a really funny way. I said after, "Oh, I thought it was really funny when you said that thing." And he was like, "That?" It was some back-pocket thing that he had done a million times, but I was like, "That was funny." And he was just like, "No, dummy, that's just how you deal with a heckler. That's not the real important part of the act."

**Jerry:** Yeah, because the thing is to have an act. If you have an act, then you can make a living.

## HOWARD STERN

**Howard:** Do you think you're in the top five? I think you do think you are. And I'm not putting you in a category with, let's say, Groucho. Groucho wasn't a stand-up. I'm talking about stand-up.

**Jerry:** Listen, a great stand-up is a victory over the self. And you are as great an example as exists. Your career is a victory over the self. The greatest obstacles are the self. It wasn't the business. It wasn't other people. It wasn't your relationships, your wife, whatever. None of that was the biggest obstacle. It was you. You conquered yourself.

**Howard:** Right. Which I totally understand.

**Jerry:** Okay, so if you've done that, how you rank amongst colleagues doesn't matter. We could do it as an intellectual exercise. But I just want to be clear.

**Howard:** But when I evaluate myself as a radio guy, I think I'm the best that ever lived. Ever. Even better than Arthur Godfrey. Better than Marconi.

**Jerry:** You know what, it'd be very hard to argue that.

**Howard:** But the reason I bring that up and I'm putting you in a category . . . Like, I think Eddie Murphy is one of the greatest stand-ups I have personally ever seen.

**Jerry:** It's Pryor, Carlin, and Cosby at the top. There's nobody who's going to argue with—

**Howard:** I don't get Cosby at all. I went to see Cosby when I was in junior high. A friend brought me. I saw him at the Felt Forum. And I wanted to kill myself.

**Jerry:** That's very personal. Comedy is personal.

**Howard:** Why is Cosby so great? I feel he drones on with a story way too long and it doesn't captivate me. Is there something wrong with me that I feel that way?

| | |
|---|---|
| **Jerry:** | No, certainly not. Comedy is more personal than food. Someone either hits you funny or they don't. |
| **Howard:** | George Carlin said that— |
| **Jerry:** | I was in the top five. |
| **Howard:** | No, no— |
| **Jerry:** | No? He didn't say that? |
| **Howard:** | In fact, he didn't even mention you. When he died, he mentioned all the comics in his will, and you were the only one he didn't mention. |
| **Jerry:** | I talked to him a week before he passed. |
| **Howard:** | Oh, you did? |
| **Jerry:** | On the phone, yeah. |
| **Howard:** | Wow. |
| **Jerry:** | Anyway, go ahead. Carlin said— |
| **Howard:** | What was that conversation? |
| **Jerry:** | I called him about his special [*It's Bad for Ya*], and we had traded calls a bunch of times, couldn't get together. We finally got together and I just wanted to talk about how great I thought it was, and we chatted about comedy. We were laughing about—somebody had died the week before, and we were laughing about it, saying, "Who's going to be next?" |
| **Howard:** | So in other words, you didn't call him 'cause you thought he was ill or something like that. |
| **Jerry:** | No, he wasn't ill. But don't lose that thought. You were going to say, "Carlin said . . ." |
| **Howard:** | Carlin said that for someone to put together a full hour of stand-up, it can only happen, like, seven times or something. You can only put together seven full hours. It was some sort of statement like that. |
| **Jerry:** | I think that's true. |
| **Howard:** | And I think Carlin disproved that point. You know what I mean? He would do a comedy special every year. I thought it was pretty remarkable. |
| **Jerry:** | Well, you know, we're getting into shoptalk here, but I could do an hour special every year. Is it as good as I want it to be? No. |
| **Howard:** | It wouldn't be classic. |
| **Jerry:** | Yeah. I like a level of refinement that brings something. . . . It's just a different thing. It's a different level of control that I have over the audience in the piece of material, and that requires time. |
| **Howard:** | So it's like a musician. You can only really write so many hits. |

"A great stand-up is a victory over the self."

## ROBERT KLEIN

**"She was something, Lucille Ball. She took me to her mother's house for dinner."**

**Robert:** I would say that my most immediate influences were Jonathan Winters and Lenny Bruce. I've been reading some of [Bruce's] stuff lately. Much of it is actually elegant. Some of it is stupid, but some of it is incredibly elegant. But that's the only thing I object to today—profanity is a terribly important part of the language, and I like it used aptly. I don't like it conversationally.

**Jerry:** Well, of course. We wish all language was used aptly.

**Robert:** But that's a generational thing. I like Louis C.K.'s work a lot. He's a smart guy. But in ordinary conversation, I wouldn't talk like that.

**Jerry:** But Winters—I never saw that in anything in the way you work.

**Robert:** It's the improvisational part. And then practically to his dying day . . . We did a thing with Paul Provenza. [Winters] could hardly get to his chair and then when he sat down he was—he can still wail. The body couldn't do anything, and it was letting him down. But he was still, "Just came back with the missus from Nanking," just out of nowhere.

**Jerry:** Give me another Pryor story, 'cause I'm fascinated by his early years. You told me he gave you some advice?

**Robert:** I think it was Pryor who hipped me to the fact that Merv Griffin is not the best lead-in person. Johnny could, as you know. And Letterman's pretty good at it too—can work in and out of a comedian's routine. So he told me to have confidence, be calm. You know, he was so funny. And he was adorable. That's the only way to describe him then. And I actually asked him, in the anteroom at the old Improv—remember the Improv?

**Jerry:** Sure.

**Robert:** Wait a minute, you imitated it. It looked like the bar on your show [*Seinfeld*].

**Jerry:** Yeah.

**Robert:** The New York one looked like the bar. Anyway, I asked him what college he went to. And he had the same reaction you just did—he laughed for about four minutes. And it was then that he told me he was brought up in a brothel. And then he disappeared. He was totally clean and adorable, got big laughs. He disappeared in '68, went out of sight. This, not coincidentally—although Richard was completely apolitical, as far as I could see—was the [time of the] assassination of Bobby Kennedy, of Martin Luther King, riots. He came back an authentic Richard Pryor.

**Jerry:** Same with George [Carlin].

**Robert:** You see, his profanity and his rhythms were extremely believable. It's like *The Sopranos* milieu. You know, to say "fuck" on *The Sopranos*—this is the way these people talk, and it was completely believable and acceptable. Have you ever seen the sanitized one on A&E? "Forget you! Forget your mother, you mother-forgetter! Forget you!" Lot of forgetting. I mean, what are they thinking? They blur out the middle finger, if somebody gives someone the finger. This is A&E. So I just thought [Pryor] had it controlled, the way he did it. One time I remember convulsively laughing when he was doing a bit about making a movie with Gene Wilder in Arizona, in the penitentiary—*Stir Crazy*. He goes, "And I see the brothers in the cell, and the brothers are there . . ." You know, I'm paraphrasing badly. "And this guy came out, about six foot seven, and I realized why there are penitentiaries." He takes you from—you think it's going to be, "The brothers . . ." to "I know why there are penitentiaries." It's like Lou Costello going from a laugh to a cry. In one motion. It was just brilliant. I really have a soft spot for him.

The last time I saw him, I was with Carlin at—you know I'm not close with anyone. I haven't seen you in years either. I'm sort of hermetic here. I belong to a Benedictine monk thing. But I was at a comedy awards thing, and despite what he had said in the *New York Times* article, hinting— Richard in a wheelchair, smoking Marlboros, watching his grandkids in Hawaii—that he wouldn't let it get too far, he was helpless. He couldn't move. Someone's dabbing his mouth and he couldn't move, and I whispered in his ear how much I loved him. He once said to me, "We get our material similarly." And he was right, because it comes, spur, and you write it down. We were completely different, but . . .

Anyway, Carlin and I took a picture with him. He was between us. We were smiling. He's in his wheelchair. And we walked away, and I was devastated. I'd been in his presence for a few minutes, but the whole thing was so down. It's exactly what you don't want to happen in your life. And I went away with George and I was just about to commiserate and say, "Isn't that a shame?" He goes, "That dude is fucked up!" And I know how he meant it. He wasn't being sentimental for the moment. "That dude is fucked up!"

**Jerry:** Isn't that a great comedian moment, though?

**Robert:** It is.

**Jerry:** It's a great comedian moment. It's like what you're talking about: the laughing and the crying. In the horror of that moment, to just kind of make a little light of it in that way.

**Robert:** Exactly.

**Jerry:** That's pure. That's pure.

**Robert:** When was the first time they understood, "Hey, you know, we're doing a sitcom. We need funny people. How 'bout using a comedian?" Like, what's-her-name, Roseanne. Was she before you?

**Jerry:** Well, go back to Jack Benny. Come on.

**Robert:** Yeah, but you can't call his a sitcom, really. Sort of.

**Jerry:** What would you call it? It was before they had a three-camera live audience, 'cause *I Love Lucy* invented that. But that was about the same year. It doesn't matter. Most great sitcoms do come from comedians.

**Robert:** She was something, Lucille Ball. She took me to her mother's house for dinner, because we worked together. And she had a voice like this [*imitating*], you know. And there was a newspaper strike, so they had "Not the *New York Times*," with television listings they made up: "*I Love Lucy*: Lucy goes to a nuclear power plant . . ." And she goes [*imitating*], "Funny." I find myself doing that sometimes. I'm too analytical. You're able to really let it go.

**Jerry:** Sometimes. But not if I'm working. If we were working, sometimes I laugh, sometimes I go, "Yeah, that'll work. Let's use that. Let's do that."

**Robert:** Rodney [Dangerfield] used to do that all the time. [*imitating*] "I'll tell you, this is funny . . ." You know, "I'll tell ya, no respect at all. Last week a hooker made me say please." He'd write them on shirt cardboards.

**Jerry:** Right. What would you guys do at night? Where did you run into each other? Was it always the Improv?

**Robert:** We smoked pot. We didn't do cocaine. Rodney did his fair share later, and I did some separately, just as an experiment.

**Jerry:** For research?

**Robert:** Budd Friedman [founder of the Improv] would give Rodney a bottle of pretty good wine and he'd do it all in. Even though he'd been smoking since 1939, he refused to smoke pot before he worked, ever. He could get crocked and he would be slurring and all that, but he could get through a show with eight or nine martinis, or a bottle of wine. He was tormented. His father had deserted, lived across the river in Manhattan. He was in Forest Hills [Queens].

**Jerry:** Rodney was in Forest Hills?

**Robert:** In an anti-Semitic neighborhood at the time. Forest Hills was pretty, you know, the tennis days. And he was a big-nosed kid selling ice cream on the beach. He was a loser. That's how he got his persona of being beaten. His mother he called selfish. He didn't really talk much about her. And unfortunately, near the end of his life, he wound up passing on bad parenting. But he has a wonderful daughter, and he has a son. He taught me a lot.

**Jerry:** Did you see each other during the day, or just at the clubs?

**Robert:** No, we'd see each other during the day too. We'd hang around.

**Jerry:** Where?

**Robert:** His place. First on Eighty-Sixth. [*imitating*] "I'll tell ya, I got an apartment on Eighty-Sixth, between Columbus and Puerto Rico." He said, "I got mugged there. The guy had a razor. I'll tell ya, it was an unusual mugger, you know? He had an electric razor. It was my own fault. I was standing next to an outlet at the time." I'm not doing it exactly, but . . . Then he had an apartment on the East Side. More we were nocturnal. A lot of trips to Chinatown. As Rodney used to say, napping between courses. Rodney was fastidious about certain things, like the fat from ribs. You know, he

was clean, but his shirts were torn and the collars were too big. He would often sit at an angle in his dressing room at the club, so that you unfortunately could see his testicles.

**Jerry:** 'Cause he loved to wear a robe.

**Robert:** He wore a robe.

**Jerry:** All the time.

**Robert:** He wasn't an exhibitionist, but he just didn't care. And, um, you don't want to see Rodney's testicles.

**Jerry:** No. No. Let me ask you, did Winters—he never really had much of an act, did he? In the old days? Was he ever a real working comic?

**Robert:** Of course.

**Jerry:** He was?

**Robert:** Of course.

**Jerry:** I remember Cosby telling me one time that they were very good friends.

**Robert:** No doubt. He liked comedians. He didn't like Bob Hope because he did a couple of those USO things and he needed the money and Bob wouldn't give him anything—you know, a taste. And Bob was making a fortune on those shows.

**Jerry:** Was he a Vegas guy? Or where did Jonathan Winters—

**Robert:** He played the big venues like Vegas. He started out with albums. He had definite set bits. But then the television thing was, "Jonathan, you have a cane and a thing."

**Jerry:** Yeah, I loved that when I was a kid. I was amazed by that.

**Robert:** I know, but it should have been better, because it seemed contrived and it didn't happen to be his—to me, his pinnacle was with [Jack] Paar and Johnny Carson. He was marvelous on those.

**Jerry:** So there's no stand-up of his that I could see? Nobody ever filmed that?

**Robert:** Oh, sure. I have a VHS. I was talking to him when he was still alive about material. But then I spoke to his daughter after he died. I said, "Do you have . . ." I had this [same] conversation with Redd Foxx shortly before his demise. He needed money desperately. He was playing dollar poker with these Jewish women in Vegas.

**Jerry:** Winters? Or Foxx?

**Robert:** Foxx.

**Jerry:** Right. That's hilarious.

**Robert:** And I said, "Well, don't you own those tapes, those old party records?" Because Eddie Murphy directed a film, which I think is very underrated, called *Harlem Nights*. And in it, Della Reese and Redd Foxx are so funny together: "Ah, get your black ass . . ." So they gave them a series [*The Royal Family*]. Which is just what he needed, because he had spent it all, either up his nose or God knows. And he drops dead, you know. They were so funny. He was a very funny man. The show was idiotic, but he was so funny in it that he brought it with him. I thought it was wonderful.

Your show had nothing in common with *All in the Family*, and yet that broke some barriers.

**Jerry:** I'll tell you what it had in common with *All in the Family*, *The Honeymooners*, and *I Love Lucy*: four people in a New York home.

**Robert:** Never thought of that.

**Jerry:** Yeah, I didn't either. I read it in an article one time, that they thought that was the secret formula for a sitcom: four people in a small New York apartment.

**Robert:** Well, *The Honeymooners* . . . My experience with [Gleason] brushing me off was not unique. He wasn't the greatest guy in the world. That's another [example] of my theory of brilliant performers and creators not necessarily being great guys. There was a guy named Wagner, and Oscar Katz. They were big CBS people in New York, and one of the things important in their purview was keeping Jackie Gleason happy. So he would do his own negotiating.

**Jerry:** Really?

**Robert:** "No, make it two limos, pal. I'm not sure which exit I'm coming out of." But you know, in the end, he screwed himself. He cheated himself, because had he had proper representation . . . They made a fortune on him. He actually made worse deals for himself than they would've.

**Jerry:** What do you mean, like with *The Honeymooners* ownership?

**Robert:** First with the variety show. They would've given him more money than he demanded.

**Jerry:** He seems like a guy who had a pretty good time.

# AMY SCHUMER

**Amy:** All my best friends are introverts. The comics. My friends from home are not, but the girls that I'm friends with, the female comics I'm friends with. We all went on a trip to Martha's Vineyard—all my girlfriends from home and the female comics that are my best friends—and we got a house. And it was good. The comics were like, "This is good and we're interacting." My friends are all teachers and nurses, whatever. It was good practice for us, it felt like. But then the last night, it was just comics—all the other girls left—and we were all in our bedrooms writing each other on GChat, like, "Is it okay I'm in my room?" We were all so afraid we were disappointing each other but so happy to be in our rooms alone.

**Jerry:** Yeah, successful extroverted comics would be a pretty small club, wouldn't it?

**Amy:** I don't know any.

**Jerry:** Would you call Colin [Quinn] extroverted?

| | |
|---|---|
| **Amy:** | You said successful. No, I'm just kidding. |
| **Jerry:** | You could've let that hang another half a beat. |
| **Amy:** | Sorry, I couldn't wait. It couldn't wait. My favorite thing to do is trash him. He's in the movie I shot [*Trainwreck*], and a guy pulls up with a beautiful girlfriend and Colin's like, "I would give it all up for that girl." And I went, "Give all what up?" He laughed. |
| **Jerry:** | Oh, that is so . . . [*laughs*] |
| **Amy:** | Making him laugh is always the best. |
| **Jerry:** | [*laughs*] That's really funny. |
| **Amy:** | Because, you know, he trashes me so hard. |
| **Jerry:** | He does? |
| **Amy:** | Yeah. No, I think he's the funniest person. |

> "Successful extroverted comics would be a pretty small club, wouldn't it?"

## STEPHEN COLBERT

| | |
|---|---|
| **Stephen:** | So who is your guy? |
| **Jerry:** | Everyone. Everyone. |
| **Stephen:** | Cosby . . . the most important comedic figure to me in my entire life. You can't see it in my work. But he kept me alive as a kid, 'cause after my father and my brothers died, I listened to [the albums] *Bill Cosby Is a Very Funny Fellow, Right!* and *Wonderfulness* every night. For years I'd end my day with that. |
| **Jerry:** | Wow. |
| **Stephen:** | And I think I might be the last guy to interview him about anything other than what he doesn't want to talk about. |
| **Jerry:** | Really? |
| **Stephen:** | I had him on my show twenty-one days before Hannibal Buress said that onstage that kind of led to the re-racking of all the earlier accusations. It's very selfish, but I'm glad I had a moment with him to just play. I just played with him for twenty minutes. I know that he was a big guy for you. |
| **Jerry:** | Yeah. |
| **Stephen:** | And what a heartbreak. A selfish heartbreak. And then Steve Martin. Those would probably be . . . Like if you chopped off my head, my mouth would still start doing those routines. |
| **Jerry:** | Yeah, yeah. Anyway, to do a guest appearance on your show— |
| **Stephen:** | Oh, we're back to this. |
| **Jerry:** | Yeah, I just want you to know— |
| **Stephen:** | You're not going to let this go. |
| **Jerry:** | It's no fucking fun, okay? |
| **Stephen:** | It's no fun? |
| **Jerry:** | No. |

| | |
|---|---|
| **Stephen:** | You'd have no fun when you're on my show? |
| **Jerry:** | No. |
| **Stephen:** | None? |
| **Jerry:** | No, it's all business. I am not going to take a chance on making an appearance on your show that does not kill. I'm going to do everything I can . . . |
| **Stephen:** | This is actually very relaxing. And I also trust you that you're going to edit this into something. |
| **Jerry:** | Exactly. So you cannot compare the pain in the ass of doing your show to the joy and pleasure of doing mine. |

## STEVE MARTIN

| | |
|---|---|
| **Steve:** | When I was hanging out with Bob Einstein, we laughed so hard twenty-four hours a day because he lived above me. We had a little house. I lived downstairs and he lived upstairs. So we were together constantly. And, you know, you'd be laughing, laughing, laughing, and then you'd just go, "Okay, we got to write a bit." It would be like this gloom. |
| **Jerry:** | That is so funny. That is such the reality of comedy writing is the gloom. |
| **Steve:** | Mm-hmm. |
| **Jerry:** | The heaviness in the air. |
| **Steve:** | When you've got nothing. |
| **Jerry:** | And you need something. |
| **Steve:** | Right. Do you feel more ease with writing now? Because I definitely do. I feel like, "Hey, you need something, here it is." That's the way I feel. Whereas . . . |
| **Jerry:** | Well, I know that everything's hit-or-miss, so it doesn't really matter. My friend once taught me a great thing. When we wrote some sketches one time and we got stuck, he said, "Let's just write the ten worst ideas we can think of in ninety seconds." We each take a pad. Ninety seconds. The ten worst ideas. And you find that whoever comes up with the ideas in there, he's not thinking that this is good or this is bad. He's just shoveling. And the batting average of that stuff is just as good your ten best ideas. There's no difference, right? Because comedy isn't really good ideas. |
| **Steve:** | No, it's not. |
| **Jerry:** | It's not. It's just what works. |
| **Steve:** | It's a mystery. |
| **Jerry:** | It's just, "That bit works." |
| **Steve:** | I was in my car the other day, and I was listening to a comedy channel on SiriusXM Radio. A guy is talking. So funny. I was going, "This guy's |

unbelievable. Who is this? This guy's going to be famous." And at the end I found out it was Mitch Hedberg [who died in 2005].

**Jerry:** Right, yeah.

**Steve:** I don't know all his stuff. I just thought, "Now, that was great."

**Jerry:** Great. What a crazy vocal style. Which I guess is kind of that Randy Newman . . . Those people who come out of Louisiana, you know, with all those crawdads. They're just so off to begin with, you know?

**Steve:** About what now? [*laughs*]

**Jerry:** Crawdads. [*laughs*] The food that they eat. They eat a lot of crawdads in Louisiana. Anything crawls out of the swamp, they eat it. Right? That's what Louisiana is to me. I think that's a good place to come from. If you could pick a place to come from to be a great artist, I would pick Louisiana. You're born there, you're nuts.

**Steve:** [*laughs*] See, that's a very good bit.

**Jerry:** Is that a fair statement?

**Steve:** I think that's a very good bit. Yeah, you're right. I mean, you don't want to offend people from Louisiana, but—

**Jerry:** Why? I don't care?

**Steve:** You're not going to play Louisiana.

**Jerry:** Yes, I do. I play anywhere.

# KATHLEEN MADIGAN AND CHUCK MARTIN

**Jerry:** I came up with a great line in another episode, which I don't think it will make the episode. It was with Steve Martin. And we were talking about— he's a total android too.

**Kathleen:** Right.

**Jerry:** Especially with his comedy. Which is why you love him, and I love him. Because we love to do the exploding diagram of a joke or a comedic concept. And I came up with this thing. I said, "All great art is like a piece of graph paper and just someone throwing some paint at it." You need both for it to be great art. You can't just have a structureless flow of madness. You can do it for a little bit, but really great art I think has both those elements. Structure and flow. Structure being right angles, and flow just being free-moving energy—or emotion. What do you think of that? Pretty good.

**Kathleen:** That's why I'd [rather] be with George [Wallace] right now. He would've never said all that.

**Chuck:** 'Cause he wouldn't have understood it, either.

**Kathleen:** He would've said, "Baby, I don't know. Just go up there and talk to them. That's what I'd do. Just go up there and talk to them." I would've went, "That's right, I'm with you, George. These two are back there structuring flow and stuff. Let's just go have a beer and go talk to some people."

## JIM GAFFIGAN

**Jim:** Hasn't Jake Johannsen done, like, thirty hours [of stand-up]?

**Jerry:** Yes. Could I just hear the best hour, Jake?

**Jim:** [*laughs*] But that's a lot.

**Jerry:** I don't give a shit, okay, about the quantity.

**Jim:** I know. Blame the British.

**Jerry:** You think I can't do that? I'll write you a fucking hour a month. That'll be you know what? Decent. It'll be decent. But what's going to happen in that room is not what's going to happen when I put the set together of what really gets the room going. That's going to be a whole different experience. That's not all about me telling my buddies, "Well, I'm doing another special. I'm done with my new hour that's mediocre."

**Jim:** Yeah.

**Jerry:** That's what I'm sick of. How 'bout an act that kills? How 'bout killing? When did killing become not important in comedy? I'll tell you when: 1994.

**Jim:** Really?

**Jerry:** When the alt scene started, yeah. That's when people decided killing didn't matter anymore. Let's fast-forward twenty-five years to when you're fifty-eight talking about how painful, uh, your life is.

**Jim:** Well, that goes back to you should make people laugh that you have nothing in common with.

**Jerry:** Right.

**Jim:** It's the Dave Attell thing of "You might not like me, but you will like this joke." And by the way, Dave Attell is very likable, you know what I'm saying? Where people are like, "Oh, I disagree with that, but I can't help myself but laugh."

**Jerry:** Right.

> "You should make people laugh that you have nothing in common with."

# J.B. SMOOVE

**Jerry:**    I had dinner with Larry David the other night. We had so many laughs.

**J.B.:**    That's a funny guy. He came to my birthday party.

**Jerry:**    Oh yeah?

**J.B.:**    My fiftieth birthday party. Larry is the funniest guy. Let me tell you something about Larry. Larry came early, right, and was walking around the party. You know, he pulls his jacket back, his hands go in his pockets, and he just rolls around the party people-watching.

**Jerry:**    Yeah.

**J.B.:**    So my party planner calls me and says, "Larry's here. He's walking around the party. I'll let you know when to come down." You know, parties, you got to make an entrance.

**Jerry:**    Right.

**J.B.:**    So Larry's walking around the party, hanging out, people-watching. By the time it was time for me to come downstairs, they called me three times: "Larry's asking about you. He said, 'How's he late for his own party?'" I'm like, "I'm not late. I'm upstairs in the hotel because my party planner said come downstairs when the party is jumpin'. Make your entrance." Larry's there *early*.

**Jerry:** J.B. Smoove style guide.

**J.B.:** He's getting irritated. He's walking around. So by the time I came down to the party—my wife and I are walking toward the stage to go onstage to welcome [everyone] to the party—Larry's on my coattails. I go onstage and they gave me a microphone, and then Larry grabs a microphone: "What's—what's going on here?" I said, "What? What are you talking about, Larry?" "I've been here for a long time, you know. What's going on?" I said, "Larry, I had to make a grand entrance. This is my party. Why would I be walking around my own party when you come in? So I'm going to be the only person standing here waiting for people to come? That's depressing."

**Jerry:** Yeah.

**J.B.:** You know? So Larry comes onstage. I said, "Larry, this is a black party. We do things differently. We hype it up. I make a grand entrance. That's how it is." He said, "Well, the invite said . . ." I said, "Larry, you turn the flyer over. You look at the back." He was like, "I didn't know there was a back." I said, "Well, it's a black party. That's how people do. We come in late, we going to make a grand entrance." And Larry says, "Well, leave earlier. See you later." [*laughs*]

# *JUDD APATOW*

**Judd:** I used to live in the valley in North Hollywood with Adam Sandler. We lived in an apartment. It was $900 a month. I paid $425. Sandler paid $475 'cause he had a room with a bathroom in it. We could just do our jokes at night and eat fettuccine Alfredo at two in the morning.

**Jerry:** Wow. So at what point did he get *SNL*? He wasn't still living with you?

**Judd:** He was. He went and did an audition at the Chicago Improv and he comes back and he said, "I got *SNL*." And I said, "How did you get *SNL*? You don't do any characters. All you do is mumble onstage. You do Elvis in the refrigerator. How's this going to work?" He goes to *SNL*, suddenly he's doing impressions of Axl Rose and he has this incredible array of voices, and then he was gone. And he didn't give up the apartment for about a year, and I just lived alone. And Sandler's so funny—he didn't even bring his clothes. He never picked them up, and then when I moved out of the apartment I had all of his clothes, and to this day I have a lot of his clothes 'cause I'm a hoarder. He left his driver's license. He just, like, left town to be a star.

| | |
|---|---|
| **Jerry:** | Maybe we need a word for positive hoarding. |
| **Judd:** | Yeah. Poarding. |
| **Jerry:** | Poarding? |
| **Judd:** | Poarding. Positive hoarding. [*laughs*] When we were making the movie *Funny People*, I remembered that Adam and I used to make phony phone calls and I would videotape them. And I said that'd be an interesting opening to the movie, to see a young George Simmons [Sandler's character]. And I went in storage and I had all of 'em, and that's the opening of the movie: Adam calling Jerry's Deli. He would always call Jerry's Deli and complain about the roast beef as an old lady. He would say it made him sick and try to negotiate how many free sandwiches he could get because he got diarrhea from the roast beef. He would say, "Can I have a free sandwich?" And they would say, "Okay, yeah. Next time you come in you can have a free sandwich." "Does it have to be roast beef? Can it be turkey next time?" [*laughs*] |
| **Jerry:** | [*laughs*] And now he's doing some stand-up too, I heard. |
| **Judd:** | He is! I forced him to come to Largo one night and he wrote twenty new songs, and now he's going on the road and doing stand-up and loving it. Don't you think you have to keep doing stand-up to stay sharp? I'm asking the wrong guy. [*laughs*] Who am I talking to? |
| **Jerry:** | Who are you talking to? |
| **Judd:** | But people who stop, I think it affects their work in whatever they do. |
| **Jerry:** | But it's very hard to keep up if you've got other big things going on. To me, stand-up is a profession. It's a full career. Okay, Judd Apatow's top five stand-up comics. |
| **Judd:** | Oh jeez. Of all time? |
| **Jerry:** | All time. Living or dead. |
| **Judd:** | That's so hard. |
| **Jerry:** | And if I'm in there, take me out. |
| **Judd:** | Okay, I'm going to take you out, but you were in there. |
| **Jerry:** | Oh, thank you. That's so sweet. |
| **Judd:** | Okay. Here we go. |
| **Jerry:** | It doesn't have to be in order. |
| **Judd:** | Okay, Richard Pryor. George Carlin. I'm going to say Maria Bamford. I'm putting her in my top five. |
| **Jerry:** | Wow. She's going to be happy when she hears this. |
| **Judd:** | Um, Steve Martin. |
| **Jerry:** | Okay. That's four. As Brian Regan says, "Go on." |
| **Judd:** | And I'm going to go with . . . then I'm going Chris Rock. |
| **Jerry:** | Chris Rock, yeah. |
| **Judd:** | That's it. That's my five. There's five more. |
| **Jerry:** | Yup. It's not really a fair question. I know. |

| | |
|---|---|
| **Judd:** | It's not fair. [When I was a teenager,] I asked if I could get a job at East Side Comedy Club, which was in Huntington [on Long Island]. It was about twenty minutes from my house, and I got a job there as a dishwasher and I just wanted to watch comedy. I would get dropped off but I'd have to take a cab home, and all of the money I made washing dishes was used for the cab home. So I made nothing. And then I realized, "I can't watch the comics. I'm in the kitchen." So then I switched to busboy, because I realized I have to be in the showroom. |
| **Jerry:** | And you were sixteen? |
| **Judd:** | Yeah, fifteen. And I would watch—Eddie Murphy was still coming in. |
| **Jerry:** | Wow. |
| **Judd:** | When he was twenty-one. Bob Nelson, Rob Bartlett . . . |
| **Jerry:** | Bob Nelson with the football helmet. |
| **Judd:** | With the football helmet and the shouldah-ma pads. |
| **Jerry:** | The what? |
| **Judd:** | The shouldah-ma pads. |
| **Jerry:** | [*laughs*] Where is he now? Do you know where any of these people are? |
| **Judd:** | I think Bob Nelson is religious and works in Branson [Missouri]. |
| **Jerry:** | Doing comedy. |
| **Judd:** | Doing comedy and clean comedy, such as yourself. And that was a great club, East Side Comedy Club. |
| **Jerry:** | Yes, it was. |
| **Judd:** | A lot of cocaine going through that club. |
| **Jerry:** | Oh, really? I never saw any of those drugs. |
| **Judd:** | So I was the busboy, and I remember Lenny Schultz came in and he had that crazy act and how it ended was they put plastic down on the stage, he would put on this Italian opera music, he would have a big thing of spaghetti, and he would lip-sync to this opera and throw the spaghetti in his face. And then it ended, like, pouring milk over his head and cracking eggs on his head. And then he would come in the kitchen and jump in the giant sink and I would have to pour buckets of water over his head to get all of the spaghetti and eggs off of him, and I could not have been happier. |
| **Jerry:** | Oh my God. |
| **Judd:** | I'm in show business, I'm cleaning Lenny Schultz's taint right now! |
| **Jerry:** | You know who loves Lenny Schultz is Letterman. |
| **Judd:** | Oh sure, those acts that go nuts. There's not many of them anymore. There's very few lose-your-mind acts. There aren't even acts like Sam Kinison anymore. You know, there was an era where there were a lot of guys like Dice [Andrew Dice Clay] and Kinison who really did something completely different than what everybody else was doing. And it's kind of like we lost the maniacs. |
| **Jerry:** | Because everybody's too career-oriented, you think? |

## "It's kind of like we lost the maniacs."

**Judd:**    I don't know. It's just, I feel like it's less . . . you know, where are the maniacs?

**Jerry:**    Well, Katt Williams. Still in the maniac category.

**Judd:**    Yeah, so funny. Couldn't be funnier. But the act's still kind of a standard act. I'm talking about the spaghetti in the face. Like Andy Kaufman. Like The Legendary Wid.

**Jerry:**    Legendary Wid, with the two garbage cans full of props.

**Judd:**    I saw Kinison in '86 at a benefit for Comic Relief. He hadn't broken big yet. So the crowd didn't know who he was. And he started his act, the place is packed at the Comedy Store. Five minutes in, every single woman in the entire club has exited the club. It's all men now, half the room and it's men, and it's the biggest laughs you've ever heard. But there was a moment when you really could clear the room with an act like that.

People forget that [Rodney] Dangerfield broke almost everybody. He took Jim Carrey on the road when Jim was, like, eighteen years old. Yeah, Dangerfield was so insanely funny. I saw him at Westbury Music Fair. You would miss two jokes for every joke you laughed at.

**Jerry:**    Right. [*laughs*]

**Judd:**    When Rodney was very old, he was in his eighties, Sandler chartered a jet, and a bunch of us went to see him in Vegas. It was an odd crew. It was me, Sandler, Rob Schneider, Carl Weathers, and Quentin Tarantino.

**Jerry:**    Carl Weathers? From *Rocky*? [*laughs*]

**Judd:**    Yes, who was in *Happy Gilmore*. And we all went to see Rodney. And someone heckled him and he just decimated the guy. And then we hung out all night with Rodney. And he's super high and so funny, and it was one of the great nights, just sitting around with Rodney.

**Jerry:**    I did that too, except I drove. Me and Mark Schiff and Steve Mittleman drove to Vegas, and we walked in and saw Rodney at the Sands. And he came out into the lobby, and Mittleman had written a couple jokes for him, so he knew him. And we were talking. He didn't know who we were, and he said, "Where are you guys sleeping?" We go, "We don't have anyplace to sleep. We just thought we'd come to Vegas, 'cause we were in LA. It seemed close. We wanted to see some comedians." So he gave us his manager's room to sleep in.

**Judd:**    Oh, wow.

**Jerry:**    But every time I saw him for the rest of his life, he loved that story, that we were so stupid we came to Vegas with no money and no place to stay. [*laughs*]

**Judd:**    That's nice of him to give you the manager's room.

**Jerry:**    Yeah, 'cause he didn't have a manager.

# NORM MACDONALD

**Jerry:** What's interesting is—this is what I've learned doing this show: you take two comics, you throw 'em in a barrel, and something happens.

**Norm:** Yeah, now, David Letterman, I realized in speaking with him, is not a stand-up comedian, and I thought he was.

**Jerry:** He never really became that. He started as that. He certainly showcased his enormous talents doing that. Or gave you a glimpse of his talents doing that. His real talent was what he did as a talk show host. And a comedian, as you and I know, is a very unique animal. That's what I've found.

**Norm:** But when David Letterman wrote a joke, his word choice, his command of the vocabulary, was without parallel.

**Jerry:** I don't agree with that, but I know what you're saying.

**Norm:** You don't agree with that?

**Jerry:** Without parallel? There are parallels.

**Norm:** Without parallel, none parallel. Who would have more command of the language than David Letterman?

**Jerry:** Um . . .

**Norm:** Is there a smarter comedian than David Letterman?

**Jerry:** Dennis Miller had a very good vocabulary in his stand-up days.

**Norm:** And Dennis Miller has in real life the ability to do those—maybe you'd call them metaphors. Like, just off the top of his head. And the beautiful part of it is, if you know [the reference], it feels so special, you know what I mean? It only hits a certain amount of the audience, but you go, "I thought I was the only guy." He knows everybody.

**Jerry:** Yes, he'll refer to the third lead in *Petticoat Junction*. And you go, "I didn't know you knew this person too."

**Norm:** Yeah, it makes you feel special. How many great comedians are there right now?

**Jerry:** Right now?

**Norm:** Yeah. Let's name some comedians. I think we both agree on Brian Regan.

**Jerry:** A hundred percent.

**Norm:** That's maybe the best comedian in the world.

**Jerry:** Maybe.

**Norm:** And yet you never mention him.

**Jerry:** I disagree. Every comedian I know mentions him.

**Norm:** Every comedian does, but not when they're asked in the newspaper, you know what I mean?

**Jerry:** That's stupid. What matters is your standing in the community. In my opinion.

**Norm:** He's right at the top. You, right at the top.

| | |
|---|---|
| **Jerry:** | Thank you. You, right at the top. |
| **Norm:** | Ah, not me. |
| **Jerry:** | Yeah, yeah. Your last *Letterman*, with the World War I and II bit. I have never heard more comics talk about a bit. For weeks and weeks. Still. When I tell people that you're doing the show, that's the first thing they say: "Oh, his last *Letterman* was so great." I heard that you put a lot of work into that. |
| **Norm:** | Goddamn right I did. Holy shit. |
| **Jerry:** | Well, it showed. |
| **Norm:** | When I saw that show ended, the Letterman show, it meant [something] to me, that show. And nothing was happening. No one was doing anything special for it. They come on as if it was just a regular show. They just had this ironic detachment. But not to me. To me it was a really sad moment in my life. So yeah, I worked really hard. I wanted every joke to be as good as it possibly could be, so I really stoked that furnace. I had eleven jokes. Five that I had in my act, and six new jokes that I worked very, very hard on. |
| **Jerry:** | That must be a great feeling, knowing that you set that goal for yourself. You loaded that arrow into your bow, and you hit the bull's-eye— |
| **Norm:** | I was very happy. |
| **Jerry:** | —on that show, which I agree with you is so important. Because for us, that was the end of the kingdom that we aspired to our entire lives. It was Carson and Letterman. That was the kingdom. |

## CEDRIC THE ENTERTAINER

| | |
|---|---|
| **Cedric:** | I tell you, one my scariest things early on, I had to open Sam Kinison. Did you ever work with Sam Kinison? |
| **Jerry:** | Many times. |
| **Cedric:** | Brilliant. He was one of my favorites, right? |
| **Jerry:** | Brilliant. Me too. |
| **Cedric:** | This was toward the end of his career. He was super-famous and rock-and-roll Sam Kinison. He was rockin'. And I was in Des Moines, Iowa. Funny Bone. Young act. I would end up being better than the middle, right? So the middle act couldn't really follow me. But I was the opening act. So Sam was in the car smashed. They say, "He's smashed, and they're getting him together. You've got to go up there and stretch." |
| **Jerry:** | After you already opened. |
| **Cedric:** | And I already opened. The middle act had went up, and he did okay. Then I went back up and kind of got the crowd back, right, thinking I'm doing the right thing. Like, "Ladies and gentlemen, I got the room back, right. |

Here's one of my favorites, Mister . . . hold on . . . hold on." Manager comes up: "Stretch, stretch, stretch." Oh, more jokes. I am completely depleted of jokes. I have no ideas. And I'm not a good crowd worker, not at that time. "Hey, so where are you guys from?" I didn't know how to do any of that. I just remember that being my scariest time onstage, man.

**Jerry:** It's so funny, 'cause I see you now, and anyone in the audience would think the same thing: I can't imagine you ever [not] being that good. I can't picture it.

**Cedric:** He finally came in, and that was one of those moments where you just felt so much relief, 'cause I didn't think he was going to make it. That makes me think of another time. Have you ever done like Chappelle? These guys that can do, like, twelve hours onstage?

**Jerry:** No, I've never done that.

**Cedric:** What was the longest?

**Jerry:** I don't think longer's better.

**Cedric:** I don't either. I agree.

**Jerry:** To me, the objective of comedy is to suck the air out of it so that it's this incredibly dense—a great joke is short. That's what makes it great: how much information is in just a few words.

**Cedric:** Yeah, I agree. I love Chris Rock's joke about a prostitute. That was one of my favorite jokes. It's a quick joke: "I saw a prostitute. She said, 'For three hundred dollars, I'll do whatever you want.' 'Three hundred dollars? Bitch, paint my house.'"

**Jerry:** Yeah, three words: "Paint my house." Brilliant. That's a great joke.

**Cedric:** I had a big joke on my special about when black shows go off [the air], they don't get the big fanfare. The final episode of *Seinfeld*, it'd be billboards. You were up everywhere. People would cry: "Oh my God, I'm going to miss them so much." When *Martin* went off, it was like he got fired on Friday. "Hey, you know, what happened to Martin? He got fired or something?" I didn't know it was the last day of *The Steve Harvey Show* until they showed up with the cake. I'm like, "What's the cake for, Steve?" He's like, "It's the last day, dog." "What?"

**Jerry:** Steve is doing great.

**Cedric:** Steve is doing amazing, man. I talk to him all the time.

# DANA CARVEY

**Dana:** One way I write is by doing the character. That's how we used to write, me and Kevin [Nealon]. We'd go for hours, just with a tape recorder. So when I do Dennis [Miller], I literally improve my vocabulary. If you give me any topic, I'd just go through Dennis. [*impersonates Dennis*] "Here, now,

*"A great joke is short. That's what makes it great: how much information is in just a few words."*

you're Seinfeld, huh? *Comedians in Cars*, okay. What's next, hang gliding with the funsters? You and Leno up there on the mountain, coming down." He's the greatest. You like Dennis, right?

**Jerry:** I love Dennis. He does not care if you know what he's talking about.

**Dana:** He keeps a Rolodex. When you talk to him on the phone, he just brings 'em out. Just unbelievable. You know, there are the classics. [*impersonates Dennis*] "I haven't seen choreography like that since the Lee Harvey Oswald prison transfer."

**Jerry:** Yeah, I love that one.

**Dana:** Never got tired of that one. You're a Robert Klein guy, right? I mean, that's probably your number one. . . .

**Jerry:** Yes. Imagine being a kid in New York, and you see this guy. He's like Robin [Williams] for you when you saw that guy and you went, "Oh my God."

**Dana:** I interviewed him for a school newspaper. I was going to San Francisco State, and he wasn't even on *Mork and Mindy* [yet]. Because I'd seen him. I'll just tell you this quick story, 'cause it's interesting. I go to an open mic, my first night ever. I'm twenty. I saw it in the paper. Too shy to do theater, acting, anything. Took some friends. Unknown comics come up—they're good, but not, you know . . . So I took out a napkin. I'm writing down the kind of shtick that I do—Howard Cosell, this and that. And then a guy comes out. Levitates the room. Ridiculous. And it was Robin. But I didn't know there was only one Robin, so I put the napkin back in my pocket, going, "I don't think . . ." I thought there was hundreds of 'em. I didn't know, you know?

But I went up that night, did five minutes. Got invited back. I interviewed Robin, and for some reason Robin had that voice, almost an English accent or something. I said, "Do you aspire to be in movies or television?" And he goes, "Oh, I just want to play for the people. Just want to play for the people." But when he would come back, I always thought, "I have to get better." He pushed me.

**Jerry:** What did you think when you heard about Robin? Were you completely surprised or no?

**Dana:** I knew there was a lot of stuff going on. I still have texts from him. He was an incredibly shy person. Part of that hyper-charisma—I have a theory about Marilyn Monroe or Elvis Presley. Crazy confidence. Totally insecure. It's this vibrating thing. I think Robin had the two. It's like the vibration of that made him, you know . . .

One night [not long before he died], I played a theater. I do the set. Now it's misty rain. It's this little teeny street. No one's around. Just a streetlight, like a scene out of a movie. And I come out the side door, and I see Robin. "Dana, can I have a minute?" This was before he left for LA. He left two days later. He said, "I just want to make amends for maybe

taking some of your material." Like, he would refer to his dick as "Mr. Happy." He thought he took it from me. I said, "Robin, no. I didn't do that. It wasn't me." And then in that moment I said, "Robin, I tried to take your whole act. I did all your voices. I had the props." So it was kind of a very real moment. And then we had lunch the next day, and we talked about our kids. The power of the word "dad." And then he left.

Then it happened, you know. Once I saw that he was in rehab in Hazelden, I thought, "He's okay." But I didn't know he was impacted on these different levels. The Lewy body dementia's very real.

**Jerry:** The what?

**Dana:** Lewy body dementia. What he had. The brain disease that can make you . . . I don't know his particular story. It can really make facial movements difficult. It'll make you hallucinate. That was too much for him. He was obviously not in his right mind. That's what the disease was.

**Jerry:** Wow, I never knew this.

**Dana:** For Robin, he felt like he couldn't be funny anymore. It was just very . . . Yeah, I'm a little emotional behind these eyes. Just . . . it's just sad.

## ZACH GALIFINIAKIS

**Jerry:** I have heard you do that somewhere: "If you didn't laugh, you're not racist."

**Zach:** I used to say it after another joke, which was, "I live in a black neighborhood"—which used to be true—"and I wear a lot of Axe body spray. But there it's called Ask body spray." The audience laughs, and then I say, "If you don't get that, then you're not racist." To put it off on the audience, I find always to be really funny.

**Jerry:** Yeah, that's funny.

**Zach:** Dave Attell does it a lot. He'll say something and go, "Or as some people call them," even though he thought it. He just throws it off. [*laughs*] He's the best. You know him, right?

**Jerry:** I do. I don't know if he's the best, but he's good.

**Zach:** He's the best live at the Comedy Cellar to me. On TV, I think he loses something. But live . . .

**Jerry:** I never saw anybody wearing two hoodies onstage. Two. I mean, I get that you feel the hoodie really is who you are. But that is underlining it just a bit.

**Zach:** Well, he's a fifty-three-year-old man.

**Jerry:** So?

**Zach:** He's just getting into the hoodie movement. I told you on the phone yesterday: that to me is the ultimate compliment. I'm not saying comedy should be clean, but it is much harder to do.

> "I'm not saying comedy should be clean, but it is much harder to do."

**Jerry:** It is. All the comedians know that. I don't think the audience cares. But comedians know that.

**Zach:** Was that a purposeful thing? That you thought it was too easy, or you just didn't want to . . . ?

**Jerry:** Well, in my day, frankly—

**Zach:** Yes, it wasn't allowed as much.

**Jerry:** Yeah, if you wanted to be on TV, you had to work clean. And then once I started doing it, it just seemed to make me do better, so I felt comfortable. I don't know. I never really thought much about it.

**Zach:** I envy it, in a way. I respect it. Being a comic who's not like that, I respect that a lot. Because of the difficulty of it. And also that it is incredibly funny. A lot of times with the clean stuff, it's too saccharine or too vanilla. Yours is different. Gaffigan's the same way. I used to perform burlesque shows all the time. In Vancouver, where I was doing a lot of stand-up, you'd go to the Ukrainian club and there would be a burlesque show, and whoever's booking the burlesque show would have a comedian. I did that a lot.

**Jerry:** That is fantastic. I would say the comedians of that era . . . See, comedians today can go up and they can give the audience an experience, let's say, that isn't necessarily result-oriented, or laugh-based. And that's okay.

**Zach:** [*laughs*] So you're saying it's not laugh-based comedy?

**Jerry:** Yes. It's doable. But not in vaudeville in the early days, in the early first half of the twentieth century, no, no. Your act has to get laughs.

**Zach:** I see what you're saying.

**Jerry:** The act has to get the laughs or you're canceled. There was no latitude. The audience gave the performance no latitude.

**Zach:** But that is welcomed in those alternative rooms—that type of stand-up. Dave Attell, I've always tried to get him to do it. He won't do it, because he has a snobbery about their snobbery.

**Jerry:** Now, what if I went there? What would happen?

**Zach:** Go tonight. You want to go tonight?

**Jerry:** I'm on a plane tonight. But I would.

# DAVE CHAPPELLE

**Dave:** I like mean comics. I like Chris [Rock] a lot too.

**Jerry:** I don't think he's mean. I don't. You see, the context of stand-up kind of negates any meanness. You're looking at a person who's just a gladiator, he's out there by himself.

**Dave:** He's not malicious, but he's mean. I can't explain it.

**Jerry:** The word I used for him is "brutal."

**Dave:** There you go.

**Jerry:** He's brutal.

## "Comedians speak in commandments."

**Dave:** He is.

**Jerry:** When he was going through his split, I was saying this is like one of the greatest things to ever happen in comedy. Because you're the most brutal man and you're now going through the most brutal circumstance. This is perfect.

**Dave:** Some of the shit he said about that divorce was some of the funniest shit I've ever heard. It's just him lamenting. But it's funny because here's this weird way where he'll take the personal element out of it and make it this bigger thing.

**Jerry:** Everything's a pronouncement. Like most comedians. Comedians speak in commandments. "Here's what you must never do. You." He's the king of that.

**Dave:** He's really good at it.

**Jerry:** I always tell him, "Your act sounds like the closing arguments of some kind of trial."

## MARGARET CHO

**Margaret:** I remember seeing Paula Poundstone [at the Other Café in San Francisco]. And it just blew my mind. She blew my mind. She was just so . . . I couldn't even describe it. It was so funny and so, like, "How do you think like that?" Somebody would get up to go to the bathroom, so she would go into their stuff. Put on their clothes and go in their purse or whatever, and just do bits and comedy about the stuff she'd find. And the audience would be dying. Then the audience member would come back and be like, "What's going on?" There's magic in comedy clubs. I'm glad that you still do sets. Can you imagine the people freaking out? You go in and then you get to see Jerry Seinfeld. That must be incredible.

**Jerry:** Yeah, I don't really think about that part. I just think the game is a wonder on every level. We could, like, do a little set here. I like this guy Sebastian Maniscalco.

**Margaret:** Oh yeah, he's wonderful.

**Jerry:** He's got a birdlike precision.

**Margaret:** It's very bird, yeah, it's very bird. Like an eye that goes all the way around.

**Jerry:** You know birds, they're very quickly in eight different directions.

**Margaret:** He's very nice too. He's very funny and sweet and surprised that you like his comedy. "Whoa, really?" You could go sneaking up on him. Like he's scared, 'cause he's just looking around all the time for predators.

## SEBASTIAN MANISCALCO

**Jerry:** Big cover story today in the Arts and Leisure of the *Times* on Lenny Bruce.

**Sebastian:** Oh yeah? When did he pass away?

**Jerry:** In '66 at the age of forty.

**Sebastian:** Forty. Of what?

**Jerry:** Drug overdose.

**Sebastian:** You ever meet him?

**Jerry:** I was eleven.

**Sebastian:** [*laughs*] I was going to do the math before I asked you, but I'm like, "Eh, I'll just ask. It's too much work."

**Jerry:** The biography of him that was done in the early '70s, this big thick book, is really what propelled me into stand-up. Because it was the first time I saw to understand how an act was created, and I went, "Oh, I think I could do that." I thought these guys just talk like that. When I would see comedians on TV I thought, "Well, that's how that guy talks all the time probably."

**Sebastian:** You didn't know there was an act behind it?

**Jerry:** No.

**Sebastian:** I thought they were just talking too. I thought they just went up there and they were reciting their day. What fascinated me was when I started to see the act over and over, how they would say it like it's the first time they're telling the story. That's when I started to think, "Oh, wow, this guy is saying the same thing over and over again."

**Jerry:** I love that part of it. I love doing the same jokes over and over. For me, it's like something good that happened to me and it gets to keep happening. "I thought of that. It's so nice to me, like I'm going to hear that two hundred times." If it was a good line, "Oh, I'm going to hear that hundreds of times."

# EDDIE MURPHY

**Eddie:** You said your comedy Mount Rushmore is Pryor, Cosby, Carlin, and Rickles.

**Jerry:** Yeah.

**Eddie:** I would change one person. I love Rickles, but I would replace him with Charlie Chaplin.

**Jerry:** He's not stand-up.

**Eddie:** But it's beyond stand-up. He has no sound. He's making you laugh with no sound, you win.

**Jerry:** I get you.

**Eddie:** No sound at all. Hey, did you get that Mark Twain award?

**Jerry:** No.

**Eddie:** You should get that.

**Jerry:** I don't like awards.

**Eddie:** You should get the Mark Twain award.

**Jerry:** I don't want it. I'm fine. You're my Mark Twain award.

**Eddie:** But you deserve that Mark Twain award.

**Jerry:** I'm more than happy with this.

**Eddie:** Mark Twain is the first stand-up comic. He's the first guy traveling around, telling his stories, and getting laughs. People are coming to hear him speak because he's funny.

**Jerry:** You know, he went broke because—

**Eddie:** Mark Twain?

**Jerry:** Yes, he went broke. He had a lot of money, he had a lot of success, and at that time, everybody was trying to figure out who was going to make the first printing press. They had invented the printing press and all these different companies were making printing presses and he invested all his money into one of these companies. And he lost it all.

| | |
|---|---|
| **Eddie:** | That's the Mark Twain story? |
| **Jerry:** | And then to survive, what he did was he booked a stand-up tour around the world. This is like 1880. A book just came out about this, and I've been reading it. Steamships, trains—he booked all through the States. Then Australia, India. He went to London, just because he was broke. He needed money. |
| **Eddie:** | The first comic. He literally is the first comic. |
| **Jerry:** | Do you know any of his bits? |
| **Eddie:** | No. |
| **Jerry:** | Well, he's not much of a comic then. Did you ever see Pryor get up in a little club? |
| **Eddie:** | You know, I had a strange relationship with Richard. Because back when I broke, the town was still doing a one-black-guy-at-a-time thing. So when I showed up, Richard had this—there was this feeling like, "Oh, this is the new one," and he kind of felt threatened. Richard would get weird. If I found out he was going to be somewhere and we all went, Richard would pull up and go "Who's in there?" "Eddie Murphy is on." And he would leave. |
| **Jerry:** | Really? |
| **Eddie:** | Yeah, he would not want to work out in front of me. It was strange. And I just wanted to puppy-dog him. I found all this stuff out afterwards. Like, "Really? He would do that?" |
| **Jerry:** | Do you think there was a racial problem? |
| **Eddie:** | There absolutely was in the 1980s. It was one at a time, one at a time. It'd be like one [black actor] in the movies who was getting all the [roles]. And Richard was like, "Oh it's not my . . . something new is going on." That was the weirdness with Cosby as well in the early days. He thought I was this new thing, and they felt threatened by it. |
| **Jerry:** | And it's so funny to me when I think back on it—that [Cosby] thought he had the power to tell you to work the way he wanted you to work. What crazy fantasy was that? |
| **Eddie:** | That's just ego. It was his ego. |
| **Jerry:** | I even in the moment thought, "Is he out of his mind, telling him how to work? He's going to work how he wants to work." |
| **Eddie:** | He had a weird thing with me that he didn't have with other comics. Because I've heard other people tell stories about, "Oh, I had this with him, and he said this to me. He gave me this advice." And the stuff that he said to me was the exact opposite. It was mean. I did this bit about somebody heckling me, and I said, "Shut the fuck up before I throw my wallet over there and crush you." And [Cosby] called me up and said, "You can't talk about how much money you have onstage." I was like, "Oh, no, you have to see the routine. It's taken out of context." He was like, "Well, you know, I don't come and see people's shows." Then he told me, "I'm in Atlantic |

*"Back when I broke, the town was still doing a one-black-guy-at-a-time thing."*

City this weekend. You should come and see how it's supposed to be done."

**Jerry:** Oh man.

**Eddie:** "And you shouldn't get on the stage unless you have something to say." That's what he told me.

**Jerry:** Wow.

**Eddie:** Yeah, he wasn't nice.

**Jerry:** That's so weird. I think he felt that he was in charge of the comedy culture. He was the president of comedy. "And I don't like what's going on in my business, so I'm going to straighten this young man out."

**Eddie:** No, it was—he wasn't doing that with everybody. He did that with me specifically. He was shitty with me, yeah. That was a whole changing of the guard, him thinking that. Because this is before *The Cosby Show*. Before all of that—1981. I think *The Cosby Show* was in '84, when it started. So he was just a comic who wasn't liking one of the new guys. 'Cause it was only a handful of black comics. It was Charlie Barnett, Barry Berry, Larry Ragland.

**Jerry:** Larry Ragland, I loved.

**Eddie:** Keenen [Ivory Wayans] was over at the Improv. Jimmie Walker and Franklyn Ajaye. You could literally count the people on two hands, that's all the black comics there was.

**Jerry:** I know, but there were only fifty, sixty comics anyway.

**Eddie:** Yeah, yeah, that's crazy. That's crazy it used to be fifty or sixty, because now it's . . . Like I said earlier, it's more of everything now. You have so many options. It's more of everything. Everything.

**Jerry:** Right. My friend calls it "the everything bubble." It's going to pop because there's just too much of everything.

**Eddie:** I don't know if it's going to pop, I just think that's the way it is now. It's because we're older, we go, "It's going to pop one day. [*laughs*] One day, all of this will pop and it will go back to a few." It's not.

**Jerry:** Yeah, but you know what? Eddie, I've got to tell you, I have heard young people also say there's too much mediocrity, but I don't care about that. Because I think comedy is an ecosystem that corrects itself.

**Eddie:** Absolutely.

**Jerry:** You don't have to do anything.

**Eddie:** The audience doesn't have the same expectation. Back in the day, most people coming to a comedy club, it was like their first time coming to a comedy club. And now you've got so many stand-up shows and so much stuff, and the audience kind of knows. That's why I say you don't have to be good to make a living. All you have to do is come in and have the beats, audience knows when you go up there that they're supposed to have this reaction, and you say that, [get] that reaction, and then it's the next comic. Like they don't know when it's special or what's special

because they were weaned on this mediocre shit. And it's always only a handful of special ones.

**Jerry:** No matter how many people we throw at this problem.

**Eddie:** Yes, if it's fifty comics back in the day, it's ten good ones.

**Jerry:** Six good ones, yeah.

**Eddie:** And if it's a thousand comics today, it's still ten good ones.

**Jerry:** I think there's more than a thousand.

**Eddie:** But it's still only ten good ones, ten special ones.

**Jerry:** Right. And that's because . . .

**Eddie:** Because there can never be more than ten special ones at a time. [*laughs*] There could never be more than ten special ones.

# FOOD

## *LARRY DAVID*

**Larry:**  If it's not free-range chicken, there's a lot wrong with it.

**Jerry:**  How much do you think these chickens really enjoy that range? You think they're going out there like a palomino?

**Larry:**  I think they're enjoying it a lot more than that little cage where they're shitting on each other.

**Jerry:**  You know what? The hell with them.

# *BARRY MARDER*

**Jerry:** I like to ask people, "What would be your last breakfast, last lunch, last dinner?" I use that sometimes as a conversational gambit in a dull, dull evening. If I'm ever at a dinner party or something, and I'm finding myself getting bored, I would challenge someone on their last meal.

**Barry:** You getting bored? You going to ask me what I would like for—

**Jerry:** No. When I do, you'll know I'm bored. You can ask anybody that and get kind of an interesting response. Don't you think?

**Barry:** Yes.

**Jerry:** What would be your last . . . I'm not bored. I'm just curious. Last dinner, what would it be?

**Barry:** If I was going to be executed? Well, as you know, I am an aficionado of those websites and I always try to read the last meals. I never see, like, a bagel and lox and capers for a last meal.

**Jerry:** No one's going to get capers in their last meal.

## JOEL HODGSON

**Jerry:** I drink coffee until my eyeballs are in front of my glasses.

**Joel:** How many cups of coffee can you drink in a day?

**Jerry:** Six. At a sitting. I'll have probably four of these while we're sitting here. . . . What do you think of this ketchup with the cap on the bottom?

**Joel:** It's great. How many fights did they have over this before someone said, "But the ketchup goes to the bottom. Put the cap on the bottom." Can you imagine?

## COLIN QUINN AND MARIO JOYNER

**Colin:** That was one of the saddest days ever, when they stopped smoking at the Waffle Houses.

**Jerry:** What do you mean?

**Mario:** They stopped smoking at the Waffle House after smoking was banned. The Waffle House was the last place to give it up. They fought it.

**Jerry:** You need that smell in the waffles, of cigarettes.

> "That was one of the saddest days ever, when they stopped smoking at the Waffle Houses."

## CARL REINER AND MEL BROOKS

**Jerry:** They know Jews are eating it, so they give you extra napkins.

**Mel:** Is that true?

**Jerry:** Well, look at the amount of napkins. Do you think a Chinese restaurant or an Italian restaurant would do that?

**Various:** Never.

**Jerry:** A Jewish deli knows: "These guys are going to make a mess."

**Carl:** Somebody said a funny line. "A chicken doesn't stand a chance."

**Jerry:** I think it was George Wallace.

**Carl:** He said that?

**Jerry:** "Not one chicken has ever died of natural causes." [*laughter*]

## MICHAEL RICHARDS

**Jerry:** One of the things we talked about was the comedy of food in scenes—comedic food.

**Michael:** Oh, yes.

**Jerry:** You did a lot of comedic eating on the show.

**Michael:** Yes, I did.

**Jerry:** But I would say—and I would like your opinion—"Not every day" with the ice cream at the beginning of "The Contest" was your greatest line reading. Remember the discussion where we were doing "The Contest" episode, which was about self-gratification? And Elaine says, "I want to be in on the bet." And George says, "No, you can't be in on the bet, 'cause it's different for girls." She says something about shaving. "Well, men shave. I shave." And your line was, "Not every day." Do you remember that?

**Michael:** Vaguely.

**Jerry:** And you had ice cream in your mouth. She goes, "I shave my armpits." And you go, "Not every day." [*laughs*]

# SARAH SILVERMAN

**Sarah:** In New Hampshire, before acid rain, we would just go outside with a bowl, scoop up snow, pour maple syrup on it out of a tree, and eat it. It's incredible.

**Jerry:** I didn't grow up like that. Aunt Jemima's was the only thing. . . . I love when people act out to the waiter or waitress. I love when they mime what they want. Larry Miller always says, "I'd like a big glass of milk." I go, "Larry, whatever glasses they have, that's what you get. It doesn't matter what you do with your hands."

# DON RICKLES

**Jerry:** So now I'm going to watch an old Jew eat a salad. That's what's coming?

**Don:** Yeah.

**Jerry:** Yeah. Have you eaten yet today?

**Don:** I had my cornflakes.

**Jerry:** Your cornflakes, you have?

**Don:** Yeah.

**Jerry:** You really are living in 1958. Nobody's eating cornflakes anymore. It's 2013. Are you in the mood for coffee?

**Don:** Yeah! What is "In the mood?" You're talking like I'm living in, I don't know, where the hell? It's America! Of course I'll have coffee. When I worked the docks, I always had coffee in the morning, Jesus Christ.

## TINA FEY

**Jerry:** I'll tell you, one of the things I like about you, besides everything, is, like myself, you enjoy eating things you're not supposed to eat.

**Tina:** The only reward for anything is food. Nights when I won an Emmy, I'd be like "What's my food treat going to be?" Like the Emmy was not a treat.

## AZIZ ANSARI

**Jerry:** So, there are a couple changes I want to make. I want to stop lying to the waiters in restaurants about how the food is. You know how they always say, "How is everything?" Isn't that what Yelp is?

**Aziz:** Yeah. Yelp is the anonymous. You don't say it to someone's face.

**Jerry:** It's like the Ku Klux Klan.

**Aziz:** [*laughs*] That's a little bit of a leap, but . . .

**Jerry:** They had a march in Paris the other day. Jews out of Paris.

**Aziz:** Get the Jews out of Paris?

**Jerry:** Jews out of France, yeah. They were marching, but they had their hoodies up. These French guys. And they were holding signs and chanting, "Get the Jews out." And I thought, "The fact that they're not showing their faces is some progress."

> "I want to stop lying to the waiters in restaurants about how the food is."

## KEVIN HART

**Kevin:** I went to KFC. I had a bag of chicken in my hand. Then a car hit me. I never let go of the chicken. I remember getting up, walking, and like a block down I just started eating the chicken. [*laughs*] I called my lady. I said, "Babe, I just got hit by a car." She was like, "Are you all right?" I said, "Wait until I get home and I guess we'll know. I'm afraid to stop walking because I don't want nothing to kick in." True story.

**Jerry:** "But I got the chicken."

**Kevin:** I got the chicken though. I felt so bad. I felt like I let my race down. I should have dropped the chicken.

**Jerry:** No, you upheld your race—your racial stereotype.

**Kevin:** There was a lot going through my mind the next couple days after I got hit.

**Jerry:** So were you hurt at all after?

**Kevin:** Yes, I was.

**Jerry:**    Yes, a car is a big heavy thing.

**Kevin:**    Very uncomfortable moment when you go to the doctor, and he says, "What happened?" And you say, "I got hit by a car." And he says, "When?" And you go, "Two weeks ago." For anybody that thinks the KFC promos don't work, they're wrong. We were in the house, we saw the promo, and I was like, "Oh shit, we've got to get that." And a KFC was close. I said, "I'm going to go right now." And little did I know that was my demise. Now that I think about it, Jerry, that commercial tried to kill me.

**Jerry:**    That is actually something that I also do that I think is one of the most fun things in life. If you see something on TV and you go, "I'm going to get it right now. [*laughs*] They've got a brown sugar Pop-Tart now with a glaze. I'm going to get it right now." I like that advertising works that well. I think whoever made that ad, they should know. I couldn't even continue watching the show. I had to get up and get that.

## FRED ARMISEN

**Jerry:** It's so easy to see how the sandwich became what it is. Nothing's easier.

**Fred:** No, it's like plates.

**Jerry:** "We figured out a way that you can hold this." Do you think the Earl of Sandwich really invented the sandwich?

**Fred:** It seems fake, right?

**Jerry:** I don't know. The guy's name is "Sandwich." First of all, people are going to go, "Come on, really? Your name is 'Sandwich'?" I would be skeptical of that.

## ALI WENTWORTH

**Ali:** I was in therapy in LA and doing some real confrontational stuff. And I came back and said to my parents, "Is there a history of depression in our family?" Both my mother and father said, "No, there's no depression in our family." And I said to my mother, "Didn't my grandparents kill themselves?" And I said to my dad, "Didn't my grandfather drink himself to death?" I consider that depression. But in their minds, no, they just died of natural causes. That's WASPy.

**Jerry:** Well, yeah. All causes are natural.

**Ali:** Right. And then, of course, whenever I'm depressed, my mother—her feeling is, a sliced tomato and an English muffin will pull you right out of it.

**Jerry:** She's right about that. I might put some cream cheese on there. I mean, if you really want to get out of a depression, cream cheese is the way. God, I'm hungry.

## JIMMY FALLON

**Jerry:** That is what you want in a pancake: you want it to be like human flesh. You want it to have the consistency of young human flesh. Does it have that?

**Jimmy:** It really does. It's spongy and it has life to it. It's got a lot going on. I'm looking forward to this. This is really, really going to be a great pancake.

## TREVOR NOAH

**Jerry:** Did you ever see my bit about how do they know when the milk is going to go bad? That's one of my favorites.

**Trevor:** You know what I hated about that joke? The fact that I learned a valuable lesson from it. Often the enemy of comedy, strangely enough, is knowledge or information.

**Jerry:** Mm-hmm.

**Trevor:** As a comedian, sometimes you must figure out your own . . . Forget Google. Just Google it yourself, in your head. Go, "I'm going to Google it myself, and this is the answer." Because when I saw that joke, I had literally just learned how they figure that out. So when I saw you say it, I was like, "But we know how they know. . . ."

**Jerry:** Oh, really? I still don't know how they know.

**Trevor:** But I don't want to spoil it for you. Do you want to know?

**Jerry:** [*laughs*] Sure. If it's funny.

**Trevor:** It's not. It's just seven days from the cow. That's how it works. It's as simple as that.

**Jerry:** Well, that's not as good as my joke.


## BARACK OBAMA

**Jerry:** Even though you seem very relaxed, you've got to go off at some point with food.

**Barack:** Yeah.

**Jerry:** What's your thing? A tray of cookies?

**Barack:** Nachos.

**Jerry:** Nachos.

**Barack:** That's one of those where I have to have it taken away. I'll have guacamole coming out of my eyeballs.


## GARRY SHANDLING

**Jerry:** I don't like eating with old Jews. I just don't. It's so difficult. Everything is difficult.

**Garry:** [I'm a] practicing, uh, Buddhist. So let go.

**Jerry:** That was some hostile Buddhism there.

# WILL FERRELL

**Will:**    See, right now, I wear a suit well.

**Jerry:**   Fantastic.

**Will:**    Right?

**Jerry:**   Fantastic.

**Will:**    Look great. If I took my shirt off, you'd go, "Ooh, not so good."

**Jerry:**   Well, that's why we have shirts.

# JIM GAFFIGAN

**Jim:**     When it's, "There's a sandwich tray. We have pastrami that's been sitting here for three hours," I don't want that. It's like a cold hamburger. Who wants a cold hamburger?

**Jerry:**   Nobody. And yet the heat has no flavor.

**Jim:**     I think if salads were warm, more people would eat them.

**Jerry:**   That sounds like a Jim Gaffigan children's book: *If Salads Were Warm*.

## "I think if salads were warm, more people would eat them."

# JOHN OLIVER

**Jerry:**   I would eat a roll off a room service tray in a hallway of a hotel well into my successful years. 'Cause I thought, "Who would think, 'Hey, let's poison this roll in case there's a comic coming home at three a.m., can we kill him'?"

**John:**    That's not happening.

# KRISTEN WIIG

**Kristen:**  It's weird what we like and don't like.

**Jerry:**   Really weird. I think food and comedy are very similar. People will go, "Oh, I like this, I hate this." It's the same thing with a funny person.

# ELLEN DeGENERES

**Ellen:**   *The Handmaid's Tale*, I just binge-watched that. That was really good. I like a lot of the Netflix stuff.

| | |
|---|---|
| **Jerry:** | Crazy company, right? Crazy what they built. |
| **Ellen:** | Insane. |
| **Jerry:** | A whole new toy. |
| **Ellen:** | I mean, it makes sense that you can just binge-watch. And now they don't even give you time to make a decision. It used to be, like, twelve seconds, and now it's about four seconds, and it goes right to the next one. Unless you turn it off, you're like, "Ah, I'll watch it. It's two a.m., but I guess I'll watch this next one." |
| **Jerry:** | Right. It's like feeding a goose pâté. You know the way they make pâté? What they do to the gooses? |
| **Ellen:** | That's a horrible thing to think about. |
| **Jerry:** | It's horrible. That's what I feel like it is. |
| **Ellen:** | By the way, they don't feed them pâté. |
| **Jerry:** | No, they make pâté— |
| **Ellen:** | From overfeeding them. It's the cruelest thing ever. Now you've bummed me out. I hope you're happy. |
| **Jerry:** | Well, just think about them feeding pâté— |
| **Ellen:** | First. |
| **Jerry:** | Because that's even crueler. "We're now going to give you the food you're going to be." The problem with human beings is, as much as you may want to dislike or disapprove of them, then they just do one wonderful thing and they get you back. Right? |
| **Ellen:** | Right. |
| **Jerry:** | And they get you back in again. It's a relationship we have here with our own species. We keep believing they're going to stop doing this, right? "He's not going to beat me again." |
| **Ellen:** | Oh, wow. |
| **Jerry:** | Right? How do you like this premise? |
| **Ellen:** | So we go from pâté to someone beating their wife. Um . . . |
| **Jerry:** | Yeah. You know that's how they do it. He's an abusive husband, but then he's so nice. |
| **Ellen:** | Then he's like, "Here, have some pâté." |
| **Jerry:** | There has never been an abusive husband who even knows what pâté is. |

## ZACH GALIFIANAKIS

| | |
|---|---|
| **Jerry:** | Let's go to Royal Donuts. Come on. |
| **Zach:** | Royal looks good. |
| **Jerry:** | Yeah, it looks good. This happens a lot of times when I'm doing this show, is I really want a doughnut. |
| **Zach:** | Well, I always want doughnuts. Honestly, doughnuts are less calories than bagels. |

**Jerry:** They are?

**Zach:** Yeah, because there's so much air in them that they're not as dense as a bagel. I don't know. I make a lot of stuff up.

> "Doughnuts are less calories than bagels."

## TRACY MORGAN

**Tracy:** You've been eating Raisinets your whole life. How did you make the switch?

**Jerry:** I just said, "Give me the Sun-Maid chocolate-covered raisins."

**Tracy:** You tried it once.

**Jerry:** The box looks better. It just looks like a higher-quality product. What I want to do now with you, let's go get both and compare them. But you don't want to eat that crap because you have diabetes.

**Tracy:** Yeah, I've got to live.

**Jerry:** Okay, forget it then.

**Tracy:** I didn't survive a Walmart truck to die of diabetes.

## "You've got to bookend your day with prunes if you want real results."

## EDDIE MURPHY

**Jerry:** What do you do first thing in the morning? What's your morning routine?

**Eddie:** I roll out of bed and I go to the treadmill. I do about three miles on the treadmill. Then I do a little exercise and stuff. Then I eat some prunes.

**Jerry:** More prunes?

**Eddie:** You start the day off with prunes. You've got to bookend your day with prunes if you want real results. Prunes and raisin bran.

**Jerry:** Prunes and raisin bran. Wow. Well, I know what the rest of your day's like.

## RICKY GERVAIS

**Ricky:** I did this joke once. I came out of the crowd and I said, "I'm eighteen years sober." And they gave me a round of applause. And I went, "The first eighteen years. Since then, I've been drunk every night of my life."

**Jerry:** That's funny.

**Ricky:** The paper picked it up. And put: "Ricky Gervais admits to being drunk every night of his life from eighteen." Shit, they knew it was a joke. They knew it was a gag. Well, why'd you do that? And then they found pictures of me at parties drinking.

**Jerry:** They've got to make a living too.

# FAMILY

## ALEC BALDWIN

**Alec:** What's it like being a dad for you?

**Jerry:** It's a surfboard on a rainbow. You're getting all you can handle of life. I used to say, "When you're single and you see someone on the street with a difficult child, and the child is crying or tantruming, it's impossible to comprehend that that parent is actually having a good time, through that struggle."

**Alec:** Yeah. They're right where they want to be.

**Jerry:** You can't comprehend that when you're single. What I like about having kids is when they're on the toilet and you knock on the door, they just go, "Come in." Nobody else does that.

## MICHAEL RICHARDS

**Michael:** How are the kids?

**Jerry:** Kids are great. Very good. Thank you for asking.

**Michael:** Are they wild? Are they wild, Jerry?

**Jerry:** No.

**Michael:** Oh. The wilder the colt, the better the horse.

**Jerry:** It's their world now, Michael.

**Michael:** Is it really?

**Jerry:** It's not my problem. It's theirs.

## SARAH SILVERMAN

**Sarah:** You have children.

**Jerry:** I have three kids, yeah.

**Sarah:** And what can they do for you is the question.

**Jerry:** They get stuff. I tell them, "Get me some water." I say, "Because that's the only reason I had you is so that you could get me things. There's no reason to have children unless you can ask them to get you things." And they believe it. They don't know that they have another function.

## DAVID LETTERMAN

**Jerry:** I look at my family now and I think, "Well, in sixty years everyone's dead here, so what's the difference?"

**David:** Good Lord, that's just—

**Jerry:** Is that horrible?

**David:** See, I worry.

**Jerry:** I know. I can see that. You're totally caught up in this generational dysfunction of parenting.

**David:** Well, yes. If I had more than one, I'd feel a little more comfortable about the decisions I would make with either one.

**Jerry:** You've used that excuse a number of times and I don't really buy it. You're going to react to two the same as one. A kid is a kid.

**David:** Right. That's what I've heard.

> *"There's no reason to have children unless you can ask them to get you things."*

# GAD ELMALEH

**Jerry:** This is the East Village. Here they like a lot of black. Everybody wears black. Here nobody calls their parents on Sunday. Nobody. They hate their parents.

**Gad:** Oh, they don't like their parents?

**Jerry:** Yeah, this is the neighborhood for people that hate their parents.

**Gad:** That's a cool neighborhood.

**Jerry:** Cool.

**Gad:** No parents.

# CHRIS ROCK

**Chris:** Here's my good jail story. My older brother was in the halfway house, in between jail and whatever, right? So one day I'm dropping him off at jail and I'm outside, waiting for him to get in, and then I realize: I'm waiting for him to safely get into jail. You know, God forbid something happened to him out here.

**Jerry:** [*laughs*] "I just want to make sure you got to jail safely."

**Chris:** [*laughs*] Yes.

**Jerry:** You know what? You're a good brother.

**Chris:** I'm a good brother.

I'm working on a bit about bullying. Everybody's trying to get rid of bullying. You want to get rid of bullying, but who's going to cure AIDS? Who's going to invent the fuel that gets us off fossil fuel? Who's going to do these things? Some guy that was bullied, that's who's going to do it. [*laughter*] Who's going to invent the airplane that gets us from New York to LA in thirty minutes? A guy that was bullied. You think Steven Spielberg was just hugged in school? And Bill Gates?

Lola had a basketball game and they didn't put her in. The coach didn't put her in. It was a real close game. She's not the greatest. They didn't put her in. Wife's pissed off. I'm a little pissed, but my thing is, "Hey, honey, you know, there's lessons to be learned on the bench too. There's a way to get in the game. There's an actual way to get into every game."

# LOUIS C.K.

**Jerry:** You know what I've decided? People talk about kids, how they grow up too fast and all that. And I feel like I can only take a year of each year. You know what I mean? I'm glad we're done. No more of you as a nine-year-old. I've had it. I need another kid. Get me a ten-year-old. I can't do more than a year. I literally get to the end of that year and go, "I need another kid."

**Louis:**     "I'm through with this."


# TINA FEY

**Tina:**     If I were Jewish, I would feel so bad that all the other kids are talking and talking about Santa Claus.

**Jerry:**    Yeah, well, that's why they came up with Chanukah. It was counter-programming. I was obsessed with Christmas trees as a kid, and I would say to my mother, "Can we get one this year?" And she'd say, "No, no, no. We can have a Chanukah bush." I go, "Oh, fantastic. When are we going to get that?" And she says, "Well, it's out front." I go, "Well, where?" She opens the door and goes, "That one. That's it." "Are we going to decorate it?" "No, not this year."


# HOWARD STERN

**Howard:**   One thing I know in my life, I can always say, "Well, I'm really proud of what I've accomplished." That to me is the greatest thing. And that's the gift I'd want to give to my children, and I would imagine you would too. To go out and, whatever that field is—I don't care if you're in show business, I don't care if you're working at a Wendy's—be the fucking greatest at it, just take such pride in it.

**Jerry:**    No, there's no greatest at Wendy's.


# SARAH JESSICA PARKER

**Sarah Jessica:**   There are things that I am sorry don't exist for my kids now. Or I don't have the strength to impose it. It's silly stuff, but like the way we communicated with each other, or walked to someone's house, or waited for an event—you know, *waited* for a special TV show—or ran to the mailbox. Or the phone ringing, and waiting for your sister or brother to get off the phone. Or a busy signal! The anticipation that a busy signal can build up and up.

**Jerry:**    Here are my three poison Ps of parenting: Praise. Pleasure—giving them pleasure. "Not those crackers. He likes *that* cracker. That's his favorite cracker." And problem solving. "Let me help you with that." One of my favorite jokes—Matthew [Broderick] has this great line that I remember from years ago about when you get your kid a spoon as a father, as you're walking across the kitchen floor with the spoon, you think, "What a great dad I am. Look at me getting my kid a spoon." That is what we think.

## GEORGE WALLACE

**George:** Your daughter's fourteen years old now?
**Jerry:** No, she's thirteen.
**George:** What's the difference.
**Jerry:** One year.

## KEVIN HART

**Jerry:** The difficulty of life presents itself in an infinite number of ways. In a way, it's going to be harder for our kids because the problems that they're going to have are much trickier. Your problem was: "Things are bad. I got to make it good." Their problem is going to be: "Things are good. Why do I feel bad?"
**Kevin:** That's very true, Jerry.

## WILL FERRELL

**Jerry:** Do you write down all the idiotic things that your kids say? Once they're, like, eleven, this is over. It's over. Then they're too smart. They don't say these things.
**Will:** See, I can only remember the dirty ones. Like this morning, the five-year-old woke up and said, "Mom, I need an ice pack." Pause. "For my nuts."

## JIM GAFFIGAN

**Jerry:** We'll be married seventeen years this December. Together nineteen years. That's pretty wild, right?
**Jim:** That's crazy. Like when you were a kid and a married couple would have their twenty-fifth anniversary, you're like, "Aren't you supposed to be dead by now?"

## JUDD APATOW

**Judd:** My daughter, who is thirteen, at night sometimes I'll lay down next to her, and she's like, "Lay with me. I want to go to sleep." It makes her feel good. And I'm like, "That's so sweet." And then the other night I said, "I can't do it, because I have to write." And she's like, "You have to. You have to do it." And I go, "Why? Why?" And then she says, "Because I don't want you and Mom to have sex." I go, "What are you talking about?" And she goes, "Six months ago I walked up to the door and I heard you have sex and it really freaked me out." And I said, "Is that why you ask me to lay down next to you every night?" She goes, "Yeah, so I fall asleep before it happens." And then I was trying to figure out, "When have I been good enough at sex to scare a child?" And she meant it.

**Jerry:** Maybe you were just trying to get a plug in an outlet?

**Judd:** I think we were watching *Narcos*. And then she heard Escobar have sex.

**Jerry:** Yeah, that would freak out a child. "My dad's a drug dealer having sex."

## NORM MACDONALD

**Norm:** Does the entitlement worry you? Is that your biggest worry about your children?

**Jerry:** No.

**Norm:** Have they shown ambition?

**Jerry:** None. None. Absolutely zero. They're just waiting to get the money.

**Norm:** [*laughs*] Yeah.

**Jerry:** But you know what? That's their problem. It'll ruin their lives. What I learned from my parents is, "We've figured our lives out. Why don't you figure yours out? I'm not figuring it out for you. And I couldn't even if I wanted to." Life is . . . life is, you figure it out. Don't you think?

Is your son like you? Does he—what do they say—favor you? Does he take after you?

**Norm:** He has a great sense of humor.

**Jerry:** Wow. That must be a good feeling.

**Norm:** Well, I do like that because it's my favorite. I wish he was funny with me.

**Jerry:** Are you funny with him?

**Norm:** I try to be. I try to show him that life is sort of a trivial thing, you know. And not to worry. Not to worry.

**Jerry:** Do you think life is a trivial thing?

**Norm:** Well, I think it's both, you know what I mean? I think that the day-to-day things are trivial, but you can find purpose. And if you find purpose, you're a very lucky person. You're a very lucky person if you find purpose.

**Jerry:** Yes.

**Norm:** You need that purpose in life. And you know, most people don't.

"I try to show [my son] that life is sort of a trivial thing . . . And not to worry."

# MUSIC

## BRIAN REGAN

**Brian:**   You ever say the wrong city onstage?

**Jerry:**   No, I never really did that. I'm pretty careful about it. It's a mistake you don't want to make. Remember when Springsteen did it a couple years ago? Screamed out the wrong city. It's much worse in rock 'n' roll, don't you think? Because they say it with such vehemence. "What's up, Rochester?! I mean . . . Syracuse."

**Brian:**   I met him backstage at a charity event. Only time I've met him. One of those guys I don't know what to say.

**Jerry:**   Yeah.

**Brian:**   And your brain just goes, "Don't say what everybody else says." But you can't think. "I love your music." "Ah, really? Yeah, I never heard that before."

## "If you have a guitar, it says a lot about you."

## JOEL HODGSON

**Joel:**   So many people think they have a good idea for a restaurant. Everybody thinks, "I've got what it takes. I've been in enough restaurants. I've had enough good experiences. I'm going to create that restaurant." And what happens is the guy that makes all the money is the guy who sells the equipment for a restaurant—stoves and all that stuff. 'Cause so many people try and they don't make it.

**Jerry:**   It's the restaurant supply guy that makes all the money.

**Joel:**   Yeah. Just like the guy who sells the guitars makes the money and not the guy in the band.

**Jerry:**   So, that Guitar Center on Sunset—they're cleaning up?

**Joel:**   Exactly.

**Jerry:**   Yeah, there's one born every day, isn't there?

**Joel:**   Yep. Exactly. Everybody wants to sing their song.

**Jerry:**   I can't believe I missed that. 'Cause I always see the Guitar Center and I think, "How are they doing it? How do they manage?" And the answer is, everybody fools themselves into thinking, "I can be in a band."

**Joel:**   Well, how many guitars have you bought over the years?

**Jerry:**   Two or three.

**Joel:**   Yeah. See? Do you play the guitar?

**Jerry:**   No. [laughs]

**Joel:**   Yeah. You know how many I've bought? Six. And I don't play the guitar. I've actually bought six guitars.

**Jerry:**   It's such a great instrument, isn't it? It's wonderful.

**Joel:**   Yeah. That's that lifestyle thing that you were talking about, like with the

sports car. If you have a guitar, it says a lot about you. You're thoughtful and you feel things.

**Jerry:**      Sensitive, yeah.

## COLIN QUINN AND MARIO JOYNER

**Jerry:**      Let me say one of the proudest moments of my comedy career. I could tell you all of them if you'd like, if you have the time . . .

**Colin:**      [*laughs*]

**Jerry:**      . . . but I'll just tell you one. I had a bit about professional wrestling—that my favorite thing in professional wrestling is when the two guys would bounce off the opposite ropes and then collide into each other in the middle. As if nothing could stop them. As if they were prisoners of inertia. So the punch line was something like, "There's nothing I can do. I'm a prisoner of inertia." Some kids started a band, and they called it the Prisoners of Inertia.

**Colin:** That's great.

**Jerry:** It's a good name, right?

**Colin:** It's a great name.

**Jerry:** That is one of my proudest moments.

## *SARAH SILVERMAN*

**Sarah:** I think about how lucky I am to be born in America at this time. But it's always good to have something to fight against when you're a comic.

**Jerry:** It's been bad for comedy, but I don't think comedy's bad now. But I think music really suffers when things are kind of flat. Have you ever noticed that every movie trailer uses '60s music? Why? Because it has energy. It has passion. I would not want to be writing music now.

**Sarah:** There's some really good music out there now.

**Jerry:** There's always really good. But there's not great.

# HOWARD STERN

**Howard:** I am my own worst critic. You couldn't say anything to me I haven't said about myself. You can hear me on the radio, the opening hour is me talking about what a witch I look like.

**Jerry:** Did you see Bruce Springsteen in a bathing suit the other day?

**Howard:** Yes, and the guy looks awesome.

**Jerry:** Amazing.

**Howard:** Makes me hopeful that maybe I could be in somewhat decent shape.

**Jerry:** It looked like his chest was shaved. Did you notice that?

**Howard:** Yeah, that disturbs me. And then it disturbed you too.

**Jerry:** A little bit.

**Howard:** Because Bruce Springsteen should not shave his chest. He's above that, you'd think.

**Jerry:** Yeah, you would think.

# SARAH JESSICA PARKER

**Sarah Jessica:** How about the song about "Hey, Dad, can I borrow your car keys . . ." Harry Chapin?

**Jerry:** "Cat's in the Cradle."

**Sarah Jessica:** Yeah.

**Jerry:** Messed up a lot of dads. It made you scared that if you don't—

**Sarah Jessica:** Pay attention.

**Jerry:** I think that song is probably responsible for some of that parent culture that's overly attentive. He had a massive coronary while driving a VW Rabbit on the Long Island Expressway. I looked it up recently, 'cause I wanted to know if they knew the exit. I thought that would be interesting when I go by the exit, to know this is where he died. I was a big fan of his.

> "Steely Dan was the music that just froze me solid."

# FRED ARMISEN

**Fred:** Growing up on Long Island, what's the music that moved you?

**Jerry:** Steely Dan was the music that just froze me solid.

**Fred:** Yes.

**Jerry:** It's the only music whenever those guys are playing I go to their show by myself. If nobody wants to go, I'll just go by myself. I love those guys, I love everything that they do, and I find that music very moving. I also find quite amusingly that there's never a woman in the theater. It's all men.

**Fred:** It's all dudes.

| | |
|---|---|
| **Jerry:** | Why is that? |
| **Fred:** | And it's not even like rock-rock. |
| **Jerry:** | No. |
| **Fred:** | And it's all dudes. I never realized that. |
| **Jerry:** | Again, we get back to not showy. Craft and technique and precision and commitment. It's like, "It's not about us. It's about the thing." The question is, what is the kinship between music and comedy? Because there is a kinship. |
| **Fred:** | Without a doubt. I think that . . . You know when you saw Peter Sellers hanging out with the Beatles? He was kind of friends with them. |
| **Jerry:** | Yeah. |
| **Fred:** | There's a picture of Peter Sellers, a really early picture where he was marketed as a drummer in England. There's a picture of him playing and they sort of advertised him that way. Something in there I think says a lot about—it's like cousins or family or something, where they're so close and . . . It doesn't happen with many other art forms, I think. |
| **Jerry:** | But you're just repeating my question back to me. |
| **Fred:** | So what is it? |
| **Jerry:** | What is the kinship? I've already said there's a kinship. |
| **Fred:** | Okay. You want me to define what it is? |
| **Jerry:** | Yeah, illuminate that for me in some way. |
| **Fred:** | Um . . . |
| **Jerry:** | Do you want me to take a crack at it? |
| **Fred:** | You want to take a crack at it? |
| **Jerry:** | I do. |
| **Fred:** | Take a crack at it. Wait. Let me take a crack at it first. |
| **Jerry:** | Go ahead. |
| **Fred:** | Let's say the common thing about them is that they're both in front of people. Let's say also that jokes and songs, sketches and songs, are about the same length. That there's a sort of burst. |
| **Jerry:** | Now you're getting somewhere. |
| **Fred:** | Let's add that there's—and I know it's been said a million times and it's a little bit of a cliché—but that there's rhythm to it. |
| **Jerry:** | There is meter. |
| **Fred:** | There's some drumming. There's drumming in it somewhere. |
| **Jerry:** | I would amend that to say there's chord changes. And I thought of this watching your stuff. Watching *Portlandia*, I'm thinking, "I love the chord changes that they make. This is here and now she's going to pick up that garbage can and smash it over his head. I didn't see that coming." You can't be sloppy in the lyrics of a song. Or a comedy bit. |
| **Fred:** | No. |
| **Jerry:** | You can't have an extra sentence in there. In a novel, a painting, there's latitude. Music and comedy must be spare. |
| **Fred:** | Absolutely. |

## JIMMY FALLON

**Jimmy:** Norman Greenbaum, you know the guy who wrote "Spirit in the Sky"?

**Jerry:** I love "Spirit in the Sky."

**Jimmy:** Great song. He was in some interview—and I might be getting it a little bit wrong—he goes, "Look, I have a home and I have a summer home and I have a little boat. I wrote one song. I have one hit."

**Jerry:** *[laughs]*

**Jimmy:** I just love that. He said that like, "That's it." He wrote "Spirit in the Sky." He's set. He's got a house. He's got a summer home. He's got a boat. He's so happy.

**Jerry:** Here's my question about "Spirit in the Sky." It's a Jesus song.

**Jimmy:** It is, right? Yeah.

**Jerry:** Yeah. And the guy's name is Greenbaum.

**Jimmy:** *[laughs]*

**Jerry:** I need more information. What is going on?

You know a lot about music, a lot more than me. And you have a deep understanding of the musical spirit. So I have to ask you this question, 'cause I don't know any real musicians. But maybe you can answer it. It's one of my life questions: Why can't these guys write a hit song later in life? Why can't Billy Joel write another hit pop song? 'Cause we can still write funny bits. I'm sixty. I still can write great bits. I've got no problems. And it's actually easier for me now.

**Jimmy:** You know the rhythm and the craft.

**Jerry:** I know the craft better, yeah. Why?

**Jimmy:** 'Cause I think pop is . . . I guess it's got to be just age. And you want to be almost attracted to the singer. Is that it?

**Jerry:** I don't know.

**Jimmy:** I don't know, man.

**Jerry:** I'll throw out a theory for you.

**Jimmy:** Help me, yeah.

**Jerry:** When the culture is in pain, the music is indelible.

**Jimmy:** Yes.

## BILL MAHER

**Bill:** I used to say the Beatles could put out an album called *The Worst of the Beatles* and it would still go to number one. I mean, I could talk Beatles all day. People always say, "Why did they break up?" I've never heard the theory that I have, which is that John Lennon and Paul McCartney grew up in an era when singles were king. In fact, they're the only group to my knowledge that didn't put the singles on the album. They made an album,

> "When the culture is in pain, the music is indelible."

and they made singles. They were not the same thing. Now, sometimes the American record companies, they would mishmash the songs they got from England and put singles on an album, but that's not how they made it and that's now how they were released in England. "Hey Jude" was not on an album.

**Jerry:** Really?

**Bill:** No.

**Jerry:** It wasn't on *Let It Be*?

**Bill:** No. No. Absolutely not. None of their singles were on albums, I'm telling you.

**Jerry:** Okay.

**Bill:** "Penny Lane" was not on an album. What was the flip side of "Penny Lane"?

**Jerry:** Uh . . .

**Bill:** "Strawberry Fields Forever." That was the B side. What was the flip side of "Hey Jude"? "Revolution." What was the flip side of . . . name any other Beatles single. Let's go through the singles.

| Jerry: | Where are you going with this, counselor? |
|---|---|
| Bill: | [laughs] My point is that John Lennon was writing amazing songs and he couldn't get the A side. He was writing songs like "Strawberry Fields Forever" and "Revolution," and they were the B sides. [He and Paul] had a competition and he was losing it. That's why I think he wanted out of that group. |
| Jerry: | Wow, I never heard that theory. |
| Bill: | And that's why they didn't put singles on an album. An album was for something else. Actually, "Strawberry Fields" and "Penny Lane" started out as the beginning of the *Sergeant Pepper* album, because it was going to be all about their childhood. And those two songs were about their childhood. And then they gave up on that and they just made a great album. But those two songs weren't on the album. |
| Jerry: | "Strawberry Fields" is not on *Sergeant Pepper*? |
| Bill: | Absolutely not. Not on any album. That's why when they put out everything on CD, they had to put out two albums called *Past Masters*. Those are the singles. |
| Jerry: | Ah. |
| Bill: | "She Loves You," not on an album. "I Want to Hold Your Hand," not on an album. "From Me to You," not on an album. |
| Jerry: | I couldn't be more impressed. |
| Bill: | "I Feel Fine," not on an album. |
| Jerry: | Do you know this much about any other area of music? |
| Bill: | [laughs] Probably not. First of all, I'm not much of a lyric guy. Lyrics are good, but the greatest lyrics in the world cannot make a song for me if I don't like the melody. Whereas there are many songs I really like, and the lyrics are shit. |
| Jerry: | Yeah. |
| Bill: | Absolute shit, including the Beatles. The Beatles wrote the lyrics: "The sun is up, the sky is blue / It's beautiful, and so are you." Now, if that didn't have a good melody to it, we would call that doggerel. |
| Jerry: | Doggerel? |
| Bill: | Doggerel, which is the word meaning really bad poetry. |
| Jerry: | Boy, that's a word you don't hear a lot in LA. That's why I live in New York. |

> *"The greatest lyrics in the world cannot make a song for me if I don't like the melody."*

## STEPHEN COLBERT

| Stephen: | Do you know the band Neutral Milk Hotel? They've got a song called "In the Aeroplane over the Sea." And the last line is: "Can't believe how strange it is to be anything at all." And I really love that idea of how strange it is to be . . . Okay, Jerry. |
|---|---|
| Jerry: | Too much. It's too much. Just stop please. |

| | |
|---|---|
| **Stephen:** | "How strange it is to be anything at all" is a perfect idea of what it's like to be alive. |
| **Jerry:** | Which do you like better? That line or Jerry Garcia's "What a long strange trip it's been," as a summation of existence? |
| **Stephen:** | I like mine more. [*laughs*] |
| **Jerry:** | I like mine. 'Cause his name is Jerry. |

## STEVE MARTIN

| | |
|---|---|
| **Jerry:** | How many banjos do you have? |
| **Steve:** | I probably have about six or seven. Not that many. |
| **Jerry:** | That's not that many for a guy who loves the banjo. |
| **Steve:** | Maybe I have ten. 'Cause I use six onstage, so I know there's four more that I don't use. |
| **Jerry:** | Wow. Ten banjos. What a life. |

## JIM GAFFIGAN

| | |
|---|---|
| **Jim:** | I was thinking of Steve Miller. What's that song? "Abracadabra." When he came out with that song, do you think anyone was like, "Look, you have a fantastic career. You don't want to do this. There's a whole generation that really identifies with you. You have this midwestern working-class kind of—look, we all want to be popular . . ." Right? Do you know what I'm saying? "Abra, Abracadabra. I want to reach out and grab ya." |
| **Jerry:** | "I want to reach out and grab ya." [*laughs*] |
| **Jim:** | It's like the Beach Boys. Come on, you guys. You're a really important musical group. We don't need "Kokomo." |
| **Jerry:** | I love "Kokomo." |
| **Jim:** | You love that song? |
| **Jerry:** | Oh, I love it. Yeah. "Montego . . ." |
| **Jim:** | "Aruba, Jamaica, baby, why don't we go. Down to ba-da-da-da-da." |
| **Jerry:** | "Come on, pretty mama." |
| **Jim:** | That song should end with the sound of a shotgun. |

# KRISTEN WIIG

**Jerry:** What else is important to you in life besides comedy? Please don't say relationships or health or anything like that.

**Kristen:** No, no, I won't. I have that answer for you. I play the ukulele a little bit, and I'm working on a ukulele album right now. So that's happening.

**Jerry:** That is very exciting.

**Kristen:** Yes. I'm very excited about it, although I don't know if it's going to have other instruments. I have to figure out how I want to structure it, 'cause I don't know if people can handle just me and ukulele for eight songs.

**Jerry:** So you're writing some songs. Are they funny?

**Kristen:** No.

**Jerry:** Not at all.

**Kristen:** No, but sometimes when I'm playing around I think of funny things.

**Jerry:** How could you not?

**Kristen:** Yeah, how could you not?

# CEDRIC THE ENTERTAINER

**Cedric:** During the recession, when it was really bad, I had a childhood friend who came up to me and was like, "Ced, I need a job." I'm like, "A job? I'm a stand-up. What do you do?" He's like, "I play the bass." [*laughs*] "I don't know if . . ."

**Jerry:** "I don't know how to work that in."

**Cedric:** What's your favorite summer song?

**Jerry:** I'll give you my two favorites: "Summer in the City," and I love Will Smith's "Summertime."

**Cedric:** Oh, I was going to say that one.

**Jerry:** For vibe. For the summer vibe.

**Cedric:** For the vibe, it's crazy. That's one of my favorite ones.

# DANA CARVEY

**Dana:** You're John Lennon or Paul McCartney, either one, and in your head you go, "I might not be the best guy in the band. I might not be." The thing I love about Paul McCartney—because he is like Jesus walking on the planet—is that he's had to develop this light persona to make everybody relax. Because people come up and they start crying. Those songs are so brilliant, but he talks about them in such a . . .

**Jerry:** Well, what is he going to do? He's got a life.

## DAVE CHAPPELLE

**Jerry:** Here's something you never thought about. Frank Sinatra, I think he decided to retire in 1970 'cause he obviously couldn't keep up with rock 'n' roll. He just seemed so over, so passé. And he realized, "Well, that's it. I'm done. I can't compete with this. I'm irrelevant. I might as well quit." So he quits. There's no plan here, right? He just does this.

**Dave:** Right.

**Jerry:** But there's an analogy to you. So he quits. Two and a half years later, he just says, "I've got to go back." So he comes back, and now in that two-and-a-half-year time, he went from being passé to iconic. All of a sudden, people saw him through a different lens 'cause he was gone.

**Dave:** Oh, that's interesting.

**Jerry:** Same thing happened to you.

**Dave:** That's right.

## MELISSA VILLASEÑOR

**Jerry:** In Brooklyn, you always have to be ironic about everything. You have to take lame things and embrace them. Embrace their lameness, which then becomes coolness. If you can un-lame something, that makes you cool.

**Melissa:** What do you listen to? Classic rock?

**Jerry:** I do.

**Melissa:** You know, that's my favorite. I've been listening to "Rich Girl," Hall and Oates, all summer.

**Jerry:** Pretty amazing song. I'm a big Beatles fan, and Steely Dan. But I don't understand how they put these words and music together. And I never will. But you know when it's right, when they hit it, and I think it's the same with us. We know when we got the right line for that joke. And you know when you don't. But I still can't get over the complexity of it. Like, you give it to this producer, and then he puts in all these other instruments. Which ones? How much of each one? I don't know how they . . .

**Melissa:** You just feel it.

**Jerry:** A good bit is kind of like a good song stanza, right? A really good bit is a whole song.

**Melissa:** Yeah.

## SETH ROGEN

**Seth:** I was with Will Ferrell recently and we were talking, and this idea of comedic regrets came up. He was telling me a story about how he was at the Grammys years and years and years ago and Prince won an award. And Prince wasn't there to accept it, but they didn't realize that. They thought Prince was going to come up. There was a moment when people didn't quite know where Prince was. And Will, in that moment, he's like, "I had the idea to get up onstage and accept the award as Prince and not make a joke about it. Just literally go up and be like, 'Thank you so much. I appreciate it.'" And it's so funny 'cause this must've been ten or twelve years ago, and you could tell that to Will it was as though it happened yesterday and has gotten if anything more frustrating over the years. He was just like, "Oh, it would've been the funniest thing that ever fucking happened."

**Jerry:** That hurts so badly.

## BRIDGET EVERETT

**Bridget:** You and me, we like '70s music. We like that yacht rock.

**Jerry:** Yeah. Why do they call it yacht rock? How did it get that name?

**Bridget:** I don't know, but I don't really understand it. I probably should have looked that up for my research point for the day. I feel like the cool thing about singing is, and not to be corny, but it's like such a love affair. And that's how I communicate. That's when I feel so alive. Do you know what I mean? I don't think I could ever lose that. But I live and die by the last game I played, the last time I was up onstage.

**Jerry:** Me too. Songwriting fascinates me. I'm obsessed with it. I love watching those videos of musicians in studios. I cannot penetrate how they do it. How they know how to confect . . . can I use the word "confect"?

**Bridget:** Yeah, sure.

**Jerry:** The elements together. "We need this instrument a little more. Different, louder, softer. This should come in here and not here. Let's have James Taylor come in and sing three words and then leave." I don't get that.

**Bridget:** Well, that's the beauty of some of those '70s things. They're all so layered. Now it's people pushing a lot of buttons. When you're back in the studio playing the instruments . . . With my band, we get in there and they just start coming up with stuff. And I'm like, "I like that." I just know if I like it or if I don't like it. They're much smarter musicians than me. I just know what I like.

*"Why do they call it 'yacht rock'?"*

## EDDIE MURPHY

**Eddie:** The suits and the way I was rolling with bodyguards and my house in Jersey . . . I bought it because it reminded me of Graceland. Yeah, I was an Elvis nut.

**Jerry:** It's so funny that you thought I was confident and I thought you were confident. That's funny.

**Eddie:** We were both right. But we didn't have as much confidence as the other one thought.

I went to see a Prince concert. I thought he was the most confident person ever and he said, "Back when I was young, I could never let the whole audience leave." It blew my mind that he wasn't confident all the time. I thought he always looked so confident. I was like, "You got on those high-heel shoes and your ass is cut out your pants and you ain't confident? You mean that you was nervous when you had your ass cut out your pants with those high-heel pumps on?" I thought, "Now, that's a fearless motherfucker there."

# THE ART OF COMEDY

# BRIAN REGAN

**Jerry:** All right, you want to hear some bits?

**Brian:** Yeah.

**Jerry:** These aren't bits. These are things. Whenever you get up in a restaurant and you're wandering around, you're only looking for one thing. And yet they still make you go through "Are you looking for the bathroom?" Just what do you think I'm doing? No one takes a walk in a restaurant.

**Brian:** Yeah, you should throw it back at 'em. They go, "Are you looking for the restroom?" And you go, "I'm looking for your corkscrews. Where are your corkscrews?"

**Jerry:** That's funny. These makeup counters in the department stores for women, there's always a chair. I always feel the chair is, like, "Honey, you'd better sit down. I can't just sell you some lipstick. There's a larger thing here that we're going to have to talk about, and you're going to need to sit down before you hear it."

**Brian:** [*laughs*] Just life in general. When people tell you, "You might want to sit down for this." Have you ever fainted? I've gotten all kinds of news and I've never actually thought, "God, I'm glad I was sitting." Why do I need to be sitting?

**Jerry:** "Are you sitting down? 'Cause people are keeling over at this one."

**Brian:** "I don't know what you're about to tell me, but I'll bet you a thousand dollars I can handle it without collapsing." What kind of news just drains all the blood from your head?

**Jerry:** People lose loved ones. Horrific medical conditions. Life is horrible, horrible things. We've all heard the worst things.

**Brian:** And I don't think people are fainting all over the place. My manager will do that to me.

**Jerry:** Really?

**Brian:** And he's on the phone. I'm not even there. Like, "Brian, are you sitting?"

**Jerry:** "I got you an extra five hundred dollars. Hello? Hello? Is there anyone there? Brian, are you there?"

**Brian:** "Thanks for the warning. Get the smelling salts."

**Jerry:** I define confidence as the people that make the toilet flushing mechanism that's mounted inside the wall. You know those old-school ones? It's not a tank. It's like in a public restroom. They plaster over the mechanism. They tile it. They grout it. What if it needs an adjustment? What if it breaks? If I worked at the company, I'd be up all night, thinking, "What's going on behind that wall?"

**Brian:** You know when you have a problem with the little handle and you have to jiggle it? It's always awkward when you have to tell your guests that. When they excuse themselves and you have to say, "Oh, you have to jiggle the handle." And I always wonder what is the highest echelon that

that has ever been expressed? Foreign dignitaries, you know? "Excuse me, Queen Elizabeth, you're going to need to jiggle the handle."

**Jerry:**  [*laughs*] That is brilliant. How high has it gone?

**Brian:**  Has a baron ever said to an earl, "You'll need to jiggle the handle"?

**Jerry:**  "Thank you, Your Excellency."

**Brian:**  I have a Cirque du Soleil bit that I'm working on. And that is the meeting of the creative director. The guy has never said no to anything. "All right, we're the new Cirque du Soleil show. I need ideas. Music, yes. Dancing, yes. Keep in mind I'm not going to say no to anything. Acrobats, yes. Streamers, yes. Come on, try to make me say no. Elephants painted gold, and they come in with helicopter launching pads on their backs, and helicopters land and monkeys come out and play kazoos? Yes. Yes, we're doing that." "No" is not in his vocabulary.

**Jerry:**  Don't you think comedians are kind of really smart idiots? Wouldn't you say in some way?

**Brian:**  I often wonder where I fall in that. Because I can do decent on a crossword puzzle. Or if I'm watching *Jeopardy!*, I know some stuff. But I don't think I know enough to really do anything other than be a comedian.

## RICKY GERVAIS

**Ricky:**  You know what Hitler did? On the last day, the Russians were advancing. They were two hundred yards down the road. He married Eva Braun, right? Secretly married her. And he had there the cake and some champagne. They retired to bed early. In the morning, he poisoned her, and shot himself, and the gardener burnt the bodies, all right? Now, say what you will about Hitler, but that's a terrible honeymoon, isn't it? That's a crapper. They should've gone to Breakers.

**Jerry:**  The funniest part of that joke is "Say what you will about Hitler." I always subscribe to Mel Brooks's philosophy, which is the worst thing you could do to Hitler is laugh at him.

**Ricky:**  I think this is the most interesting joke of all time, on so many levels. A Holocaust survivor eventually dies of old age and goes to heaven. And he meets God and he tells God a Holocaust joke. And God goes, "That's not funny." And he says, "I guess you had to be there." Isn't that amazing?

I like to analyze a joke and see if it works and then hone it. But stand-up's slightly different than everything else. When you do a film or a sitcom, you go, "That's how I want it. Now I hope they like it." If they don't, that's it. Whereas during stand-up, there's more of an evolution. They choose your best hour for you.

**Jerry:**  Yes. The audiences creates the show.

> "Don't you think comedians are kind of really smart idiots?"

**Ricky:** It's not your selection.

**Jerry:** You're a mouse in a lab experiment. I always tell people that.

**Ricky:** "Every time I do this, I get food. I'll keep doing it." Until the only things you're doing are getting you food. Every line gets a laugh.

**Jerry:** That's right. Your act is created by hundreds of audiences prior to this one.

**Ricky:** Yeah, and they're all the same. Whether you're playing to five thousand people or whatever. They're all the same, outside there being any language barrier. What makes a bigger difference than towns or countries is the day of the week and the venue.

## *DAVID LETTERMAN*

**Jerry:** Do you remember the guy who said to you, "Dave, have you ever had the hump of a camel?"

**David:** "No, but when I was younger, I was pretty good." Or something like that. Yeah, I do remember that.

**Jerry:**   Yeah. And it was that long beat. I wonder if you had it right away, or it came as—

**David:**   What I do remember was: Is the double meaning that I'm leveraging this joke on going to hold up?

**Jerry:**   So you thought that?

**David:**   That's what I thought. Because I knew it was a setup, but I didn't know that "hump" would be the fulcrum, you know?

**Jerry:**   Right. And that's what it was, because it was really a complicated joke. And you think, "Gee, I don't want to waste this fat pitch on something." But it really was so great.

# DON RICKLES

**Don:**   You know how they call me "hockey puck"? For the life of me, maybe forty years ago in a joint, my ad-lib joke was, "Don't be a hockey puck." They think that's the cleverest thing I ever said. My house is loaded with hockey pucks and I never use it.

**Jerry:**   That's funny.

**Don:**   It's unbelievable. It really is.

**Jerry:**   I love everything you've ever done. I know guys, friends of mine, we sit and talk about you, and we really analyze some of the little things that you do that make your stuff work, that make you work. The thing that's so great about you is—I don't mean to embarrass you—is that your personality comes out so far beyond any act. There's no act. It's not like, "You should hear what Don says about this or he says about that." You have to be so much funnier than most guys to do what you do, because you're not bringing up a subject and talking about a whole thing. You're just using your raw funny all the time, which is a very difficult thing to do, any comedian knows that. But I love when you would say to somebody, "And what is your heritage, sir?" Because it's so respectful. You said "heritage." "Well, he's asking me about my heritage. He obviously has respect for my ethnic background." And then of course, as soon as you have it, he's finished.

**Don:**   Yeah.

# CHRIS ROCK

**Chris:**   The ability to talk to a lot of people at one time is a freakish talent. It really is. You know in the old movies, the alien would come from outer space and they would hide him because they were scared the government's going to put him in a cage and have observation? That's what they should

| | |
|---|---|
| | do with comedians. The fact that you can talk to a lot of people at one time . . . You think Superman could talk to a thousand people at one time? |
| **Jerry:** | Superman could, yeah. |
| **Chris:** | He can get their attention 'cause he has to bend something first. But to just get up in front of a thousand people and start talking? Probably not. |
| **Jerry:** | They would give him a few minutes, and then if he's not funny— |
| **Chris:** | Yeah, every time they'd lose their attention he'd have to break something— |
| **Jerry:** | Or he would lose the room. He would eventually— |
| **Chris:** | —burn something with his X-ray vision or something. |
| **Jerry:** | "Folks, folks! Over here. I'm not done yet." |
| **Chris:** | He'd fly, come back. "Okay, I got your attention." |
| **Jerry:** | That is really funny. Superman trying to hold people's attention. Larry David would love that. |
| **Chris:** | You know, forget the fact that we're funny or not funny. That's always up to the bit. The fact that we hold people's attention—it's spellbinding. It's ridiculous, when you think about it. |
| **Jerry:** | Somebody was saying the other day about comedy and how you've got to be funny or they'll turn on you—it was a regular person telling me, "They will turn on you." I go, "They *should* turn on you." |
| **Chris:** | They should, if you're not funny. |
| **Jerry:** | There's justice in show business. |
| **Chris:** | Oh, there's justice in comedy. It's really fair. It's disturbingly fair. You have more in common with a great truck driver than a shitty comedian. Only people who are really good at what they do for a long period of time know what it means and know what it takes. |
| **Jerry:** | No matter what it is, they come down to the same things. |

## *PATTON OSWALT*

| | |
|---|---|
| **Patton:** | I remember you did a bit when you were on the Rodney Dangerfield *Young Comedians Special*, and it's about seeing a hair in a shower— using someone else's shower and there's a hair. |
| **Jerry:** | Right, right. |
| **Patton:** | And you do this really awkward process of putting the water to make the thing go down. And you watch it and realize, "Oh, that is a very awkward thing that he clearly did a lot of times without thinking about it, and then one time paused to go, 'Is this crazy?'" It's almost like you're presenting this behavior to the world, going, "It's not just me . . ." And if you watch that segment, how the crowd responds is this wave of laughter—confessional laughter, like, "Yeah, I do actually do that, and I look just as dumb doing |

that." But that's crucial. "I don't want to touch it. I can't die from touching another person's hair, but it's another person's hair." It couldn't be more symbolic of "Please accept this behavior. Please understand me. You need to understand this about me, 'cause otherwise I can't live. 'Cause I'm going to keep doing this." The best comedy is the moments that we just ignore because we do them so often and they're so mundane and embarrassing. If you can pause and nail that—

**Jerry:** Well, you're pickpocketing their life.

**Patton:** Oh, wow.

**Jerry:** That's what you're doing. They're going to you, "How did you know that was in my pocket?" You walk out there like, "Here's what's up." And they're like, "Please, someone tell me something, 'cause I don't know what's going on." So you go, "I'm going to pretend I know so well, you're going to believe it." But only for the purpose of laughter. That's the only thing you're really extracting. But the scam is, "I know what's up." That's the scam of stand-up comedy: "I know what's real. I know what's fake. I know what's true. I know what's a lie. I know what's funny. I'm not telling you about anything that isn't funny, by the way. Because there's a lot of that. I already wrote that and threw it out." It's a happy scam. It's a good scam.

People are laughing before they stop to think, "That didn't make any sense, what he just said." I used to tease Leno about this. He had these two bits, which escape my memory at the moment, and he would link them: "And it's the same thing with insurance . . ." and he would do his insurance bit. I said to him one time, "You know, those aren't really the same thing at all." And this was a big discovery for me in comedy: if the syntax sounds right, that's right enough.

**Patton:** Yeah. And every new bit is exciting because there is a moment when it's not funny. It's just an idea. It's a thing you're looking at, like, "Well, is there anything funny?" And then when you unlock it, it's such an endorphin rush.

**Jerry:** Yes. I don't wonder what it feels like to be a surfer and slip into the tube. I know what that feels like. Onstage. And that's really what I live for.

## GEORGE WALLACE

**Jerry:** So how was the show for you tonight?

**George:** The show for me tonight was good. You know, it's always different. I never know which direction I'm going every night with different jokes. Lot of new stuff I didn't get to work with. That's why I brought you. I was supposed to work on some new stuff and go over it with you. We can do that at the coffee table.

**Jerry:** Oh, okay. Tell me how that same-sex marriage joke goes.

**George:** Everybody's talking about same-sex marriage. People always ask me, "What do you think of same-sex marriage?" My joke is usually, "Look, I live at 1602 Chestnut Street. If it ain't happening in my house, it ain't my business." And then I follow up: "Everybody's worried about same-sex marriage. What difference does it make? After you get married, ain't no sex, you know?"

**Jerry:** I just thought there's something funny, because it's always the same. Because you're with the same person. That's what they mean by "same-sex." You know what I mean? There's a joke in there.

**George:** There you go. I'll make that work—because you're with the same person and it's the same thing. A good same five minutes and you're done. That's going too far?

**Jerry:** This is what I say to the audience when a bit gets interrupted, if somebody drops a glass or something. I say, "You ever see one of those stunt drivers with the motorcycle and there's a train going by, and there's one empty car and that's the hole he jumps through on the motorcycle? That's what it's like when you're doing a joke. Once the train goes by, I can't jump the motorcycle anymore. That was my hole." So once you screw up a bit that someone's trying to do to entertain you—

**George:** The hole's gone.

**Jerry:** That's what it's like. That's why comedians get angry, by the way. Because I'm trying to give you a gift of this laugh, and you're interrupting my gift.

**George:.** We are approaching the Riviera Hotel [in Las Vegas]. In 1977, Jerry Seinfeld and George Wallace drove out to California. And we went to see Bob Newhart [here at the Riviera]. And he told that joke about the two Polish airline pilots.

**Jerry:** Let's tell the joke. We'll tell it together.

**George:** Okay.

**Jerry:** Bob Newhart told this joke, and he closed the show with it, right?

**George:** Yes, he did.

**Jerry:** It was two Polish airline pilots, and they're bringing the plane in for a landing, and the plane hit the runway and it smashed through the lights.

**George:** And hit the control tower.

**Jerry:** Hit the control tower, and the two pilots finally got it back under control. And then one pilot said, "Man, that was a short runway."

**George:** And the copilot said, "But . . ."

**Jerry:** ". . . it was wide though, wasn't it?"

**George:** Okay. Well, you tell the joke different than I do. He closed his show with that.

**Jerry:** Oh, that brought the house down, that joke. Now, Bob Einstein used to go on *The Tonight Show* with Polish jokes. He would always talk about, "They have finally put a stop to these horrible jokes that are prejudiced against ethnic groups like the Polish, and it's horrible, and I'm glad that they've been outlawed now. Nobody can tell them. I just want to give you some examples of what they were like." That's how he would do it.

**George:** That's great.

## ROBERT KLEIN

**Jerry:** I think one of the legendary Klein bits is the opera pimp. One of the great bits. What was the gist of the opera pimp bit? That she was making a lot of money.

**Robert:** Making money. Yeah, my wife is an opera singer. She makes money. She makes some good money. She gives me the checks. Makes me feel good. Like an opera pimp. "Where's the money from that *Così fan tutte*, bitch? You holding out on me? I got two girls doing an oratorio in San Diego. I don't need this bullshit. . . ."

I was picking up my new car yesterday at the dealer, and the kid, he's showing me how to do the stuff. And I said, "I have to call Jerry Seinfeld." Which I did, right from there. He says, "I'll leave you. . . ." And then just before he said good-bye, he said, "Hey, you know the difference between a Jew and a canoe? A Jew don't tip." I go, "José! Not funny to begin with." We're not hip enough for that. In other words, this kid is maybe first-generation, second-generation Dominican. Nice kid. There's no hate behind it. I don't think we're hip enough for some of that stuff yet. We've come a long, long way.

**Jerry:** It's mostly a really bad joke. It's just not a funny joke. If it was funny, you would excuse it. But it's weird that he would say that to a guy named Klein.

**Robert:** Stewie Stone, for example, would say a joke like, "Waiter approaches a table of Jews and says, 'Is anything all right?'"

**Jerry:** That's a good joke.

**Robert:** It's a good joke.

> "Waiter approaches a table of Jews and says, 'Is anything all right?'"

## KEVIN HART

**Kevin:** I don't sit down and write. I can't. I can't sit down and, "This going to be my joke. Let me just write it out." I have two guys that have worked with me and started with me from the bottom, Harry Ratchford and Joey Wells, and what I have them do is take notes while I'm onstage.

**Jerry:** Oh, really?

**Kevin:**   I have an idea of what I want to talk about basically in my phone. Stupid stuff will happen. These are my notes.

**Jerry:**   [*reading Kevin's phone*] "I try my best to avoid long conversations." This is my kind of stuff. "I will avoid going to certain locations if I know a long talker is in that venue."

**Kevin:**   I'm not going if I know there's a long talker there. You know you're talking to a long talker when they say, "Let me talk to you real quick."


# BILL BURR

**Jerry:**   Your "Gold-Digging Whore" bit is one of the great pieces of material I've ever seen. Not only the material itself but the way you perform it, with such confidence. You know what I really love about it? The way you take your time and then you make the audience's discomfort part of the bit. I can't think of anyone who's ever done that. That's greatness. I have never seen anybody do it. Not like that. Not in a fun way. You make it fun.

**Bill:**   Do you know how I started doing shit like that? I used it as a tool to get the crowd to shut up and listen to me. Because I would go onstage and start going into my bit, leading them like they thought I was going to land on sexism, I was going to land on racism. I would deliberately lead them down. They think you're going to say something like that, they would shut up.

**Jerry:**   Right, 'cause we think, "Hey, we may need to report on this."

**Bill:**   And this is back before there was even this blogging crap. And then at the last second, right before you hit the wall, you break 'em over to what you were going to say anyway. It started as a technique to shut 'em up. Like, I'm doing a bit right now where I'm just basically discussing how you can't get mad at the president because he makes $500,000 a year.

**Jerry:**   Is that what he makes? I thought it was $200,000. Oh, I think they doubled it to $400,000. Anyway, that's really funny. You can't get mad at the president 'cause he makes—

**Bill:**   He makes $500,000 a year, and getting mad at that guy is like yelling at the person behind the counter when your flight gets canceled. Like, "I'm never flying your fucking airline again." And the person's like, "My airline? Yeah, yeah, I'm running shit. My last name is 'United.' I don't even have health insurance." But how I get into that to shut 'em up, I would just say, "You know there's people out there that actually think a woman being president would be a good idea?"

**Jerry:**   That's great.

**Bill:**   So I go into it like, "This is some caveman who's going to say this sexist thing." And that's what all those fucking bloggers tap out—the second

> ## "You take your time and then you make the audience's discomfort part of the bit."

I say that, they're already writing. But what I'm doing is getting them to shut up, thinking that I'm going to say this sexist thing, and what I bring it back to is, "You know what he's making a year, and basically if you truly wanted to effect change, you would have to do it the way it's been done throughout history, which is you would have to go out and basically Moe Greene a bunch of people."

**Jerry:** But what does that have to do with the woman president?

**Bill:** Because people think to have a woman be president, that would change things. No, it would just be another person making $500,000 standing behind that counter and getting yelled at and getting blamed for all this shit.

## CHRISTOPH WALTZ

**Christoph:** The talk show situation is a lot of pressure. You're sitting there in front of an audience, pretending to be so relaxed. And all that's really happened is very uptight one-upmanship. And sometimes that's funny. Because it's like sparring a little bit. But overall it's a lot of pressure.

**Jerry:** See, comedians love that pressure.

**Christoph:** Is it an adrenaline thing?

**Jerry:** Yes. It's a sport.

**Christoph:** I can understand that. Do you think it's a sport that's slowly, slowly, let's say altering its appearance or requirement or it's sort of overall cultural entropy, as I observe it?

**Jerry:** Entropy?

**Christoph:** Yeah. You know, it kind of all dissipates and trickles to the bottom. Meaning: Is the standard of comedy and the craft aspect and the wit and intelligence—is all of that in progress or regress?

**Jerry:** There's no way to tell. It's too large an amoeba. It's kind of like movies. It's kind of hard to tell what the trends are because it's such a big, amorphous organism. Comedy's never easy, but there's a different kind of culture of support around comedy now. It's nurturing. Which is not good, I think.

**Christoph:** Yeah, exactly. It strikes me as uncritical—sort of a consumer attitude more than intellectual participation. And that's what I enjoy in great comedy: if I'm asked to participate.

**Jerry:** Right. Now when you played, uh, Hans Landa in *Inglourious Basterds*, did you think of it as, "There's something funny about this guy?"

**Christoph:** I'd love you to correct me if I'm wrong, [but] I think funny is a result. Funny is not the process. You laugh as a release of something. It's like an explosive release.

**Jerry:** Right.

**Christoph:** There are sort of mechanical things that facilitate the flow, that will result in that release. But always as a result. That's why people trying to be funny are unbearable.

**Jerry:** Well, all artists are concealing of the art. But that character, to me, was funny because he was enjoying himself so much.

**Christoph:** Well, yeah. And it's the context that makes it.

# ALI WENTWORTH

**Ali:** Do you know when I first met you on the set of *Seinfeld*, you were trying to remember the joke about the lemon meringue pie.

**Jerry:** No, it's Bavarian cream pie. Here's the joke. I'll tell the short version. The point of the joke is how long it is. But it's exhausting if you tell the full version. The actual joke is: So a man is a soldier in World War II. He parachutes in. He's working his way across the German countryside and he stops into a little German bakery, has a piece of Bavarian cream pie. It's the greatest thing he's ever had in his life. The war ends. He goes home. He gets married. Raises a family. The kids go to college. The wife eventually passes away. He goes to the doctor. The doctor says, "You have six months to live." He's done everything he wanted to do in life. There's only one thing that he would like to experience again—and that is to have another piece of that Bavarian cream pie that was the greatest dessert he's ever had in his life. So he books passage on an ocean liner. Halfway across the Atlantic, the ocean liner hits an iceberg and sinks. He falls out into the water in a lifeboat. He starts paddling the lifeboat. He can see the coast of France. He keeps paddling. The life raft runs out of air and he falls into the water. Now he starts to swim, but he's getting eaten by sharks. His legs and arms are both completely eaten off and he's lost a lot of blood. But he lands on the coast of France, and he begins to crawl. He crawls across France, across Switzerland, finds his way into Germany asking directions. There in the distance he sees it: the same little German bakery where he had the Bavarian cream pie so many years ago. He crawls into the bakery. He's lost all his blood and the will to live. But he still has the fight left in him. The cancer, of course, has been eating away at his body this entire time. He crawls into the bakery, pulls himself onto an empty stool. No arms, no legs. Cancer riddled through his body and brain. And with the last ounce of energy of life that he has left—remember he's lived an entire life. He's an old man. Eaten by sharks and riddled with cancer.

**Ali:**      It's a bad day, yes.

**Jerry:**   It's bad. He's in bad shape. The waitress says, "May I take your order?" He says, "I would like a piece of Bavarian cream pie." The waitress says, "Oh, gee, I'm sorry. I just sold our last piece." He goes, "I'll have peach."

**Ali:**      This is how we had this conversation the first time I met you. I said to you then I think it's funnier if he says, "I'll just have a cup of coffee." I think it's better.

**Jerry:**   It is. You're right. It is better. You're good. That's how you got on this show.

## JIMMY FALLON

**Jimmy:**  I was talking to Jay Leno about this. I was thinking about getting a cool old car.

**Jerry:**   Yeah, I think we talked about that.

**Jimmy:**  And he goes, "Why don't you just get a truck?" I go, "I could get a truck, but I want to get something old and cool like what you have." And he goes, "Do you like fixing cars?" And I go, "No. I don't. I don't have a clue about fixing cars." He goes, "Then you won't like this. Because that's why I do this. I like fixing cars. I like maintaining them. That's what I like. If you don't like that, then don't."

**Jerry:** Yeah, I like fixing jokes. I love a broken joke. "This doesn't quite run. It's a beauty, but we can't get it running." I like to get in there with my tool kit and go, "Let's decide . . ."

**Jimmy:** It is fun, right? It is exciting. I do like doing that. I like fixing jokes. I love any problem. I love when somebody goes, "We can't use that because . . ." And I go, "Okay, we can't do that. All right. But now we have a three-minute hole in the show. What do we do for three minutes that's going to be something? We've got to figure it out."

**Jerry:** What is that? What is that gift? I think that's the greatest gift you can have in life, I'm going to tell you right now, what you just said. I love fixing. I love any problem. Those are the people that do well in show business, because it's all problems. It's endless, constant, crippling problems.

**Jimmy:** It's always something, yeah.

**Jerry:** If you like that, you'll like this business.

If you think something's funny, it probably isn't. But you're willing to keep working to find it. That's how you do it.

**Jimmy:** There's probably something funny in anything, right? You can make anything funny.

**Jerry:** No.

**Jimmy:** You don't think?

**Jerry:** Somebody has a bit probably about everything. You think anybody has a bit about, like, the thinness of forks and knives? You could tell the restaurant about the thinness of the metal. I would start with that. Thin metal. I think that would be a funny detail in a bit. "So I take this girl to this restaurant and the forks are thin. It's a thin-fork place." You're on your way to something else.

**Jimmy:** A thin-fork place.

**Jerry:** Right. You throw that in. "And already I can see she's not having a good time because the fork is thin."

## "I like fixing jokes. I love a broken joke."

## STEVE HARVEY

**Steve:**    I was born to this. I tell people about comedy all the time: comedy is the one profession that's nontransferrable. You know, comedians can become great actors. Great actors can't become comedians.

**Jerry:**    No, no.

**Steve:**    You can go to school, and you can take a lesson on everything. How to bungee jump, how to parachute, how to fly a plane, how to be an engineer. You can go to school to be a doctor. You can go to school and learn how to play football. You can go to basketball camp.

**Jerry:**    You can get better at anything you want to get better at, except this.

**Steve:**    You're born to this.

**Jerry:**    Do you think it's teachable? Do you think that you could explain, "Here's the fishing bit. Here's the way I broke it down. Here's how I created it."

**Steve:**    No, man.

**Jerry:**    Why?

**Steve:**    'Cause they're not even going to get it. If you explain it to 'em, it will make no sense. This is the most senseless profession on earth. You can't explain to anybody how you got into this. You can't tell a person, "You have two eyes. I have a third one that sits right here, and this one in the middle sees everything totally different from the rest of y'all. I was born with this eyeball that sees everything differently. It all has a comedic turn to it."

**Jerry:**    That's so funny.

**Steve:**    You can't tell a person that. Tragedy strikes, but I got news for you: we have the jokes that night. Now, we know that we can't bring this to the public yet, 'cause we'll get hammered. But in the room alone, when it's just us, we have the jokes already ready.

**Jerry:**    I was once asked to talk at a comedy class.

**Steve:**    Oh boy.

**Jerry:**    And I went in front of the class and I said, "The fact that you're even here is a very bad sign. 'Cause I wouldn't be part of any of this." Right?

**Steve:**    The same thing happened to me. They have me come to a comedy class. I said, "Listen to me. None of you have what it takes. 'Cause why you in this class? If you had what it takes, there would be no need for this class. What are you wanting me to tell you that you have to already have? You have to have it." A lady got up and just started packing her stuff up, this black lady. I said, "Are you walking out on me?" She said, "No, I'm going to get a job. I'm through with this here. I ain't got what it takes. That's all I need to hear." The guy that was running the class was in the back going, "What are you doing? These people paid good money for this." I said, "Good money for what?" This thing about comedy is you cannot fake funny. You can't play it off. You know, dude may go, "I don't get him." All we need is five million people to get us. Which is a huge number. But if

> *"This is the most senseless profession on earth."*

you get five million people who get you, you can have a wonderful life. What was your ratings share at the top of the show?

**Jerry:** Thirty million a week.

**Steve:** Shut your ass up. Thirty million a week.

**Jerry:** Yeah. But that means 90 percent of America doesn't like it. Three hundred million people. We got 10 percent.

**Steve:** The rest of 'em don't give a damn about the Jerry Seinfeld show, which just goes to show you. But do you know what you had to do to get thirty million people?

**Jerry:** Mm-hmm.

## JIM CARREY

**Jim:** Don't you find when you were a kid, maybe you weren't the toughest kid in school but you could be the funniest?

**Jerry:** No. I never saw it as a defense or as a means to an end. I just thought they were the most interesting contraptions. I thought jokes were interesting mechanisms.

**Jim:** Well, that's what I always felt about you. I always thought, honest to God, I used to watch you at the Improv when I was starting out, and I was like, "This guy is a mechanic. He's an amazing mechanic."

**Jerry:** Yeah. I like to construct a little machine.

**Jim:** But you are funny too. It's not just mechanical. You made me laugh so hard because I had just started learning to scuba dive, and you did that bit about scuba diving and how the whole point of the sport is not to die. "Oh, what a beautiful fish . . . don't die. Oh, look at that coral . . . don't die." And it's so true.

**Jerry:** "There's a fish, there's a rock, who cares, don't die." It was a song. I made it into a song.

## BILL MAHER

**Bill:** A joke is like a balloon. You have to pop it. The surprise has to come all at once. If it dribbles out, you got nothing.

**Jerry:** That's good. I've never heard that before. Is that yours? Or is that from a French movie?

# TREVOR NOAH

**Trevor:** Who was the famous inventor—the American one?

**Jerry:** Thomas Edison?

**Trevor:** Yeah. He said, "I didn't make mistakes. I just learned a hundred ways to not do the thing."


# STEPHEN COLBERT

**Jerry:** My favorite piece of advice. I heard Rodney Dangerfield talking with a young comic one time at the bar in Catch a Rising Star. The kid was peppering him with questions. "How do you learn this? How do you learn that?" Rodney had a drink in his hand, and he just looked at the kid and went, "You'll figure it out."

**Stephen:** Or not.

**Jerry:** Or not. And that's what it is.


# STEVE MARTIN

**Jerry:** Give me a bit that you're doing now that you really like.

**Steve:** Okay, here's a joke I just recently used. Some people get it, some people don't. I use it right off the top. I say, "By the way, I recently turned seventy." They clap. "And also I just recently turned five-nine." You get it?

**Jerry:** Yes. If I may, I would change—

**Steve:** Five *foot* nine?

**Jerry:** No. "Got down to five-nine."

**Steve:** "I recently got down to five-nine."

**Jerry:** Yeah, because that's the joke, right?

**Steve:** Yeah. You shrink as you get older.

**Jerry:** But you want to say "recently turned" twice. That's . . .

**Steve:** Yes, that's what I want to do. But I could just change the joke completely and say, "I recently lost ten pounds. And I recently got down to five-nine." But I don't know.

**Jerry:** That disturbs the beautiful simplicity of it.

**Steve:** Yeah, it does.

**Jerry:** How long a set was it when you were doing these giant places?

**Steve:** I did one hour and six minutes. I'll tell you why. I had an opening act, Steve Goodman, who was fantastic.

**Jerry:** I remember him.

**Steve:** Yeah. He wrote "City of New Orleans." And nobody could open for me, it was really hard, because the place was abuzz. But he killed them, just killed them. He would play a song, and he hit the guitar really hard or played really hard, and usually he would break a string. And you can't intentionally break a string, you can only accidentally break a string. But he seemed to break one every night. And he could continue with the song and change the string. And still play. So he'd go blah-blah-blah-blah-blah, strum-strum-strum-strum, and put the string in. And the audience would go insane. But I think it's hard for comedians to do more than an hour.

**Jerry:** It is. This is the stuff I love. People have no idea that you think about it. I was talking to somebody about you last night. He saw one of your shows at the Hollywood Bowl, said it was unbelievable. He's a big fan of yours. Also a comedian. And I was saying, I think the thing that's most amazing about you is the confidence. The bits that you do are sitting on this mountain of confidence. That is what makes them so funny. A lot of bits rely on cleverness or surprise or all different kinds of things, obviously. But your comedy, as a performer . . . I think people think, "Well, that's just kind of an easy thing to do." There's nothing harder than taking an idea like that and performing it with that level of confidence.

**Steve:** When I first started, when I was really intellectualizing comedy and what to do and how to do it, I decided to fake confidence. Cause I thought it was important. I write about this in [*Born Standing Up*]. If I was the slightest bit nervous about something, they could smell it, and then they would become judges. But if I was confident—like, "I don't care what you think"—that worked.

# GARRY SHANDLING

**Garry:** One time I was watching George Wallace onstage at the Comedy Store. I've never forgotten this, and I don't think I have a good memory. George was up there talking about his dog and how when he'd go on the road he'd have to put the dog in the kennel and how excited the dog was. And he came offstage and I said, "George, did you get a dog?" He said, "I didn't get a fuckin' dog, man. I was writing some jokes about dogs with somebody."

**Jerry:** I do this whole thing about Pop-Tarts, how much I love them.

**Garry:** Oh, I see. Okay.

**Jerry:** Somebody saw my set and they go, "I got you some Pop-Tarts." I don't like Pop-Tarts. It's just a bit.

**Garry:** How much people misinterpret from your act. It's a discussion.

**Jerry:** But that's a compliment to your selling of the material. You actually seem to feel this way about these things you're saying. That's a compliment . . . There's an answer to a joke.

| | |
|---|---|
| **Garry:** | Well, I don't think [Albert] Einstein bounced it off a crowd. Am I right? I don't think he said— |
| **Jerry:** | "What do you think of this?" |
| **Garry:** | "What do you think of this? A plus C equals D squared. No? That doesn't seem to get anything." |
| **Jerry:** | Right. Did Einstein bounce it off of Oppenheimer? "So, tell me if you think this is scientific. . . ." |
| **Garry:** | Well, that's what happened. It's in the movie about Stephen Hawking. He would pitch his theories, and the other scientists would go, "No, no, no." But he had the right answer, Stephen Hawking, who I always wanted to get into my basketball game. You know I have that weekend basketball. |
| **Jerry:** | Yeah? But he's in a wheelchair. |
| **Garry:** | He's always on. |
| **Jerry:** | Hawking? Yeah, always pitching. |
| **Garry:** | We'd watch a football game, and they'd have a time-out, and he'd say, "You know time doesn't exist." I'd go, "Oh, just drop it for a minute and enjoy the game." |

## SEBASTIAN MANISCALCO

| | |
|---|---|
| **Jerry:** | Remember we talked about that bit about the basement, the den—you bring the girls into the den. Did that ever grow on anything? |
| **Sebastian:** | Yeah, going downstairs and nothing matches in a basement in the '80s. That was a piece to the puzzle of the dancing bit, because then you'd ask the girl out, you'd take her out, you'd take her back to the place, you end up in the basement with the bleach and the smell of Tide and mold and you're trying to be sexy and all that. |
| **Jerry:** | Yeah, that's funny. |
| **Sebastian:** | I think what people relate to is the nostalgia—how it is today and how it once was. |
| **Jerry:** | I think one of the most powerful bits that you have hit upon in your young career is the "Company" bit. Do you hear that from people? |
| **Sebastian:** | Yeah. The "Company" bit is the one that really resonated with everybody online, and that's kind of what propelled me. |
| **Jerry:** | Isn't that amazing? It's a tremendously powerful bit. No one ever talked about that before. The word doesn't exist anymore. |
| **Sebastian:** | "Company"? |
| **Jerry:** | Yeah, it doesn't exist. |
| **Sebastian:** | Or having company. Yeah, you're right. It's a word that kind of got lost. |
| **Jerry:** | "That's for company." Everybody grew up hearing that in the house. You don't know it's gone. |
| **Sebastian:** | "We're going to have company." It's funny, I never even thought of that. |

*"'That's for company.' Everybody grew up hearing that in the house."*

| | |
|---|---|
| **Jerry:** | Really? |
| **Sebastian:** | I thought of the word just 'cause I grew up with it. But when you really look at it, nobody goes, "We're having company tonight." |
| **Jerry:** | Do you write on the computer? |
| **Sebastian:** | There's no writing involved with me. |
| **Jerry:** | You just do it. |
| **Sebastian:** | My process is, a lot happens with telling stories to my wife and my mother. If I see that they're laughing, it doesn't come off as a bit. I don't want to be like, "I'm the bit guy." |
| **Jerry:** | Right. |
| **Sebastian:** | We went to Turkey, and we went to a Turkish bath. Now, the experience in the bathhouse, I'll come home, I'll tell my mother about it, and in telling the story I'll see where the beats are. And then I'll take the story onstage, I'll record it, and then I'll listen to it, and I'll go, "Oh, that would be funny there"—in my head, as I'm listening to it. Nothing is written. No writing to it. . . . So it's really hard to kind of make you laugh, right? |
| **Jerry:** | Hopefully. |
| **Sebastian:** | Because I feel like your barometer for humor's pretty high. |
| **Jerry:** | I believe that's the business we're in. |

## JIM GAFFIGAN

| | |
|---|---|
| **Jim:** | Do you camp with your kids? |
| **Jerry:** | No. |
| **Jim:** | I'm not a big camper either. |
| **Jerry:** | I don't leave Manhattan. |
| **Jim:** | I had jokes all about camping. Like, "There's a reason why we keep bugs out of our house." |
| **Jerry:** | My other thing was, "The space shuttle was estimated to have twenty million horsepower. Why are we still comparing it to the horse? Is there any chance that we would go back in case the shuttle broke and say to the horses, 'Do you have twenty million friends?'" |
| **Jim:** | When my mother died, my dad didn't even know where the dry cleaner was. He was like, "Do we have a dry cleaner in town?" I'm like, "Yeah we do. That's where we go to pick up the dry cleaning." |
| **Jerry:** | Here's an idea for a bit about dry cleaning. When you take your dry cleaning to a store, you can take it to any dry cleaner you want. But when you pick it up, you can only go to one. |
| **Jim:** | That's true. |
| **Jerry:** | Now, that is not a joke but that's a good example of how comedians think. |
| **Jim:** | It's interesting. I think it's also interesting when you go into a dry cleaner, |

we have a certain expectation. There's nothing of looking at a dry cleaner that will indicate whether they're good at it or not.

**Jerry:** Not really, no.

**Jim:** You walk in and you have the hanging clothes. When they first open a dry cleaner, are they like, "Let's put some dry-cleaning stuff up in here so we look like we know what we're doing?"

**Jerry:** What's the first day when you open a dry cleaners? There's not one thing hanging in there. Who trusts them?

# J.B. SMOOVE

**J.B.:** You know what I love? When people laugh at the premise before you even get to the punch line. And you're saying to yourself, "Oh, you wait. You freaking wait till I tell you the punch line."

**Jerry:** Yeah, when the premise gets something, that's the greatest thing in comedy.

**J.B.:** That's the greatest feeling.

**Jerry:** I had a bit about chopsticks. And the beginning of the premise was, "I see the Chinese are hanging in there with the chopsticks. . . ." I haven't even started the bit. I just observed that we have this.

This is what I think the career is. You are born with two or three of the five pieces you need. Your success depends on learning those other two pieces. Do you agree with that?

**J.B.:** It's like building a comedian Frankenstein.

**Jerry:** Yes, that's what it is: comedian Frankenstein.

**J.B.:** I absolutely agree. You're born with certain things. You got two or three already built. You need five. And other ones come in a different form. Stage presence.

**Jerry:** Material. Persistence, night after night.

**J.B.:** Timing.

**Jerry:** I think a comedian has to have a toughness to withstand the brutality. 'Cause the failure of comedy has a brutality that other kinds of failure do not have.

**J.B.:** It does not match it.

**Jerry:** When you were in school and you got an F, that was one thing. When you're on that stage and you get an F from the audience, that's a different thing.

**J.B.:** That's a different F. You have to have something built in you. You've got to be thick, you know. Like rhinoceros ass. I love people who—there's this thing I use about performing with no net. And that's what I feel like I'm at sometimes. I like the challenge of knowing I could fall to my death.

**Jerry:** Who's got a net? Who has a net? A singer? A musician? A guitarist?

> ## "The failure of comedy has a brutality that other kinds of failure do not have."

**J.B.:** A singer does because here's what a singer has as his culture: When they sing a song that people love, that's what people do. They start singing with you. That's a net.

**Jerry:** That's a net. When you act in a movie or a TV show where you're doing multiple takes, that's a net.

**J.B.:** Right. That's a net. But that allows you to get what you need, what the director wants.

**Jerry:** It's a different energy though than a live show.

**J.B.:** Now, when we're onstage as comedians, we don't have that ability.

## CEDRIC THE ENTERTAINER

**Jerry:** The greatest opening bit I've ever heard of, and I don't know whose it is—maybe you saw this guy—there was a guy used to come out with a cup of coffee onstage. He would shake the sugar, put it in, stir it, put a little cream in, take a sip, then go to the mic and go, "Oh, like when you show up at work, you start right away."

**Cedric:** That's brilliant right there. I love that. I got a guy who opens for me. He does a joke in closing and says, "All right, y'all, good night." And then he goes, "Oh, so you expected some big joke. Like when you leave your job, all of a sudden you just start doing it extra good. No, you just get your stuff and you leave. Good night." And he just walks off.

## BOB EINSTEIN

**Bob:** I have an Eleanor Roosevelt joke. Eleanor goes into Franklin's office and he's working. "Darling, look at me." He said, "Not now, sweetheart." "Look at me. There's something different." He looks at her. "Oh, you got a new dress." "No." "New shoes?" "No." "Your nails are a different color." "No." "Well, what's different?" "I'm wearing a gas mask."

**Jerry:** Here's a question that intrigues me. Can you remember where you heard any of these jokes? Who told them to you?

**Bob:** No.

**Jerry:** No memory?

**Bob:** No.

**Jerry:** Because, you know, you don't hear a lot of these great jokes anymore, right?

**Bob:** You don't.

**Jerry:** People don't tell you jokes. When we were young, we would hear them all the time.

**Bob:** Yes.

**Jerry:** And for some reason now, they've gone out of vogue, and very rarely does someone say, "Hey, did you hear the one about . . ." and they tell you a wonderful joke like you've told me today four times.

**Bob:** Do you know what I find? And you'll agree with me. I'm going to tell you something that I found. You and I are very lucky in that we do all different kinds of humor.

**Jerry:** We do?

**Bob:** Yes, I think we do. I think we experiment. I like physical comedy. I like everything.

**Jerry:** Right. Joke jokes and bits and funny sketches, physical things. Okay, I'll accept that point.

**Bob:** But a great joke, or a great physical piece, makes you laugh harder than anything. Don't you agree?

**Jerry:** No. But what I love about great jokes—

**Bob:** Why did you say no?

**Jerry:** Because I don't agree.

**Bob:** Why?

**Jerry:** Because my personal favorite is a fantastic, brilliant, inventive piece of stand-up comedy. I love a great stand-up comic. I'm watching Bernie Mac now on YouTube and just loving every second of it. When a great joke teller like you—and that's a rare, rare gift that you have, amongst many, many comedic gifts that you have—makes you laugh in the telling of the joke.

**Bob:** You're a hundred percent right. You're a million percent right. An Arab's crawling along the desert, burning up. "Water, water, water." He comes up to a Jewish tie salesman, Fagin, and he says, "Water." He said, "I don't have any more. I got a tie. You want to buy a tie?" He says, "No. I need water." He said, "Forty miles west, there's an inn you can get water." Arab goes. Three days later, crawling back, his face is on fire, "Water, water." Fagin said, "Didn't you get any water in the inn?" He said, "They wouldn't let me in without a tie."

This is not a scream, but it's good enough. Father walks into his older daughter's bedroom. Sees a vibrator on the bed. Daughter comes out of the shower. He said, "What the hell is going on?" And she said, "Listen, Daddy. I'm forty-two years old. I hate my job. I don't have a man. I have to have a life." Shrugs his shoulders, walks out. Next night, five o'clock, she comes home from work. He's sitting at the bar with a cocktail in one hand and a vibrator in the other. She said, "What are you doing?" He said, "What do you think I'm doing? I'm having a drink . . . with my son-in-law."

**Jerry:** Do the punch line again. Don't take a pause before.

**Bob:** I couldn't help it. I lost my breath.

**Jerry:** Do the punch line again.

| | |
|---|---|
| **Bob:** | I don't want to do it again. |
| **Jerry:** | I want it right. |
| **Bob:** | Use it twice. Show how I didn't do it and then how I did do it. |
| **Jerry:** | Okay. The pause is . . . you don't want that pause. |
| **Bob:** | All right. Daughter comes home, sees her father at the bar with a cocktail in one hand and the vibrator in the other. She says, "Daddy, what are you doing?" He says, "What do you think I'm doing? I'm having a drink with my son-in-law." |
| **Jerry:** | Great. |
| **Bob:** | Just show it both ways. |
| **Jerry:** | So much better. |
| **Bob:** | Show it both ways. |
| **Jerry:** | You think people are interested in those kinds of subtleties? No. |
| **Bob:** | No. This is fun. I don't know what the fuck we're doing here, but it's fun. |
| **Jerry:** | It's fun. |

# JERRY LEWIS

| | |
|---|---|
| **Jerry S.:** | The complexity of your work . . . What I love when I'm watching the stuff now, you can be appreciated on so many different levels. You can be a complete moron and just watch and laugh. But as a comedian, when I watch it now . . . There's some rehearsal footage from *The Bellboy* that you can find online, working out the phone bit with all the phones, how you originally were going to do it on your feet. And then you decided to do it seated. The rehearsal is really, really funny. |
| **Jerry L.:** | Yeah. And [the scenes] didn't fit in any chronology. That's what made it tough to find out where I was Wednesday, and this is already Monday. But I am the only one that knows, so I'm the only one that's going to get the answer. |
| **Jerry S.:** | So there's not another writer on that set. |
| **Jerry L.:** | No. Never has been. |
| **Jerry S.:** | And you're directing it. |
| **Jerry L.:** | Right. |
| **Jerry S.:** | And you're acting in it. |
| **Jerry L.:** | Yeah. |
| **Jerry S.:** | That seems like a lot. |
| **Jerry L.:** | It is. |
| **Jerry S.:** | Yeah. How did you get Kathleen Freeman? She's great. |
| **Jerry L.:** | I needed a Kathleen Freeman. And found her. And she was with me for twelve or thirteen films. I'll tell you the kind of an actress she was. I called her on a Wednesday night and told her, "Tomorrow we're going for a 19A." That happened to be a nine-page screenplay by itself. And then |

# "Comedy makes everyone feel weightless."

something happened with an actor that made me change the plan. And Thursday morning at seven, I called her and told her, "Forget 19A. We're shooting at nine. And you better look at scene 16B, all through to 19." She came through at the studio two hours later, and did this first run-through with me without a mistake.

**Jerry S.:** Wow. You still don't mind schlepping around to do shows?

**Jerry L.:** No!

**Jerry S.:** Really? It's not a pain in the ass?

**Jerry L.:** Four thousand people are waiting to laugh.

**Jerry S.:** You don't want to sit at home, right? So it never ends, that's what you're telling me. It never ends.

**Jerry L.:** It never ends.

**Jerry S.:** You always want to go out and perform in front of people

**Jerry L.:** You bet.

**Jerry S.:** And how long a show can you do these days?

**Jerry L.:** Two and a half hours.

**Jerry S.:** Come on! That's a lot!

**Jerry L.:** I don't get warmed up until two hours.

**Jerry S.:** [laughs]

**Jerry L.:** When you're scoring, it's not a lot.

**Jerry S.:** You're right, you're weightless. I think that comedy makes everyone feel weightless. The weight of whatever their troubles, or the weight of life, and in that moment, when you're laughing, it's like you're free of earth's gravity.

**Jerry L.:** Yep. Absolutely.

**Jerry S.:** Do you like political comedy?

**Jerry L.:** No.

**Jerry S.:** No. Why?

**Jerry L.:** It's not funny.

## KATE McKINNON

**Kate:** Do you think writing is the worst thing? The hardest thing?

**Jerry:** Mm-hmm. For sure, no question. No contest. Writing comedy is the hardest thing. And if you have any doubts about that, just press the on button on your TV. Press on. And you will see how hard it is, because everything is horrible.

# DAVE CHAPPELLE

**Jerry:** To me, comedy is like trying to get the butterfly on those pins. It's out there flying around. Everybody knows butterflies and likes them, and I'm going to catch it. I'm not going to damage it. I'm going to get it on pins in a glass case. That to me is what we're trying to do.

**Dave:** I'd be a jazz musician. It's the same lifestyle.

**Jerry:** Not much money. You'd have to adjust to that a little bit.

**Dave:** Yeah, the poverty of it all would drive me fucking nuts, but I wouldn't mind sleeping on a couch, dating a stripper, all the stuff they do.

**Jerry:** I like things you can do when you're really old.

**Dave:** Well, didn't Paul Newman race cars all his life?

**Jerry:** He did. I went with him one time to a go-kart track. I met him at a party, we started talking about cars, and—this is one of the great regrets of my life—he called me and left a message on my machine: "Do you want to get together and go to this go-kart track?" And I didn't save it.

**Dave:** But you went.

**Jerry:** But I went, and we raced go-karts. And I said to him, "You know, car racing is really just a sperm flashback, isn't it? That was your first race. And you won it."

**Dave:** That's fucking hilarious.

**Jerry:** Comedy is hard, but we created something. That's why you are suffering.

**Dave:** For your art.

**Jerry:** For your art and to contribute something with the skill set that you are blessed with.

**Dave:** Yes.

**Jerry:** And now we're free of that, okay? Now you don't have to do that. But do you feel a little obligated? If you're able to contribute that, maybe you should do it?

**Dave:** If I had an idea that is a driver, it's a good idea, the idea says, "Get in the car." And I'm like, "Where am I going?" And the idea says, "I don't know, but don't worry. I'm driving." And then you just get there.

**Jerry:** That is great. The idea's driving. And you're in the passenger seat or in the back seat?

**Dave:** Sometimes I'm shotgun, but sometimes I'm in the fucking trunk. The idea takes you where it wants to go. And then other times it's my ego, like, "I should do something."

**Jerry:** "I should be driving." That's not good.

**Dave:** No, 'cause there's no idea in the car. The idea is, "I think I'm so dope that people should be watchin' me do something." That formula doesn't work.

**Jerry:** Dave, this is one of the greatest things I've ever heard.

**Dave:** Really?

**Jerry:** Yes. I am someone who appreciates nothing more than a great analogy, and that is the greatest analogy for how and why you should or should not do a project. If the idea is in the car honking, going, "Let's go . . ." The idea drives. You navigate. And make sure that we have gas and food in the car. We're going to work together.

**Dave:**   Right. And ideas should get some rest.

**Jerry:**   Yeah, but when you're driving by yourself looking for an idea, it's like picking up a hooker. This relationship isn't going anywhere.

# *NEAL BRENNAN*

**Neal:**   Jewish people being funny, Irish people being funny, black people being funny—people that have been through something. You need it.

**Jerry:**   Right. But I grew up in a very comfortable, middle-class environment.

**Neal:**   I did too. Extremely comfortable.

**Jerry:**   So how do you explain that?

**Neal:**   My parents didn't. My father's one of thirteen kids of Irish immigrant parents.

**Jerry:**   My parents didn't also. Both orphans.

**Neal:**   Yes, and that gets in you.

**Jerry:**   It does?

**Neal:**   There's something called imprinting, which is like your grandparents' stress levels end up in you.

**Jerry:**   Really?

**Neal:**   There's a thing about Holocaust survivors and stress levels in their ancestors.

# *TRACY MORGAN*

**Jerry:**   Now, the young people today—and I don't want to get into this attitude, but I'm going to—we're not interested in amusing anecdotes from your journal, okay? So you went to the doctor and there was some confusion. I don't care. Make something up. Make the pipe talk.

**Tracy:**   Period.

**Jerry:**   Don't just tell me you're a crack addict. That's not funny. If the pipe is talking, now we've got something.

# EDDIE MURPHY

**Eddie:**   I had somebody come onstage once. I was doing some kind of joke about a funeral or something—I was working with Dave Hawthorne, because afterwards they did impressions of that guy all the time. The guy came onstage and he had just buried someone and I was doing some funeral bit. He didn't just go at me. He was like, "Ladies and gentlemen, I just want to say"—it's on the mic—"I lost my so-and-so very recently and then I have to see this young bastard onstage. . . ." I was kind of standing there. For years Hawthorne would do that: "I'd just like to say, ladies and gentlemen . . ." He was so formal. "Ladies and gentlemen, I just want to say sorry to interrupt the program. But I've just got to tell you this young whippersnapper stepped over the line. You're a marvelous audience. Thank you and good night."

**Jerry:**   Oh my God.

**Eddie:**   Oh, how we laughed on the way home. We just laughed and laughed. It wasn't like, "Oh no. I fucked up. I said this thing." I was laughing onstage while he was doing it, and the comics were screaming. It just became this funny moment when this guy came on the stage. I've seen footage now where they come onstage and fight. They've attacked comedians.

**Jerry:**   Yeah?

**Eddie:**   There's footage of comedians doing their set and people come on and there's a physical fight onstage.

**Jerry:**   Steve Harvey had a thing he said about what people don't understand about us is there's nothing that's not funny to us. Nothing. All this "careful" thing—that's just for the audience and for the public. Amongst ourselves, we don't care about anything. Somebody died, it's funny two minutes after they died.

**Eddie:**   The funny idea comes in.

**Jerry:**   Right away.

**Eddie:**   And you go, "Hmm," depending on who's around you. But everything is funny at first. We see the joke in everything first.

**Jerry:**   Yes. We have feelings that normal people have, regular humans have, but we don't care about them as much. You know what I mean? You feel sad if somebody dies, but you're just as happy to make a joke about it.

**Eddie:**   Yeah, I think we care about them as much. We're just wired to see the joke, we're wired to hear the joke. You have no control over it.

**Jerry:**   Right. But I also think we view it differently. I think we view life like we're not really part of it. We're here to just comment on it. I've had people say to me, "So-and-so died," and I went, "Eh, that's enough of him anyway."

**Eddie:**   That's funny.

**Jerry:**   That's funny unless I put a name in there, then it's not funny. If it's another comedian, you could say that. "Eh, enough of him anyway."

*"We view life like we're not really part of it. We're here to just comment on it."*

**Eddie:** That's funny, period. That's funny because that's not the response that people have. A good sense of humor is like an acute sense of proportion. A comic is the first one who notices everything. We're the first one. "It's cold in here." Or, "What's that smell?" Somebody pulls up in a new car. The comic would say, "Hey, it's nice. You know you got a little scratch right there?" We're just wired for that.

# JAMIE FOXX

**Jamie:** I did Fallon. I did seven jokes. All killed. I did a pit bull joke. The joke was, "You know, pit bulls can be cantankerous." I used "cantankerous." I should get credit.

**Jerry:** I like that.

**Jamie:** I said, "Those pit bulls can be cantankerous." And the pit bull community was up in arms. They said pit bulls are nice animals. I've been around pit bulls. I've owned pit bulls. Even my own pit bulls would scare the shit out of me, and I've known them for years.

**Jerry:** That's funny.

**Jamie:** Every time I go to feed them: "You good?" "Yeah, we good. Just put that shit down where you need to." I'm feeding one. The other one's behind me locking the gate. "Hey, did you just lock the gate?" "Yeah, we just want to talk about our surroundings, B. It's all good. Just got to talk about this whole thing. We need bigger . . ."

**Jerry:** That's so good.

**Jamie:** I watch Chappelle, and he's like, "I was incensed." I love Dave because he always uses a very intelligent word to go with his hood. "I was incensed. I was beside myself. I was chartreuse."

**Jerry:** "The perspicacity of these people."

# SARAH SILVERMAN

**Jerry:** Jay Leno used to say comedy isn't talent, it's temperament. I mean, you've got to have a talent, obviously, but I think there's a point in there that's very important. I used to say being a comedian is like being a murderer. No matter what people tell you, you're probably going to do it. You don't care that you're not supposed to do this.

**Sarah:** Yeah, if you can quit, then you're not a comedian.

## JAY LENO

**Jay:** I meet a lot of guys that go, "I don't know if I want to do stand-up or be a writer," and I go, "You're a writer." If you don't know, you're a writer. You're not a stand-up. If you can sit down and give your jokes away, these children you've given birth to, if you can hand them off to somebody else, then you're a writer. And there's nothing wrong with that.

## BARACK OBAMA

**Barack:** What's your theory of handling hecklers?
**Jerry:** Sympathy. I say, "You know what, you seem upset."
**Barack:** [*laughs*]
**Jerry:** "I'm so sorry. I know that's not why you came in here. Let's talk."

## STEVE MARTIN

**Jerry:** Do you think there's any truth to this comedian depression thing? I don't.

**Steve:** I don't either. Everybody's a little depressed.

**Jerry:** Yeah.

**Steve:** And some comedians aren't depressed at all.

**Jerry:** Right.

**Steve:** So, yeah, I don't buy that. There may be some truth to [have an] unhappy childhood, go into the arts. There may be some truth to that.

**Jerry:** What would be the connection? Looking for a little love?

**Steve:** Searching.

**Jerry:** Searching.

**Steve:** For recognition, you know? Or maybe in an unresponsive family when you're young . . .

**Jerry:** Right. Actually, you had a line in your book I read this morning where you said the answer is "Who wouldn't want to be in show business?"

**Steve:** Yeah, mm-hmm.

**Jerry:** That would be my answer.

**Steve:** I just assumed everybody wants to be in show business.

**Jerry:** Yeah. I just thought, "Well, this seems to be the most fun thing around."


## NORM MACDONALD

**Norm:** You know, public speaking is the biggest fear in the world. And I suppose it is. But so many times I rented a cab, and the guy's the funniest guy I've ever heard in my life. And then he's like, "What do you do? Ah, by God. I could never do that." And I'm like, "Hey, guy, you sure can."

**Jerry:** It's true.

**Norm:** Because I wouldn't have a job if all those really funny guys went onstage and tried and learned how to do it. Because if a cabbie can—

**Jerry:** Being funny in a cab and being funny in front of an audience are two completely different things. Here's a question I asked a professional baseball player—top pitcher for the Angels. I said, "How many guys coming up that you saw had the talent but could not do it in front of the big crowd?" He said, "Eighty percent."

**Norm:** Wow.

**Jerry:** He said, "I knew guys that could throw it a hundred miles an hour. But when the lights were on them, couldn't do it." And that is I think the measure.

# LORNE MICHAELS

**Lorne:** You can't hide behind art. When you're playing the real game and you're taking a full swing at the ball? There's no denying that you missed. And so I think that's a bigger-stakes game, and I think New York just forces you into that faster.

**Jerry:** And comedy triply so.

**Lorne:** Yes, more than any other forum.

**Jerry:** There's no, "Well, I got it. Nobody else did."

**Lorne:** Right. If you're painting and show paintings and everyone you know likes it and you believe in it, it doesn't much matter whether an audience likes it or not. But in our world it is "It worked" or "It didn't work."

# MONEY

## LARRY DAVID

**Jerry:** It's a Jewish thing: tip anxiety. Wouldn't you say? Or it's across the board?

**Larry:** I definitely think about the Jewish thing when I'm tipping. I used to do a bit on that.

**Jerry:** Oh, really?

**Larry:** Yeah. You're representing the tribe, in a way. You need to leave a decent amount so they won't think you're a cheap Jew. But you can't leave too much 'cause you don't want them to think you're a show-off Jew. You got to straddle the line, 'cause they'll get you on either end of it.

## SETH MEYERS

**Jerry:** So I was thinking about this bit. I don't know if you've had any fifties recently, but if you give someone a fifty, it's a big thing now where they check it quite a bit. And it's like, "Well, I used it. Why can't you use it? Why can't we all just use it?"

**Seth:** Right. Do you think they check it more than a hundred? 'Cause I know what a hundred looks like way more than I know what a fifty looks like.

**Jerry:** Right. But it seems like we're all just kind of going along with this "paper has value" scam. So why don't we just go along with it? Why are you stopping me?

# CHRIS ROCK

**Jerry:** Have you ever heard Adam Carolla do that bit about similarities between really rich guys and really poor guys?

**Chris:** No.

**Jerry:** My favorite bit. Really rich guys and really poor guys both drink brands of alcohol you never heard of. They both have ways of bathing outdoors. They both do not drive themselves; other people drive them.

# LOUIS C.K.

**Jerry:** How would your life be different if you had a hundred times the amount of money that you have?

**Louis:** I'd probably use it to make stuff. I'd make movies with my own money probably.

**Jerry:** Really?

**Louis:** Yeah, TV shows and movies. That's probably what I'd do with it.

**Jerry:** Max Bialystock [in *The Producers*] said, "Never put your money in the show."

**Louis:** Yeah, well look, he's not a great role model.

# JAY LENO

**Jerry:** Let me tell you how people hear that. When you say, "I bank this and I live on that," here's what they hear: "This guy's rich."

**Jay:** Right. I see what you're saying. But when I was a kid, I always had two jobs. I worked at McDonald's and I worked at the auto dealership, and I would bank one and I would spend the other. And then when I started to make it, I worked at the car dealership and I was a comedian, and I would spend the comedy money and bank the car money. And then when I got

## "The real motivation of being a comedian is if you really love the sound of a laugh."

*The Tonight Show*, I just continued to do that. Because to me it was a good form of discipline. It kept me working, and it made me take gigs I might not normally take.

**Jerry:** Here's what's funny to me about you. That you think you need this little game to motivate yourself, that you worry that you might suffer from a lack of motivation.

**Jay:** Yes.

**Jerry:** That will never, ever, ever happen in the life of Jay Leno.

**Jay:** But that's what keeps me going.

**Jerry:** No, it isn't.

**Jay:** It is.

**Jerry:** It's a dumb game that means nothing. The real motivation of being a co-median is if you really love the sound of a laugh. If you love that, you will never want to stop writing and working and traveling and doing it.

## GEORGE WALLACE

**Jerry:** What makes you think I care about money?

**George:** Well, why don't you come over here tomorrow night and work a second show? You deserve all the money.

**Jerry:** We never did it for money.

**George:** Never did it for money, right?

**Jerry:** Never.

**George:** Never did it for money. That's what it's all about, making sure you enjoy your life. If you honor your essence, you don't have to worry about the money. As long as you doing what you do and you love it, the money will come.

**Jerry:** You've been wearing that gold—the ring and the bracelet—

**George:** For twenty years.

**Jerry:** At least.

**George:** And I really need to get rid of it, don't I? I need to get rid of it. I need to take it off.

**Jerry:** Well, since the money has come to you, as you said, perhaps . . . How about Michael Jackson making more money now than he did when he was alive?

**George:** Same thing's going to happen to you when you die.

**Jerry:** Really? Who's going to do it?

**George:** We going to make money on your ass like you won't believe. I'm going to be selling all your shit. When you die, we're going to just be selling all kinds of paraphernalia. I'm just going to make up stuff. T-shirts and belts. "Jerry Seinfeld wore this."

# KEVIN HART

**Kevin:** This is going to make you laugh. I got a deal for $225,000. I think, "I just made it. I'm fucking rich."

**Jerry:** "Forever."

**Kevin:** This is a real conversation I had with my brother: "All right, first things first. I'm going to get you and Mom a house. I'm going to square Dad away, throw him in a house. So that's three houses, let's knock that out. I got to get me something, so let me go ahead out to LA, probably find me something. Just know we all set. Everybody's set." Twenty-one years old. I get another deal right after. I got, like, three deals in a row and something like $225,000, $150,000, $175,000. No conversation about taxes. "All right, look, cars . . . who want what? Hey, Mom, you trying to get something? You good, okay. Kenneth, get my brother something. Dad, you been talking about a truck. Done. I'm going to go ahead and get me something." Listen, have you ever seen a credit score underneath 500?

**Jerry:** No.

**Kevin:** I broke that record. [*laughs*]


# BILL BURR

**Bill:** My brother, he was talking about boats, but it was really a philosophy on life. He said, "Bill, you don't want to be the guy that owns the boat. You want to be the guy that has the friend that owns the boat."

**Jerry:** Right.

**Bill:** Let him deal with the docking fees and scraping the barnacles off and all that shit. He goes, "You just show up with a twelve-pack, you're a hero. You get on it, you enjoy it, and when it's done, that's it, you're out." I keep my debt low. I don't buy flashy shit.

**Jerry:** I do.

**Bill:** Yeah, but I think you got the means. [*laughs*]

**Jerry:** No, I did it since I was five years old. When I had thirty-five cents when I was five, right to the candy store. "What do you got that's thirty-five cents?"

**Bill:** Oh yeah, you always enjoyed it?

**Jerry:** Yeah. I always spend every nickel I ever had.

## JIMMY FALLON

**Jerry:** Your whole youth is watching *SNL*, you love this show, and then you're in it. I don't know how your head doesn't explode.

**Jimmy:** It does. It did. It totally exploded. It was like, "Oh, this is insane." My sister would be like, "Dude, that's Don Pardo saying your name." My friends said, "They're paying you to do this? I can't believe you're getting away with this. You should be paying them." Like a fantasy camp. Seriously, I would pay them. So I never renegotiated my contract.

**Jerry:** Wow.

**Jimmy:** Turns out, a very stupid move. No one cares. There's no romance in that. No one finds that charming. They just go, "Great, you're an idiot." Someone renegotiated. They have a boat now.

## STEVE HARVEY

**Steve:** Guy tells me, "Are you afraid of being oversaturated?" I said, "With what, money?" He said, "No, fame." I said, "I'm oversaturated with fame?" He said, "You're everywhere." I said, "Man, I'm not everywhere. I'm on a lot, but I'm not everywhere." He said, "Well, there is a danger of being oversaturated." I said, "Excuse me, sir, everywhere I go I see the Nike swoosh. I see it everywhere I go. Dubai, London—I don't give a damn where I go, I see the swoosh."

**Jerry:** Can't get away from it, yeah.

**Steve:** Are they oversaturated? Ask 'em. Reebok would love to be that oversaturated. I said, "Man, you got to be kidding me. Oversaturated? See, you're thinking too long about this thing. I'm just doing everything I can do while I can do it." 'Cause after a while, these windows, they close.

**Jerry:** Mm-hmm. And they bring in fresh troops.

## STEPHEN COLBERT

**Stephen:** When I was younger, living in Chicago, the one thing I would never deny myself is books. If I couldn't afford anything, if it was books I would buy them. I'm like, "This'll pay for itself somehow. I will buy this book."

**Jerry:** That's really pretentious.

## SEBASTIAN MANISCALCO

**Jerry:**      Why is tipping done as if we're not supposed to be doing this? It seems like the people receiving the tip are happy about it. I want to give a good tip. It feels nice. Why the subterfuge around it? Why the whispering? I had a bellman tell me a Frank Sinatra story in Chicago.

**Sebastian:** Oh, tell me. I've got to hear it.

**Jerry:**      We were standing in front of the hotel, waiting for the car, and I said, "What's the biggest tip you ever got?" The bellman said, "You know who asked me that question one time? Frank Sinatra." I said, "Really?" He said, "Yeah, Frank Sinatra said to me, 'What's the biggest tip you ever got?' And I said, 'A hundred dollars.' And he gave me a hundred dollars." Then Frank said, "Who gave it to you?" The bellman said, "You did, sir."

**Sebastian:** Oh, wow. [*laughs*]

## JIM GAFFIGAN

**Jim:** Oh my gosh. I didn't even think they made people like Jerry Seinfeld pay for food anymore. It's a formality, right?

**Jerry:** I pretend. I don't really have to. It looks good for the show. It looks like, "Wow, he's so normal."

**Jim:** Oh, look at that, it's all cash. Is it true that you don't believe in credit cards? I'm just starting some rumors. You don't believe in credit cards and you don't believe—wait a minute, do you have the metal AmEx?

**Jerry:** Yeah. I'm the reason that it exists.

**Jim:** No way.

**Jerry:** Yeah. I was doing a commercial for American Express back in the '90s and some crew guy comes over to me, and he says—this is when the gold card was the top card—he says, "So, do you have the black card?" I go, "What's the black card?" He says, "There's only three in the world. The sultan of Brunei has one. President of American Express has one. I thought you would have the other one." And I said, "I will."

I called the president of the company the next morning. And he said, "It's just a rumor. It doesn't exist. We've never made it . . . but maybe we should." I go, "Yes, I want one. Make it. Make a black American Express card." And that's why the black American Express card exists.

"We're not in the money business. We're in the fun business."

## JUDD APATOW

**Jerry:** As I always say, and I'll say it again—I don't think I've said it on this show—if you want money for whatever reason, the best way to get it is never make a decision based on money. We're not in the money business. We're in the fun business.

**Judd:** Yeah.

## NORM MACDONALD

**Norm:** I was in the elevator, and I'm always interested when I hear just a small snip that explains a big, long story. So it was just a man and his wife. And the man says to his wife, "I don't care what I told you. Give me the money."

**Jerry:** And then the husband yelling at the wife: "How do you lose a hundred fifty dollars at a slot machine?" And she says, "You lost fifteen hundred dollars." He says, "Yeah, but I know how to gamble."

**Norm:** That's right. The guy who says, "My God, I've had a terrible day. I lost fifteen out of fifteen in college football. I lost eight out of eight in baseball. I lost six out of six in soccer. I don't know what I'm going to do." And the other guy goes, "Well, there's a hockey game on tonight." He goes, "I don't know anything about hockey."

# ZACH GALIFIANAKIS

**Jerry:** Do you think it's possible to have started out in comedy if you didn't have to worry about money? Let's say you just had money—your parents gave you a bunch of money.

**Zach:** Oh, I didn't have any money.

**Jerry:** I know, but if you did, could you have done it?

**Zach:** I don't think so. I think for me specifically, when I first did stand-up, it was such an aha moment because—

**Jerry:** Oh, please, you're not really going to say "aha moment," are you?

**Zach:** My vocabulary's too weak to come up with something else.

# HASAN MINHAJ

**Jerry:** Doesn't Bitcoin sound like something the comedians made up?

**Hasan:** Yeah. "That's five Bitcoins."

**Jerry:** "How much for that bit? I want to buy that."

**Hasan:** "Yeah, well, that's a closer. That's at least a hundred fifty Bitcoins."

# EDDIE MURPHY

**Jerry:** I feel like when you add money to a project, you're tampering with the comedy. You could get less funny real quick 'cause all of a sudden we're building big things, taking time, taking the fun out of it. Comedy is good a little sloppy.

**Eddie:** With a little pressure.

**Jerry:** Yeah, a little pressure, a little cheap, a little sloppy.

# JAMIE FOXX

**Jamie:** The worst thing a comedian can do is start to think he looks good and start dressing a certain way. Any kind of leather or, you know, dialing the hair in. If you look too good, hard to get to the jokes.

**Jerry:** Yeah.

**Jamie:** So I start making a little money. And I went onstage and I started doing rich jokes. "Got that Range Rover. Anybody else? Those things are cantankerous, huh? Ha-ha-ha. You know, when you get the square footage of your home and it's less than five thousand square feet, that can be kind of cramped. Ha-ha-ha." And people are looking at me like, "What the fuck?" I'm like, "I'm Jamie Foxx." In my mind, they're going, "Ah." And when I get offstage and walk out, I'm standing outside this little club in LA and somebody opens the door: "Waah!" "The fuck is that in there?" And when I open the door, it's a skinny black kid with a little tank top on. His name was Chris Tucker. And he was hungry. He had a comedy samurai sword. Took it out, and he did like this and cut everybody's heads off, put them in a bag like this. They're all laughing.

**Jerry:** *[laughs]*

**Jamie:** And he walked past me, like, "Muthafucka, you think you're rich?" The next night, I went up somewhere, I bombed again, 'cause I was behind my gate. And then I remember getting a little embarrassed 'cause I'm thinking everybody knew who I was. I'm at the Comedy Store hanging out. And this girl walks up to me: "Oh my God, oh my God." I'm like, "Yo, what's up?" "Do you know who Chris Tucker is?" "I think he's in the, uh, main room." And the girl said, "You look so familiar." I was like, "Oh, shit." I had gained a little weight. I had a little fame face. [One night] I finish a joke, and while I'm getting my breath for my next joke a girl goes, "Why your belly so big?" I was in a funk. So I lose the weight. I get back on my shit. As a matter of fact, we win the Oscar for *Ray*. But when I win the Oscar, I don't take the Oscar home. I give it to my manager. "You take this." "You don't want it?" "Nope. Because if I take that, I'll buy into the Oscar shit and I won't be funny anymore."

# SPORTS

## LARRY DAVID

**Jerry:** Do you still rely on baseball as a palliative? Can I use that word? Is baseball a palliative in your life?

**Larry:** By the way, fantastic word. I've never heard it come out of a human's mouth in my life. No, I don't think it is. I don't think it serves that purpose for me. But I'll tell you what I'm struck by. The way the brain worked when I was a kid. For example, baseball. I could give you the numbers of all the players on the Yankees when I was a kid. I'm a Jets fan now. I can't tell you the numbers. I don't know the numbers.

**Jerry:** Well, your brain is too cluttered now.

**Larry:** Is that it?

**Jerry:** Yes. When you're a kid, it's like a hotel thing with the keys. You've got tons of empty boxes. Now there's junk in all those boxes.

---

*"I'm so annoyed by these tall guys that love basketball. It's so lame."*

## BOB EINSTEIN

**Jerry:** Give me your three favorite sports.

**Bob:** Pro basketball.

**Jerry:** 'Cause you're tall. I'm so annoyed by these tall guys that love basketball. It's so lame. You show me a short guy that likes basketball, that's a fan.

**Bob:** Steve Nash.

**Jerry:** He's a player. I'm talkin' about a fan. . . . Look at how close you live to where you grew up. That's weird.

**Bob:** I'll tell you a quick story that's a great one. My stepdad was very sick. He was just a great guy. And he loved the Dodgers. I called my mom and I said, "Turn on the Dodger game. I'm going to call Vin Scully and ask him if he'll say hello to Bernie Bernstein." So I called him and he said, "Look, unfortunately I get a thousand of these requests. I just can't do it." I said, "I totally understand. Thank you." At the end of the pregame show he says, "And one more thing. A big hello and get well to Bernie Bernstein, a big Dodger fan." I called the hospital, thrilled out of my mind, I said, "Mom, did he hear it?" She said, "Honey, I turned the radio off. I'm talking to the doctor."

## DAVID LETTERMAN

**David:** I think football should get rid of time-outs. I think they should get rid of punts. And also I think they should be allowed to play as many guys at once as they would like.

| **Jerry:** | I see. |
|---|---|
| **David:** | If you've got a play for forty guys, send them in. |
| **Jerry:** | If you can have forty guys, there's going to be a lot of those good plays. Those are going to be very successful plays, by the way. If the other team has eleven and you have forty, you're going to move the ball quite well. |
| **David:** | The other team would know something was up, you know? |
| **Jerry:** | When forty guys come on the field. I see. |
| **David:** | The Indianapolis 500 would be a nightmare for you. Really. People literally would want to lick you, you know? And it'd be a lot of "Hey, Jerry!" It's three hundred thousand people. And they can all see you. |
| **Jerry:** | So how do you navigate that? |
| **David:** | Well, I just stay down in the pits and put the headphones on so you can't hear anything. It would either be the drunks yelling and wanting to lick you, or it'd be the guys in the suite: "Hey, Jerry, look, do you use under-coating? Here's my card." It would be that all fucking day. |

## DON RICKLES

**Jerry:** I know you're a baseball guy. Me too.

**Don:** Mainly the Dodgers. I used to go down in the dugout with Lasorda. Put on the uniform one night—Appreciation Day. He said, "Go out and take the pitcher out." I'm in a uniform. I said, "Come on, Tommy, I can't." "No, I'm telling you, go out there." "You'll get fined." "I don't give a shit. Go out and take the pitcher out." I walk out to the mound. Fifty thousand people. "Gimme the ball." "What the hell are you doing out here? You don't even play." I said, "Shut up, give me the ball!" Having an argument on the mound. Harry Wendelstedt, who was the head umpire, comes racing out. It's a true story. Rips off the mask. "What the hell's—Don, can you get me four seats in Vegas to Dean Martin's show? Just four seats."

## SETH MEYERS

**Seth:** In 2004, I went to Game 1 [of the American League championship series] in Yankee Stadium when the Red Sox lost, and then I went to Game 3 at Fenway when the Red Sox lost, like, 19 to 8. And I had tickets to Game 4, which was the Dave Roberts steal. And I didn't go. I was going to bring my dad to the game. And I said, "I can't do it again. I can't see them lose." I flew home to New York and I landed, and I remember I went and turned on the TV and it was, like, the tenth inning and I watched it. And I was so fine. I never have regretted not being there. I truly believe if I was there, it would have gone a different way.

**Jerry:** Really?

**Seth:** Yeah.

**Jerry:** That's really egotistical.

## PATTON OSWALT

**Patton:** The one thing I love about baseball is when the manager walks out to the mound. It's like silent-movie acting. The manager will always walk out, he's got his head down, and the pitcher's got his chest flared 'cause he's taking his power position, and as the conversation goes on they both kind of change and then the pitcher is sort of starting to deflate, and then the manager just struts back like, "Did my job. He's coming out."

**Jerry:** How about the ball thing? "Give me the ball." Like that's the only ball. "We got a million balls here, but give me that one you got. I want *yours*."

**Patton:** 'Cause it's the symbol. It's like, "Your gun and your badge, put them on my desk. Right now. You just wrecked eight cars. Gun and your badge, right now." "Really? 'Cause there's other guns here." "I don't give a—give me *your* gun."

# GEORGE WALLACE

**George:** Baseball people are crazy. And the Chicago people especially. You go to Wrigley Field, forty-two thousand people standing up [singing] "Take me out to the ball game." Where the hell do you think you are?

# KEVIN HART

**Jerry:** I'm a little crazy with my comedy sports analogies, but comedy's the NFL. The second you can't play, the whole stadium knows it.

**Kevin:** Everybody knows it.

**Jerry:** And I like that.

**Kevin:** Philadelphia's the toughest place. . . .

**Jerry:** A tough town, I know.

**Kevin:** I saw a dog get booed at halftime of the Eagles game because he dropped a Frisbee. Like literally. "Boo."

**Jerry:** My aesthetic role model is Mike Tyson. When Mike Tyson was at his peak, do you remember his robe?

**Kevin:** I remember. I remember.

**Jerry:** He would cut the hole in the hotel towel. No socks, no robe.

**Kevin:** That's how he came into the ring.

**Jerry:** No stool.

> "I saw a dog get booed at halftime of the Eagles game because he dropped a Frisbee."

# JIMMY FALLON

**Jimmy:** I know you're a Mets fan.

**Jerry:** They offered me a partnership for me to invest in the Mets, and one of the benefits that they said—I'm not making this up. This is not a joke.

**Jimmy:** Okay.

**Jerry:** Access to Mr. Met.

**Jimmy:** I mean, come on.

**Jerry:** And of course my first thought was, "You mean I didn't have access to Mr. Met?"

**Jimmy:** I went to a Yankees game once—World Series—with Lorne Michaels and Jack Nicholson. Jack Nicholson's the coolest guy. One of those guys where his voice is his voice. So we order a hot dog and a beer and I get Cracker Jacks. I'm eating Cracker Jacks. He looks at me. He's got sunglasses. And he goes, "Did you get the prize yet?" I swear to God. I go, "Not yet." So I get it out, I open up the prize, and I go, "It's a sticker. It's a picture of a snake."

He goes, "You know, when I was a kid, we used to get metal things like tin whistles—stuff like that." And without even looking at me—he was looking out at the game—he goes, "Now you get a picture of a fucking snake."

## STEVE HARVEY

**Steve:** I was talking to somebody on the golf course. He said, "Do you know that Tiger Woods played a round with a buddy with a seven iron the entire round, putting and everything, and he beat him?" I said, "Yeah, that's cool. But I tell you what: you give Tiger Woods a mic and you put Tiger Woods in front of five thousand people, tell Tiger Woods to give you forty-five minutes of good laughter, I will show you a person that sucks to the highest hilltop."

## BARACK OBAMA

**Jerry:** What sport is politics? Is it chess? Is it liar's poker?

**Barack:** That's interesting. That's a good question. It's probably most like football.

**Jerry:** Football?

**Barack:** Yeah, because a lot of players, a lot of specialization, a lot of hitting.

**Jerry:** A lot of attrition?

**Barack:** A lot of attrition. But then every once in a while, you'll see an opening. You hit the line, you get one yard. You try a play, you get sacked. Now it's, like, third and fifteen. You have to punt a lot. But every once in a while, you'll see a hole. And then there's open field.

## GARRY SHANDLING

**Garry:** What I want at my funeral is an actual boxing referee to do a count. And at five, just wave it off and say, "He's not getting up."

## JIM GAFFIGAN

**Jim:** I watched *The Wire*. I'm sucked into the dramas. You don't watch anything?

**Jerry:** Baseball.

**Jim:** Baseball.

**Jerry:** I always say I have no time to watch these shows but I can watch four hours of baseball a night, no problem.

**Jim:** And so 160 games, how many will you watch or listen to?

**Jerry:** A hundred.

**Jim:** Really?

**Jerry:** Yeah.

**Jim:** That's a commitment. That's a lot.

**Jerry** I like it. It's interesting. It's real. No one's trying to pretend to be anything. I can't take any more pretending. The acting—I can't take it.

## JOHN OLIVER

**John:** I met David Beckham once. I was the most nervous I have ever been.

**Jerry:** Are you a fan?

**John:** I'm a fan. I mean, not of the team. I hated the team he played for.

**Jerry:** What'd he play for?

**John:** Man United. But when he played for England, he was incredible.

**Jerry:** I'm just tired of him scowling at me from the bus shelters. He's always scowling at me.

**John:** It's 'cause he looks better in his underwear than you do.

**Jerry:** What's he mad at me for?

## CEDRIC THE ENTERTAINER

**Cedric:** I used to live in this building in Hyde Park, in Chicago. I was dating a girl who lived in that same building, and I was coming up. There were people taking stuff out of a truck—two guys sitting still by the truck. It looked like they needed some help. So I walked up and he turned around, and it was Muhammad Ali. You just don't expect it. He was so regular. It was such a regular-day kind of situation. He was just super cool. I helped him get one thing out. He was like, "I got it, thanks a lot." It was before the whole cell phone thing. I didn't even know what to do—I think I tried to get an autograph, but he was picking up the boxes. I didn't even bother him.

## LEWIS BLACK

**Lewis:**   I don't want to go to the Super Bowl. Would you?

**Jerry:**   Never.

**Lewis:**   Why?

**Jerry:**   There's people there.

**Lewis:**   The problem with football is there's so much going on around it. Between me and [the players] are all of these cheerleaders who are now dressing up in those kind of slutty Halloween outfits. It's just too much stuff. I don't need a slutty outfit. I need to see the game. I need slutty outfits for another time.

## BRIAN REGAN

**Brian:**   It's the social part of golf that I enjoy. I like the game as well, but I like hangin' with friends, and smokin' a cigar, and listenin' to music. Some people don't like the music, but I like the music. Some beers, some friends, some cigars. You play lousy, who cares? You're havin' a ball. I have three, four golf weekends a year that I do. I schedule them. They're with brothers and friends.

**Jerry:**   I talked to you one weekend, you were doing one.

**Brian:**   Golf during the day, Texas Hold-'em at night. Wonderful. Mm-mm-mm.

**Jerry:**   You ever think about your children sitting home crying while you're doing that?

## HASAN MINHAJ

**Hasan:**   So why white sneakers for you?

**Jerry:**   Cosby.

**Hasan:**   Really?

**Jerry:**   Cosby on *I Spy* in the '60s wore clamshell Adidas. And Joe Namath in '69 was the only guy in the NFL with white shoes. It was the coolest. And he predicted that he would win the Super Bowl and did. Why do you like white sneakers?

**Hasan:**   They're just clean. They look amazing. They look pristine. Especially for guys like us when we're onstage.

**Jerry:**   Right.

**Hasan:**   The way the light hits them, they look awesome. They just look so cool.

**Jerry:**   My first *Tonight Show* I wore these kind of light taupe shoes, 'cause you couldn't wear sneakers on *The Tonight Show* in 1981.

# MATTHEW BRODERICK

**Jerry:**  Nothing beats your Ralph Kiner story. Have you ever told that on TV?

**Matthew:**  I don't think so.

**Jerry:**  Oh, tell your Ralph Kiner story.

**Matthew:**  Well, Ralph Kiner, great baseball player and announcer. He would call the game on the radio.

**Jerry:**  No, on TV.

**Matthew:**  On TV. And Bob Murphy and Lindsey Nelson. And he came backstage when I was doing *The Producers*, Ralph Kiner.

**Jerry:**  Wow, that's really cool right there—that he would get off his butt and come see a show.

**Matthew:**  I was so excited to meet him. Very tall. You know, you meet those guys and you're like, "Oh yeah, you're a professional baseball player. You're a big guy." And I told him a heartwarming story about how my father when I was little would say, "Oh, I don't like when Bob Murphy takes over. I feel like then the Mets lose. I think they do better when Kiner is talking." So I got to tell Ralph Kiner that. And he said, "Well, we didn't really have very much effect on the outcome of the games when we were calling 'em."

**Jerry:**  Do you realize how stupid he thinks you are?

**Matthew:**  How stupid do you think I am? How stupid do you think my father was?

**Jerry:**  Yeah, and he's trying to be nice about it.

**Matthew:**  Very nice. "No, I'm sorry to break it to you, our calling the game didn't have much effect on the game outcome."

**Jerry:**  One of the things I wanted to talk to you about today was baseball words and phrases that we like. I always like when they have a slugger coming up, he's always "looming" on deck. They never use any other word. I also like their "vaunted" defense. It's always "vaunted." Which nobody in the world uses for anything. Nobody.

**Matthew:**  "Vaunted." You're absolutely right. And that means, like, people talk about how good it is or something like that?

**Jerry:**  Of repute.

**Matthew:**  "An outfield of repute." Yeah.

**Jerry:**  Another thing I like is, "He looks like the Justin Verlander of old." Like *Canterbury Tales* . . . Okay, two people that I hate almost as much as anybody in the world: when Hank Aaron hits home run number 715, those two guys who ran next to him between second and third. What the hell are you doing there? You didn't do it. Let him take his home-run trot.

# MARIO JOYNER

**Jerry:**    I feel bad for these martial artists—people that study martial arts their whole life that never get into a fight. You ever think about that? They'll tell you they're a black belt. "You ever been in a real fight?" "No." But they're ready for it.

**Mario:**    But you feel sorry for them?

**Jerry:**    I feel sorry that they put all that work into being ready for something that never happens.

# SEINFELD:
# THE TV SHOW

## LARRY DAVID

**Jerry:** I think I would like a show where there's no problems.

**Larry:** No, you wouldn't. I remember the first show. Even the pilot. It was just the barest thread of a story.

**Jerry:** The girl coming over.

**Larry:** The girl coming over. The barest thread, for the most part. There were no other stories involved.

**Jerry:** There wasn't?

**Larry:** No, that was the only one. I think Kramer was taping a game and you ruined the game by giving it away. That really wasn't a story. That was just a bit. George was talking to you in the laundromat, but everything was about this girl. The one bare, flimsy story on this girl. And it wasn't a very good show. It wasn't as good as our other shows.

**Jerry:** Right. Because we thought the overexplored flimsy thing would work.

**Larry:** Yes.

| | |
|---|---|
| **Jerry:** | But it didn't really. |
| **Larry:** | Not really. |
| **Jerry:** | Right, you need a bigger thing. And then the smaller things live underneath it. |
| **Larry:** | Absolutely. But in the end they combine with the bigger thing. They're attached in a way. |
| **Jerry:** | Yeah. Do you feel that you really learned all this stuff as we were doing it? Or you feel you knew it coming in? |
| **Larry:** | No, I knew nothing coming in. [*laughs*] Nothing. |
| **Jerry:** | Well, you put on a pretty good act, 'cause I thought you knew everything. |
| **Larry:** | I don't know why you would even say that. |
| **Jerry:** | Because you had written that script. |
| **Larry:** | Big deal. One script. That was just luck, you know. I knew nothing. [*laughs*] |
| **Jerry:** | Well, that was pretty exciting, then, that we learned. |
| **Larry:** | Yeah. We figured it out. |
| **Jerry:** | As we were doing it. |

_____

## *"I knew nothing coming in. Nothing."*

## MICHAEL RICHARDS

| | |
|---|---|
| **Jerry:** | Remember we played each other—where I played you and you played me in that one episode 'cause we switched apartments? And I came in the door. Did you ever see that moment where I was you? "Oh, I'm stressed." |
| **Michael:** | Yeah, I kind of vaguely remember that. |
| **Jerry:** | The Kenny Rogers Roasters— |
| **Michael:** | Oh God, I'm awful at this. |
| **Jerry:** | The orange sign? |
| **Michael:** | Nuh-uh. |
| **Jerry:** | I was thinking the other day, one of my favorite bits you ever did—and obviously you did millions of bits that will live forever—but you opened the door and that orange light hit you, and you leaned backwards. That was one of the funniest bits. Because they had put a big neon sign outside your window. |
| **Michael:** | Oh my. And it hurt me? The light hurt my face? |
| **Jerry:** | You were sunburned. |
| **Michael:** | Oh, it sunburned me? |
| **Jerry:** | Yes. [*laughs*] I mean, it was so bright. |
| **Michael:** | Oh my. Those were good days. |
| **Jerry:** | Those were good days. |
| **Michael:** | Those were really great days, Jerry. Yeah, I appreciate all that. You gave me the role of my lifetime. You know, I have a confession to make. I never |

watched *Seinfeld* until after the show was over with. I couldn't bear to watch them.

**Jerry:** Oh, I know that. I still haven't watched it.

**Michael:** Oh, really?

**Jerry:** No.

**Michael:** I knew I was going to get the part. I knew it the first time I met you.

**Jerry:** Really?

**Michael:** I knew it. I never said a thing.

**Jerry:** And I never said it to you.

**Michael:** I knew when I started reading with you. I just [*snap*] said, "They can't pass that up, 'cause I've got a chemistry. I can feel him. He can feel me."

## SETH MEYERS

**Jerry:** I took some acting classes. They're horrible. It's the worst thing you could do to a comedian is put him in an acting class.

**Seth:** Yes.

**Jerry:** You're like a lizard in the circus.

## TINA FEY

**Jerry:** One of my writers had a great line about the way we worked. He said, "The only way I knew what day it was is Sunday. I stepped over the big paper."

**Tina:** Yeah, you really have to give in to it. You have to be like, "This is my entire life."

**Jerry:** Yeah.

## PATTON OSWALT

**Patton:** When I did your show, which was the first acting job I ever got—

**Jerry:** Really?

**Patton:** First acting job I ever got was your show. That show spoiled me for sitcoms, because I believe it was season six and at that point, you guys were filming that show in essentially real time. It was [director] Andy Ackerman with his little wheels on the podium, and we just go and do a scene, one quick take and, boom, wheel it down, let's do it. You guys had it so down and you barely rehearsed because you just knew each other's rhythms.

| Jerry: | By season six, yeah, we had it pretty good. |
| Patton: | It took an hour to shoot the show. It took an hour. |
| Jerry: | Really? |
| Patton: | It took an hour. I'm not kidding. I told my manager, "I want to do sitcoms. That was so easy." "No, no, dude, no, that's not how sitcoms go. That's not how those things work." |

## HOWARD STERN

| Howard: | Are you friends with those guys [the *Seinfeld* cast] still? |
| Jerry: | Well, what do you mean "friends"? |
| Howard: | I mean, when's the last time— |
| Jerry: | I saw Julia two weeks ago. I talked to Larry David yesterday. |
| Howard: | Oh, you did? |
| Jerry: | Yeah, what do I got to do? |
| Howard: | Well, that's interesting. I feel Larry left you on the last year of the show. |
| Jerry: | Two years, he left. |
| Howard: | He shouldn't have. That was mean. |
| Jerry: | He needed to do it. I ended up getting a lot out of that. I became a different person. That was one of the scariest moments of my life, when he left. |
| Howard: | I can't imagine what that was like for you. |
| Jerry: | Because we were the team that did everything together. But he got to that point. It's a very tough thing to do, a show like that. |
| Howard: | But how fulfilling was it when he left and the show was just as successful if not more successful? |
| Jerry: | I was grateful. |
| Howard: | That's life-changing. |
| Jerry: | It was. |
| Howard: | Because you realize you weren't tethered to Larry. |
| Jerry: | Well, I was, but I made the best of it, and I'm grateful to him for giving me that experience. |
| Howard: | But you weren't at first, when he first said he was leaving— |
| Jerry: | I accepted it. |
| Howard: | You did? You weren't angry with him? |
| Jerry: | A little bit. |
| Howard: | Oh, come on, of course. |
| Jerry: | A little bit. Just because I thought, "This is a pretty special thing we have." |
| Howard: | Yeah, and, "Where are you going? What are you doing?" |
| Jerry: | Everybody has to go where they've got to go. |

## JIMMY FALLON

**Jimmy:** I took a toothbrush from your set.

**Jerry:** [*laughs*] Oh, you did?

**Jimmy:** Yeah. I snuck onto the set, obviously your last episode, with Barry Sobel. And I sat behind Rob Reiner. And I watched the whole courtroom scene being shot. So I took a toothbrush out of your bathroom. It was a blue toothbrush with white bristles.

**Jerry:** Do you still have it?

**Jimmy:** I have it in a *TV Guide* with your face on it. Was it a cartoon face?

**Jerry:** That's so funny.

**Jimmy:** And I owe it to you.

**Jerry:** I don't want it.

**Jimmy:** What do you mean? You have to have it.

**Jerry:** No. It's yours. You stole it.


## JULIA LOUIS-DREYFUS

**Julia:** This is one thing I was thinking about yesterday, in terms of us and our history. Do you remember—

**Jerry:** I love anything you're going to say today that starts with "Do you remember." [*laughs*]

**Julia:** Do you remember when I was pregnant the second time . . .

**Jerry:** Yes.

**Julia:** And we were shooting on New York Street, and I was about five months pregnant with my youngest, and you came up.

**Jerry:** Uh-oh, I know where this is going.

**Julia:** All right, here we go. So I'm about five months pregnant. Big as a house, 'cause I gained a lot of weight in my pregnancies. And you came up to me, and you said, "I have a great idea. How about if we write it in this season that Elaine just gets fat?" Don't get in a car accident from that reminiscence.

**Jerry:** [*laughs*]

**Julia:** And so what did I do? Burst into tears. Automatic. It was as if you told me—it was like a death sentence. And so there are two things I have to say about that.

**Jerry:** Okay.

**Julia:** One is you have no interpersonal communication skills. Number one.

**Jerry:** That's not true, or I wouldn't have this fantastic show that I have [now]. Which is all interpersonal communicating.

**Julia:** Okay. No, no, but wait. And this is the second thing, much more importantly.

| **Jerry:** | Okay, yeah. |
| **Julia:** | The second thing is it was a great idea and we should've done it. |
| **Jerry:** | I can't believe you're saying that. |
| **Julia:** | That's exactly right. Well, you know it's true. |
| **Jerry:** | I did know it's true . . . |
| |    I was excited about everybody we cast. But you were the last one, and I remember coming home and we were talking, an agent or somebody. I'd heard something, and we were saying, "It looks like it's going to work out." But it hadn't happened yet. |
| **Julia:** | Yeah, we had to make that deal over the weekend. |
| **Jerry:** | Yeah, and Larry was in my apartment, and I said to him, "If we could just get her. Gold." |
| **Julia:** | Isn't that something? |
| **Jerry:** | I knew it. I didn't know it before then. I didn't know what we were doing. But when you came in, then I saw it. Then I said, "Ah, I see that works. Now I see the whole thing." You. |
| **Julia:** | That's a lovely thing to say, and I'm very grateful. Thank you very much. |

# CARL REINER AND MEL BROOKS

**Carl:** If he had spent his time with [*Get Smart*] he would have never done *The Producers*.

**Mel:** I knew that. I kind of knew if I got stuck in a sitcom, it's a swamp.

**Jerry:** You're telling me.

**Mel:** It's quicksand. And it makes money.

**Jerry:** And you're telling me I should have kept going.

**Mel:** Well, I would have for the money, but I mean, it's quicksand. You're never going to get out of it.

**Carl:** No, if you do the best in anything—

**Jerry:** If you've done your best work, to watch it fall apart is not good.

**Mel:** How do you know?

**Jerry:** You don't. You don't know.

**Mel:** How do you know? It may still have been, five years later, number one best—

**Jerry:** You're right, it may have. So what do you go by? You go by how you feel when you eat a sandwich.

**Mel:** That doesn't apply.

**Jerry:** You know what people said to me? A lot of times people would say to me, "How you going to know when to end the show?" I said, "You ever sit in a restaurant? You've had the meal. You've had the dessert. You've had the coffee. You're sittin' there. How do you know when to leave the restaurant? All of a sudden somebody goes, 'All right.' And everybody goes, 'All right.' And that's when you leave."

**Carl:** True.

**Mel:** I never thought of it, but that's absolutely true.

**Jerry:** And that's how I ended the show. We had the check. We had the coffee. Let's go.

# GETTING OLDER

> *"Here's what a lot of people think about bald men: that they put no work or effort into their hair at all."*

# LARRY DAVID

**Larry:** I find conversations with strangers increasingly harder as I get older. I never remember having that problem when I was a kid. I don't remember feeling that way. Like being scared of or nervous around a person I don't know. I don't remember that feeling of "I'm not going to have anything to say to this person" when I was younger. Do you?

**Jerry:** No, I don't.

**Larry:** And now all of a sudden it's torture. For example, we've talked about this: the kids' parties. Right?

**Jerry:** Yeah.

**Larry:** The kids' birthdays where you have all these parents around.

**Jerry:** Really rough.

**Larry:** Brutal. Oh, wait a second. I think for the first time I'm seeing the first signs of gray in you.

**Jerry:** Oh yeah?

**Larry:** Yeah, look.

**Jerry:** Well, you accused me one time of coloring it.

**Larry:** No, I didn't accuse you.

**Jerry:** You asked.

**Larry:** I asked. That's not an accusation.

**Jerry:** Well, it's pretty close.

**Larry:** I don't think so.

**Jerry:** Pretty close. [*laughs*]

**Larry:** It is not an accusation. An ask. How old can you be before I see a gray hair on you?

**Jerry:** Things just happen, Larry.

**Larry:** I know, but it's unusual. You're in, like, a one or two percentile of hair.

**Jerry:** Nothing could interest me less than hair. I used to love those bald conversations. I tried to sell you on it, remember?

**Larry:** On what?

**Jerry:** On the virtues of baldness.

**Larry:** Yes.

**Jerry:** That it's a future look.

**Larry:** But here's what a lot of people think about bald men: that they put no work or effort into their hair at all. People think that the bald man just towels off and doesn't even think about his hair. "Because you don't have any, what are you even thinking about?"

**Jerry:** Right.

**Larry:** But by habit, you have never gotten out of the hair habit. There's always something. As long as you have it on your head, there's always something to do to it.

## *BRIAN REGAN*

**Jerry:** Have you heard these commercials on the radio where they have this music and it's about retirement? The guy goes, "And the first day . . ." and they have this kind of lyrical sound. The campaign is for your first day of your retirement. It's about how somebody helps you plan for your retirement. And the excitement of—"Imagine that first day." Have you heard these playing on the radio?

**Brian:** No, no, no.

**Jerry:** I listen to the radio a lot. He goes, "It's the first day, and I realize I don't have to do anything." It's the stupidity of people. That this is their fantasy. "The kids were in the car. And I realized my brain had turned to mush. That's when I realized—" [*laughter*]

**Brian:** "That all my motor systems were starting to shut down. Three weeks later, I was dead."

**Jerry:** Yeah.

| | |
|---|---|
| **Brian:** | I have that fantasy, though. |
| **Jerry:** | Of not working? |
| **Brian:** | Yeah. |
| **Jerry:** | Come on. |
| **Brian:** | I do. |
| **Jerry:** | Where are you in the fantasy? What are you doing? Where are you sitting? |
| **Brian:** | It's very specific. And I don't know why. It's a second-story one-bedroom apartment in Alaska. Like, Juneau, Alaska. Or, you know, not a big city in Alaska. With an Italian place right near there where I can get meatball sandwiches. |
| **Jerry:** | Meatball sandwiches. |
| **Brian:** | And I just sit in my place and—I've got enough money. You don't need a lot of money for meatball sandwiches. |
| **Jerry:** | I don't think so. |
| **Brian:** | And I eat meatball sandwiches. And watch the news. |
| **Jerry:** | The news? |
| **Brian:** | Yeah. Forever. |
| **Jerry:** | And that's something you think about? |
| **Brian:** | Yeah. |
| **Jerry:** | What appeals about the setting of Juneau, Alaska? |
| **Brian:** | Away. Just away. |
| **Jerry:** | But you're watching the news. So you're caught up in all the stress and strife that everybody else is going through. |
| **Brian:** | Yeah, but I'm away from the business, away from family drama, away from negotiating your way through that stuff. Like, "I'm done with that. I've done my best at it. And now I just want to chill." |
| **Jerry:** | And do you think it's possible? Even remotely? |
| **Brian:** | I'd need a lot of money. [*laughs*] Do you know what one-bedroom apartments go for in Juneau, Alaska? |
| **Jerry:** | Well, I've done my homework. I've googled that. Pricey? [*laughter*] |
| **Brian:** | Oh no. |
| **Jerry:** | Especially above a meatball sandwich store. The only way that that's appealing to me for you is the guy's only making sandwiches for you. There's nobody in there but the cook, the coffee, the waitress, and they're just waiting. You've got a direct line that just says REGAN over a beat-up old phone. And when that rings— |
| **Brian:** | They've got to prepare it all? |
| **Jerry:** | Yeah. I mean, you're talking about money, that's the money. You bought the restaurant, you pay for these people. Because if you're doing that for that sandwich, when you order you want that sandwich. You don't want, "You know what, we're a little busy. It's going to take an hour." "No. I need it. It's got to be here in ten minutes. It's meatball time." |
| **Brian:** | I love that. The red hotline. Like the Batphone. And there's a whole restau- |

rant of workers that have to facilitate. That'd be good. You know, I see a lot of people in show business who just work forever. And that's good for them. That's not my attitude. I want to get in and get out.

**Jerry:** First of all, my perception of you is a very hardworking guy. I've looked at your schedule and I know your output of material. I think it's clear that you're successful because of that. You have a wonderful talent. But you put all the work in—the sets, the writing. So, do you think—

**Brian:** That's why I like to see a finish line.

**Jerry:** Yeah, but are you dumb enough to think that you can turn that off? That there's an off switch on your drive? Your drive, young man. You have drive.

**Brian:** But I like finish lines. I like to work. I love doing what I do, and I want to do that. And set myself up, and have the kids set up.

**Jerry:** You don't want to do sets? You don't feel that you need that? See, to me . . . I happen to like Chris Rock. He does his tour, and then he just shuts it down for, like, three years. I can't nutritionally—my emotional nutrition of the set . . . You know what I mean. Like, the only thing that could make this [day] better for me is if you and I had a gig in about three hours and we're going to hit the stage.

**Brian:** You might be right about that. In fact, when Johnny Carson retired, I remember him being interviewed. This was six months after his retirement or something. And he didn't do a lot of interviews.

**Jerry:** No.

**Brian:** But he said the hardest thing for him was thinking of something funny in the day, and not having the stage that night to do it. So I can see missing that. And I opened the Juneau comedy club. I'm not giving up on that fantasy.

**Jerry:** When I was a kid, I always thought the plumber wants to be a plumber. I thought the guy who drives a truck loves driving the truck. That's why he's doing it. Why would he do it if he didn't love it? That's what I thought. As you get older, you realize that's not always the case.

**Brian:** Well, what's interesting about the economy is that those jobs people wouldn't necessarily want to do, the price has to keep going up to a line where somebody goes, "I don't want to do that." And then one penny more, "All right, I'll do it."

**Jerry:** That's right. That's what psychiatry is. I don't want to hear somebody else's shit. But there's a number at which, "You know what? How long you going to talk—forty-five, fifty minutes? How much? Okay. All right. I'll tell you what I think."

**Brian:** "All right, all right, for that? I'll pretend like I'm listening, and then I'll give you a couple of little tidbits." I had a high school teacher my freshman year who said, "The clothes you like now are the clothes you're going to like for the rest of your life."

> **"All dads essentially dress in the clothing style of the last good year of their lives."**

| | |
|---|---|
| **Jerry:** | Really? What a funny thing to say. |
| **Brian:** | He said the way you think, you're pretty much set. |
| **Jerry:** | Freshman year in high school. What subject? |
| **Brian:** | Sociology. He was trying to say we get to a certain age and we start locking in. You get what you like, you get what you don't like, and you ride it. Some people change, but most people just go, "All right, these work for me. I'm riding this ride for my life. I like this football team, I like that political party . . ." |
| **Jerry:** | Right. "I like this hobby." |
| **Brian:** | When he said that, it was eye-opening. |
| **Jerry:** | Yes. Teachers say things that really stick in your head. |
| **Brian:** | I'll give him a shout-out. Mr. Burris. He still teaches at the high school that I went to. |
| **Jerry:** | It's similar to my dad bit. All dads essentially dress in the clothing style of the last good year of their lives. They just freeze that moment in fashion history. |
| **Brian:** | Right. They look in the mirror over and over and over again, but there's one time when they look in the mirror and they go, "This is it. I'm riding this." |
| **Jerry:** | If you were a cop in LA, would you want to be in a squad car or on a motorcycle? |
| **Brian:** | Squad car. |
| **Jerry:** | Why? |
| **Brian:** | Because of the safety aspect. I'd want to be a safe cop. I'd want to have bubble wrap all around me. And be seat-belted in. And only do white-collar crime. |
| **Jerry:** | So you want to be a cop in a squad car going into office buildings, sayin', "Everybody on the floor." |
| **Brian:** | Yeah. I actually saw some people riding around the other day on a motorcycle, and I thought, "Am I at the place in my life where I should just take chances like that, and have fun with it?" You know what I mean? You only get the one crack at life—should I go without ever having ridden a motorcycle by myself? Maybe not. |
| **Jerry:** | You've never ridden a motorcycle? |
| **Brian:** | I've been on the back. But behind another guy. I've never ridden one by myself. |
| **Jerry:** | How did you like puttin' your arms around that guy? |
| **Brian:** | I do a bit about it. |
| **Jerry:** | What is it? |
| **Brian:** | Because I put my arms around him, and he said, "No, no, no." And I'm like, "What do you mean, 'no'?" And he's like, "No, you've got little handles down by your seat." |

| Jerry: | Yeah. But that's an interesting thing: Is there a point in your life where you don't worry about safety anymore? Because you kind of look at your life and you go, "Well, I've had a good life. Why not take a little risk at this point if it makes life better?" |
|---|---|
| **Brian:** | Yeah. For the thrill of it. "Maybe I should just zip around on a motorcycle between these cars and see what that feels like." |
| **Jerry:** | It feels great. I did it for years. |
| **Brian:** | Really? |
| **Jerry:** | Yeah, loved it. |
| **Brian:** | You'd ride around on the streets of New York on a motorcycle? |
| **Jerry:** | Yeah. But I found that I was getting the thrill of risk and adrenaline from performing which took the place of that. So I said, "Why do I put myself in physical—" |
| **Brian:** | Right, and the fear of death is a lot less. |
| **Jerry:** | Now, if I wasn't a comedian, I'd probably still be on the motorcycle. I think there's an adrenaline addiction that we have—I know I have. I have to get that buzz. |
| **Brian:** | Yes. You get the butterflies. |
| **Jerry:** | Oh, I need that. |
| **Brian:** | I always say that the things you remember in life are the things that happen right after you had butterflies. |

# *JOEL HODGSON*

| Jerry: | Joel, I want you to put your mind on this dilemma. Or at least give me some insight, some perspective. Why are we looking back all the time? The people that built this diner were looking forward, right? |
|---|---|
| **Joel:** | Well, you know what I think? |
| **Jerry:** | Just answer me. |
| **Joel:** | Yes, they're looking forward. |
| **Jerry:** | So why are we looking back? |
| **Joel:** | Because when you look back you know what you're going to say. That's why. You know what to say about the past. And you don't know what to say about the future. |
| **Jerry:** | Damn it, you're smart. Are you enjoying your life? |
| **Joel:** | I do, man. |
| **Jerry:** | I'm doing my part to brighten it. |
| **Joel:** | I know. I appreciate it. I definitely said, "It always kind of works out when I'm with Jerry. It's never really that bad." |
| **Jerry:** | That's as faint a compliment as you can possibly pay someone. |

## CARL REINER

**Carl:**   I heard a good one. Two old Jews on a bench. One said, "Guess how old I am?" "Ninety-eight." "How'd you guess?" "You told me yesterday." I get up in the morning, first thing I read is the obits. You don't do that yet. You'll see.

**Jerry:**   No, I read them. I like them. I like that they boil the whole guy's life down to "Invented the ballpoint pen spring."

## MIRANDA SINGS [COLLEEN BALLINGER]

**Jerry:**   So what do you think will happen to Miranda as she gets older?

**Colleen:**   You know, I don't know, because I never thought it would even get to this. Five years ago when I was starting all of this craziness, I thought it would last a week or then a month. I never thought it would keep snowballing to what it is. Now that it's continuing to, I just don't know. One of the top questions I get on Twitter is from kids saying, "What are you going to do when Miranda gets pregnant—when you get pregnant?" Like, "What's your excuse going to be?" They're just so excited about me getting pregnant lately. Which I don't know why [*laughs*], 'cause I'm not working on that. But they're very excited to see me get pregnant and see me get old. They want Miranda around. So she'll live as long as the audience wants to see her. She can be around. I'm fine with that.

**Jerry:**   It's very interesting when the audience gets ahead of the performer. That's a brilliant projection. Pregnant Miranda. Who can't wait to see that?

**Colleen:**   [*laughs*] Awful.

**Jerry:**   Oh my God. It's going to be fantastic.

**Colleen:**   It'll be awful.

**Jerry:**   Miranda with kids.

**Colleen:**   Yeah. Horrible.

# CHRIS ROCK

**Chris:**   Now, have you been going into the city to work on stuff during the week?

**Jerry:**   I try to. I can't go out. I'm too tired at night.

**Chris:**   I'm tired at night too. I have to take a nap to really work.

**Jerry:**   I take a nap and I'm still too tired. I'm [almost] sixty.

**Chris:**   But you're a rich sixty. You know what they always say, "Money is the best lotion in the world."

# SARAH SILVERMAN

**Sarah:**   I don't know if this is sad or not, but I plan on dying in a nursing home for comedians. I think there must be nursing homes that are mostly comedians, right?

**Jerry:**   Not good comedians.

**Sarah:**   You're going to have children to care for you when you die.

**Jerry:**   No.

**Sarah:**   Yeah.

**Jerry:**   Are you going to care for your parents? No. That is the really tragic thing. You're not going to escape that. No one can escape that. You have this wonderful experience of raising kids, but no one will escape the fact that your kids eventually don't want to be around you. Maybe that's how the holidays got invented. We'll designate a few times a year that we'll just put ourselves through this. . . . I was talking to my manager, George Shapiro, about this yesterday. We were talking about how comedy makes comedians age so slowly, and I think it's giving and receiving laughs all the time. Chris Rock, of course, quite cynically says that richness is the ultimate face lotion.

**Sarah:**    Yeah, but not all comics are rich.

**Jerry:**    No. But hearing laughter is like getting extra sleep, don't you think?

**Sarah:**    Yeah. It makes my arms itch, at its best. I don't know why. Do you know what I mean?

**Jerry:**    Of course.

**Sarah:**    That feeling.

**Jerry:**    It's worth all the struggle.

## DON RICKLES

**Don:**    I was very pleased that you called. As you get older, as you'll find out, you start to say, "Nah, I don't want to do that." I remember when I was young, if a guy called me, "Yes! Oh God, yes!" You know? "How much is it? Four dollars? I'll do it! Four dollars, oh God!" Everything becomes so different, you know.

**Jerry:**    So what is it that you still really like to do?

**Don:**    Well, doing the stand-up, I do like to do. Believe it or not, sitting on the couch—a lot of couch. A lot of dinner at night with friends. I like that very much. We have a beach house. My family's down there now, my daughter. I love the beach.

*"It's not about age. It's about your mindset."*

## PATTON OSWALT

**Jerry:**    You've ruined this whole neighborhood for yourself, do you realize that?

**Patton:**    I know.

**Jerry:**    Now you can't move down here.

**Patton:**    Well, they wouldn't have me here 'cause I'm too old. I'm forty-four. I have the kid. I'm just too boring.

**Jerry:**    That's not true. Just be cool, man.

**Patton:**    Just be cool.

**Jerry:**    Yeah. It's not about age. It's about your mindset. Where's your mindset?

**Patton:**    Well, here's my mindset. Forty-four. If I could wait till I was sixty, then I'd be the cool, weird old guy that they were like, "Oh, look at the old guy down here."

**Jerry:**    Who is your favorite superhero?

**Patton:** I think my favorite superhero is Spider-Man. As I get older, it's Spider-Man.

**Jerry:** As you get older?

**Patton:** Yeah, because it is the one superhero comic where they are never not aware of, "Rent is due, shouldn't I be in a better apartment? If I want to get married, then I have to improve this part of my life. Should I be out crime-fighting if I want to have a family? Maybe I should stop. Does the city really need me?"

**Jerry:** So you like all that self-doubt?

**Patton:** Yeah. It makes the action that much more shocking. It's like that moment in *Huck Finn* where Huck Finn just goes, "Well, then I'll go to hell." Like, "I'm going to go save Jim, I don't care." So, it's this guy Spider-Man going, "I have these powers. I could just hang back, make money, and be—no, you know what, I'm going to put it on the line." There's something so heroic and optimistic and futile about what he's doing that's great.

## JAY LENO

**Jerry:**  How old are you now?

**Jay:**  Sixty-three.

**Jerry:**  Sixty-three. I love when people turn away when they say their age.

**Jay:**  I don't mind being sixty-three. Because I'm in better shape against other sixty-three-year-olds than I ever was against [my peers] as a twenty-five-year-old.

**Jerry:**  Really, you think so?

**Jay:**  Yes! I don't drink. I don't smoke. I try to run a couple miles every day. I keep in shape. I don't go crazy. I don't knock myself out. But all my friends at twenty-five were working out all the time.

**Jerry:**  So they were in better shape than you then.

**Jay:**  Yeah. Now their knees are bad because they played football, or they have headaches all the time, or their rotator cuff is . . . whatever it is. Whereas I go, "Want to fight now, Bob?"

**Jerry:**  So is there anything you want to do differently about doing your stand-up now, when you're free to really concentrate on it?

**Jay:**  I don't know if I'd do anything different. It's interesting to watch your act sort of evolve with your age. I used to see that with comics who used to talk about sex. Everything changes. And it's fun. The aging process, the whole going through life, it's real. It's what I call the thirty-nine-and-a-half rule. Did we ever discuss that?

**Jerry:**  Only about a thousand times.

**Jay:**  Okay, so you know the thirty-nine-and-a-half rule.

**Jerry:**  I love the thirty-nine-and-a-half rule. What is it?

**Jay:**  The thirty-nine and a half rule is when you're thirty-nine years old and you're onstage and you say the word "pussy," girls laugh. When you're thirty-nine and a half and you got that bald spot in the center and you're wearing the leather pants and you say the word "pussy," they go, "Eww! That old guy said the word 'pussy,' eww! Eww!" . . . I said the other day— it was when the Rolling Stones were announcing their tour—"Wow, they still look pretty good." And these interns go, "Because they're old! They don't look good! You're old! You think they look good 'cause they're your age! They don't. They look ridiculous."

## JON STEWART

**Jerry:**  How would you like to be buried? Do you want a traditional funeral or cremation? Have you ever thought about it?

**Jon:**  I have not thought about it in any way. Have you started to think about that?

**Jerry:** It doesn't bother me to think about it.

**Jon:** But why would you think about it?

**Jerry:** Just for fun. So you've never thought about how you would like—

**Jon:** What do I care? Here's the way I look at it. What if you die in the summer? Now the beach is crowded. People go out there. "What are you doing?" "Oh, I'm, uh, spreading Jerry Seinfeld . . ."

## GEORGE WALLACE

**Jerry:** These old men. Let me tell you something about old men. They don't know when change has come. This is the first sign of oldness: when change comes and they can't tell.

**George:** The first sign of old is, you ever drop something on the floor and you just look at it? Your hair is turning gray. I think you should dye it. I think you really would look better.

| Jerry: | No. I'm a comedian. I don't have to lie. |
|---|---|
| **George:** | It's not that you're lying, just that you might look better. |
| **Jerry:** | I don't need to look better. I have things to say. |
| **George:** | You do need to look better! |
| **Jerry:** | No, I don't. I look good. |
| **George:** | You ugly. |

## STEPHEN COLBERT

| **Stephen:** | I'm betting on making it to a hundred, because I'm enjoying myself. |
|---|---|
| **Jerry:** | What's the flavor that you want to taste in your mouth—the last thing you taste? |
| **Stephen:** | Probably razzleberry. |
| **Jerry:** | Razzleberry? |
| **Stephen:** | I don't know. Maybe coffee. |
| **Jerry:** | Coffee. You really want to perk up right at that moment? |
| **Stephen:** | What's the option, then? Hemlock. It cures what ails you. Which is existence. |
| **Jerry:** | That's really funny. |
| **Stephen:** | When I die, I don't want to be thirsty. And I don't want to be in pain. |
| **Jerry:** | You're a genius. |

## GARRY SHANDLING

| **Jerry:** | Garry, we represent a time. And I don't know if anybody cares about it. I don't care. But it's just nice. |
|---|---|
| **Garry:** | It's right around sixty you get reflective. That's exactly when it happens. I was sitting there watching CNN, and they broke in and said, "Robin Williams . . ." And I was frozen. They said he killed himself. And I sat there and I was frozen. This is totally true. I was in that kitchen of mine, by the island. And then Wolf Blitzer says, "Sixty-three is so young." And I looked up with a little hope, 'cause I'm the same age as Robin. And then I realized, "Sixty-three is so young" is a phrase you never hear relative to anything but death. |
| **Jerry:** | Yeah. You have to die in your sixties for them to say, "Boy, he was young." |
| **Garry:** | I went in to get a CT scan last Wednesday. I'm totally clear. I'm totally fine. And I go in there and the tech guy—a smart guy, midforties, focused—he says, "Hey, Garry Shandling, I'm a big fan. I did a CT scan a year ago of you. Do you have cancer?" I said, "No." He said, "Oh, good, I was wor- |

ried. We took a CT scan once and there was a thing on your pancreas." I said, "Yes, it was cysts and they got rid of it." And he said, "Oh, good, so you're still alive. Because I was watching the news and it seemed like if you'd passed away I would have heard about it on the news." And I said, "Well, I don't know, man. I mean, I don't know if they would have broken in or anything, but . . ." You know, I didn't know what to say to the guy. He kept at it, and he said, "That's so great that Garry Shandling's still alive."

**Jerry:**  [*laughs*]

## SEBASTIAN MANISCALCO

**Jerry:**  One of the things of our profession is it's kind of an age-free profession. I don't even know how old you are. I think I know, but if I guessed I could be off fifteen years.

**Sebastian:** You're not good with the age?

**Jerry:**  Not with comedians. Like, I'm sixty-one.

**Sebastian:** Would have never known.

**Jerry:**  Right, you wouldn't know. Comedians, they just get frozen. If a guy's brain's working, and his mouth is working, that's what's got your attention. In your sixties, the percentage of things out of your mouth in a day that are just "I don't care" goes up. It just goes up. When I was in my forties, I'd say, "I don't care" 10 percent of the time. In my fifties, 30 percent of the time. In my sixties, 80 percent of the things I say are versions of "I don't care."

> "In my sixties, 80 percent of the things I say are versions of 'I don't care.'"

## NORM MACDONALD

**Jerry:**  This hot sauce is so hot.

**Norm:**  Do you like really hot things?

**Jerry:**  I do, but that is unbelievably hot. Do you like hot sauce?

**Norm:**  Oh, I hate it. But you know, you've got to try new things in life.

**Jerry:**  No, you don't.

**Norm:**  Yeah, you're right. Now that I grow older, I realize it's not like you become fearless when you become older. It's the opposite. You're fearful.

**Jerry:**  Right.

**Norm:**  And you just want to sit in your chair. I remember my grandmother. I walked into the room once and she had a bruise the length of her wrist all the way up to her shoulder. Big purple, yellowish bruise. And I said, "My God, Grandma. Where'd you get that?" "The wind."

## CEDRIC THE ENTERTAINER

**Jerry:** I'm not one of these people that cares about age. I don't care. I'm happy to be old. Happy to be out of it.

**Cedric:** I just read this whole article on Sumner Redstone.

**Jerry:** He just looks like a bag of leaves, doesn't he?

**Cedric:** Yeah, I don't want to do that.

**Jerry:** When your neck can't touch the shirt at any point, it's time. That's not how I want to go. I don't want to be that. I don't want to look like somebody else [knotted] the tie, you know?

## JOHN MULANEY

**John:** I have a joke I was just trying this past week. I'm not old yet, but there's a phase before "old" called "gross." And I'm getting gross. I'm damp a lot more. I have hair on my shoulders. And I talk through burps. Which I never did when I was a kid. And I won't take a pause.

**Jerry:** Yeah, when you're a kid you really make the most of that burp.

**John:** A burp was like, "Everyone be quiet."

## NEAL BRENNAN

**Jerry:** It's so fun at my age. The older you get, I really think the more fun life is. Because you see and understand so much. Like, I can watch John Lennon now on *Dick Cavett*, and I go, "Oh, I know who that is." But when I saw it in '74, I said, "Oh my God, John Lennon." You know what I mean?

**Neal:** Yeah. I always say that by the end of life, you will have been every person. You're the loser, you're the winner, you're the cheater, you get cheated on, you're the criminal. You're every part. And as you watch John Lennon, now you go, "I think I know what he's going through."

## TRACY MORGAN

**Tracy:** I got a million dollars set to the side for me, my wife. I bought a plot on the top of Mount Everest.

**Jerry:** You can buy a plot on the top of Mount Everest?

**Tracy:** A million dollars for the Sherpas, which is the tribe that lives at the bottom of Mount Everest. We're going to be cremated—me, my daughter, my son, and my wife—and taken to the top and just leave us there, top of the world, baby. It was either that or the Mariana Trench.

**Jerry:**   Where's that?

**Tracy:**   I forget where it's at in the Pacific, but it's the deepest part of the world, thirty-eight thousand feet. Only James Cameron, two people, ever went down there.


# EDDIE MURPHY

**Jerry:**   What do you miss about New York?

**Eddie:**   I don't do a lot of pining for the good old days. Right now is the best it's ever been. It only gets better. You think at eighty you'll still be going up?

**Jerry:**   Yeah.

**Eddie:**   Wow.

**Jerry:**   Why not? I mean, it depends on how you look.

**Eddie:**   I'm lazy. I'd like more than anything to be doing nothing with my family and my kids.

**Jerry:**   They won't be kids at that point.

**Eddie:**   At eighty, I'm thinking I just want to just sit [in the] backyard. Just relax and wait on the reaper.

**Jerry:**   Can you sit still now?

**Eddie:**   Absolutely.

**Jerry:**   Really?

**Eddie:**   That's what I do most of the [time]. Doing nothing is my favorite dish.

**Jerry:**   You could do nothing all day.

**Eddie:**   I could do nothing all day. For years on end.

**Jerry:**   Wow.

**Eddie:**   And I have. And I mean, really nothing. Like, nothing. Don't watch the news. Don't know what's going on. Totally disconnect.


# MARTIN SHORT

**Martin:**   Would you ever retire?

**Jerry:**   That's kind of a dumb question.

**Martin:**   Tough one or dumb one?

**Jerry:**   Dumb one.

**Martin:**   Yeah. I think so too, completely. I think if you have a horrible job you hate your whole life, fantastic. But this idea that you would stop doing what you adore because of a number? It's insane.

**Jerry:**    Did you have something that you liked to do that was fun that was outside of show business?

**Martin:**   Well, I told people I did. "What do you do, Marty, when you're not in show [business]?" "Oh, tennis. Love tennis." Couldn't care less about tennis.

# JAMIE FOXX

**Jamie:**    You know how I talk about fitness? In my world, it was always about the pump. You get older, your shit is different. I pump the fuck out of myself. Looking in the mirror, I'm pumping, pumping. But then I walk to my car and I hear *ssssss*.

# MISCELLANEOUS WISDOM

# CHRIS ROCK

**Jerry**  Comedians have wisdom. Great jokes always have wisdom buried in them.

**Chris:**  Right. They require observation. Eighty percent of your job is just paying attention to shit.

**Jerry:**  I know, but it's deep.

**Chris:**  At a level that most people don't pay attention. We're detectives. We're always on the case.

**Jerry:**  [*laughs*]

**Chris:**  Always on the case! That's all it is. . . . I say everything's about company.

**Jerry:**  Yes, it is.

**Chris:**  All life is about the company you keep. All enjoyment is about the company you keep. A gourmet meal with an asshole is a horrible meal. A hot dog with an interesting person is an amazing meal. Yes, we're in a million-dollar car. But if we were in a yellow cab and you were driving—

**Jerry:**  We'd have just as much fun.

# BRIAN REGAN

**Jerry:** What is that about comedians? That comedians, we're not bothered, we don't feel vulnerable. You know what I mean? The way regular people feel very vulnerable. Most people, they come up to me and I go, "Really, that's your shirt? You're wearing that?"

**Brian:** And then they're crushed.

**Jerry:** You could see the look of terror.

**Brian:** They're going to go and sit down.

**Jerry:** That's what bothers me the most about regular people. I can't tell them, "That's the most idiotic thing I've ever heard."

**Brian:** And just have them go, "Yeah, I guess so." [*laughter*] That should be the reaction.

**Jerry:** It should be.

**Brian:** Yeah. It is kind of dumb.

**Jerry:** It is kind of dumb. And that's why this is—to take something from Colin Quinn—a whole crock of shit, "the insecure comedian." None of us are insecure. None of us. You get them onstage by yourself, and just talking. You have no stories, no instruments. No. You're not an insecure individual. Sorry.

# AMY SCHUMER

**Jerry:** Here's my secret trick for talking with people. Which you need.

**Amy:** Okay.

**Jerry:** Numbers. Ask them a question to which the answer is a number.

**Amy:** Wow.

**Jerry:** This is the Seinfeld secret technique for talking to regular people. "So how long have you been around here?" Or, "When did you do that?" Or, "What time do you start work?"

**Amy:** That's great. Why numbers though?

**Jerry:** There's always an answer. It gets them going. And it's easy to inquire about. "How long have you lived here?"

**Amy:** "How many of your grandparents are alive?"

**Jerry:** Right. [*laughs*] Yeah.

**Amy:** "What age were you when you lost your virginity?"

**Jerry:** Yeah.

**Amy:** Like maybe even more general.

**Jerry:** Maybe more general. Yeah. [*laughs*] That's my little trick.

**Amy:** That's really good.

> "All life is about the company you keep. All enjoyment is about the company you keep."

> *"The truth ends every conversation. If you just tell the truth, the conversation's over."*

## SETH MEYERS

**Jerry:** Someone told me a story the other day. They were driving in the city and there was this car just driving completely crazy, not signaling, just swooping across, like, three lanes and then back and making turns, and the guy was like, "What is going on with this person?" This is Chris Mazzilli. Do you know Chris Mazzilli?

**Seth:** No.

**Jerry:** He owns the Gotham club. And he pulls up alongside at a light and it's a middle-aged Asian woman. He says to her, "What are you doing?" And she goes, "I don't know."

**Seth:** [*laughs*]

**Jerry:** The more I think about that story, the more I think, "You know, I don't think he can improve on it." It's perfect. Its simplicity is perfect.

**Seth:** Yeah, she just told him the truth.

**Jerry:** The truth ends every conversation. If you just tell the truth, the conversation's over.

## JULIA LOUIS-DREYFUS

**Jerry:** You have things. I could go through your little closet and find so many. 'Cause I know that you do love your things.

**Julia:** I love my things.

**Jerry:** So what's wrong with that? If they make you happy and you're not hurting anyone, what's wrong with it?

**Julia:** Okay.

**Jerry:** You just don't want to argue, or you're taking my point?

**Julia:** I'm taking your point.

**Jerry:** It's not healthy to think things are more important than the other bigger, really important things.

**Julia:** Right, in terms of profound happiness, I'm not sure it's a pursuit worth going after.

**Jerry:** Well, if you're going to throw in the word "profound," that completely screws the whole thing.

**Julia:** It screws it all up for you?

**Jerry:** Well, profound happiness is almost arrogant to expect.

**Julia:** Arrogant?

**Jerry:** [*laughs*] To expect to be that happy—that's a very American concept.

**Julia:** So perhaps I shouldn't say "profound." What's the word I'm looking for? True happiness. Is "true" a better word?

**Jerry:** Yeah, it probably is.

| Julia: | Okay. That's what I meant. |
|---|---|
| Jerry: | It won't bring true happiness. But . . . |
| Julia: | I wish I'd worked out with that woman today. Talk about not being happy. I didn't work out today. |
| Jerry: | You didn't work out today? |
| Julia: | No, I didn't. |
| Jerry: | What's your excuse? |
| Julia: | Do your goddamned show, that's my excuse. |

## STEPHEN COLBERT

| Stephen: | How do you feel about happiness? Are you a fan? Where do you rank happiness on your priorities? 'Cause you said you like suffering. |
|---|---|
| Jerry: | Very low. I think it's a foolish thing to pursue. |
| Stephen: | I agree. Well, I don't know if it's foolish. It's pleasant. I think happiness is pleasant. |
| Jerry: | I think it's irrelevant. |
| Stephen: | But so is liquor. |
| Jerry: | Huh? |
| Stephen: | I think happiness is pleasant, but so is liquor. You know? |
| Jerry: | That's right. Yeah. |
| Stephen: | You can't take too much of it. |
| Jerry: | No, people try to go for that. They don't realize, the only way to get that is to do something. There's a mechanism. |
| Stephen: | Suffering is actually a pretty good way to get to happiness. |
| Jerry: | Exactly. That would describe my whole perspective on life right there. |
| Stephen: | Really? |
| Jerry: | What you just said. That's what I meant when I said I know when I'm suffering, I'm headed to something good. Number one, I'm probably making someone else happy if I'm suffering. |
| Stephen: | Mm-hmm. |
| Jerry: | Like I'm suffering right now trying to make you happy. |

## BARACK OBAMA

| Jerry: | What is it that you really want to do that they don't let you do? |
|---|---|
| Barack: | I would love to just be taking a walk, and then I run into you. You're sitting on a bench, right. And suddenly I say, "Hey, Jerry. How you doing?" And you say, "I'm doing pretty good. What are you doing?" "Uh, nothing. Just a Saturday morning." |

| Jerry: | Right. |
|---|---|
| **Barack:** | That moment when you lost your anonymity. And anonymity is not something you think about as being valuable. |
| Jerry: | With all due respect, I remember very well not being famous. |
| **Barack:** | You think it was okay? |
| Jerry: | It wasn't that great. |
| **Barack:** | You think being famous is better? |
| Jerry: | Yeah. |
| **Barack:** | How did you keep perspective? |
| Jerry: | I'll give you the real answer. It's got to be similar to your life. I fell in love with the work. |
| **Barack:** | Mm-hmm. |
| Jerry: | And the work was joyful. And difficult. And interesting. And that was my focus. So that's that. |
| **Barack:** | So now that you're like a quasi-retired man of leisure— |
| Jerry: | I work a lot. |
| **Barack:** | Do you? |
| Jerry: | Yeah. |
| **Barack:** | Are you still doing stand-up? |
| Jerry: | Are you still making speeches? |

# SEBASTIAN MANISCALCO

| Jerry: | Don't say, "Six of one, half a dozen of the other." Okay? Don't say that. It's not a fresh expression. We've all heard it too many times. "You know, it's kind of six of one, half a dozen . . ." Yeah, we know that that means they're similar. We know that. Don't say these things. |
|---|---|
| **Sebastian:** | So you don't want people going to stock phrases. |
| Jerry: | My wife now, when someone will say, "It is what it is," she'll say, "Don't say that in front of him." My wife will intercede now, 'cause she knows I'm going to lose it. Why are you saying that? 'Cause you heard someone else say it? And that sounded good to you? So you thought you would incorporate it into your little patter?<br><br>The little things. That's all I care about. I think the big things are dull. |
| **Sebastian:** | The big things are dull. |
| Jerry: | The details are interesting. The details of life are interesting. |
| **Sebastian:** | Yeah, like that's a small detail there. You took the wallet out. You readjusted the cash. Was the cash not sitting well? |
| Jerry: | It was not sitting well. [*laughs*] |
| **Sebastian:** | Now, why would you move it from the back to here? Was it bothering you? |
| Jerry: | I'm sitting on it. I don't want to sit on it. It's uncomfortable. |

**Sebastian:** Okay. See, those little things.

**Jerry:** We should write a book or do a show. We would call it *The Art of Living*.

**Sebastian:** *The Art of Living*.

**Jerry:** Put some art into everything you do. Put a little art into it.

**Sebastian:** Absolutely.

**Jerry:** Don't say, "Oh, I'm not creative. I'm not perceptive." Everybody has a little gift. Put it in the earth.

# JIM GAFFIGAN

**Jim:** You ever consider how lucky—I mean, 'cause there's stability in our lives, economic stability, but there's also the opportunity to do what you enjoy. That's insane, right?

**Jerry:** Um . . . no. No, because you take that risk.

**Jim:** You have choice.

| | |
|---|---|
| **Jerry:** | You get some guts, you get some balls, and you go, "You know what?" You had a job. You left. |
| **Jim:** | Yeah, yeah. |
| **Jerry:** | Nobody else left. So why are you so lucky? |
| **Jim:** | Because you had the courage to do it. |
| **Jerry:** | And that's just luck too? |
| **Jim:** | You're right, Jerry. |
| **Jerry:** | I'm asking. I find this interesting. It's a very difficult thing to analyze. People say to me, "Well, what about your talent?" Was that just luck? What about the gift of being able to work hard? Is that luck? When do I get any credit for doing anything now? |

## SARAH SILVERMAN

| | |
|---|---|
| **Jerry:** | When you say men are pretty much born gay— |
| **Sarah:** | Not all men. |
| **Jerry:** | The "pretty much" bothered me. |
| **Sarah:** | Why? I've been working on this bit about Scientology. It's only weird to us 'cause it's new. We make fun of it because it's batshit crazy, but it's no more batshit crazy than Catholicism or anything, right? And it's new to hear people worship a guy named Ron. In our ears [it] feels weird. We know Rons. And he had to make his name "L. Ron" 'cause there was another Ron Hubbard in the Writers Guild. That's how recent of a religion it is. And that's why we feel weirded out by it. It's no more weird than fucking everything. |

## MELISSA VILLASEÑOR

| | |
|---|---|
| **Melissa:** | I went to my brother's wedding on Saturday and I didn't get a plus-one. I don't have a boyfriend, you know? But it made me think like, "Am I just going to be a comedian in the family that doesn't have anyone at the family parties?" |
| **Jerry:** | No, I don't think that's going to happen. |
| **Melissa:** | I know, I know. I just need to be patient and keep my heart open. That sounds so funny coming out of me. |
| **Jerry:** | I know. What is that horrible piece of jewelry? "Keep your heart open, and love will find a way." Who was that actress doing a bland infomercial? Jane [Seymour]. You never know what's going to happen. |
| **Melissa:** | I know, that's it. |

**Jerry:** See, the dumbest thing is to try and figure it out, or plan it. That's a complete waste of your mind.

**Melissa:** I'm going to write that in my journal today. The dumbest thing is to try to figure it out.

**Jerry:** Yes.


# CARL REINER

**Carl:** [In the play] *God Almighty*, I'll never forget the one scene at the end of Act I. This is so brilliant. This man dies and meets God, and the Archangel Gabriel is there and Michael. And they're in heaven. He says, "I'm here." [God] says, "Who are you?" He says, "I'm man. I'm a man." [God] says, "I don't know who you are?" He says, "Man. Man. You made man. In your image." [God] says, "No, I don't remember making you. I remember the ants. That was good. You know, they can carry 1,800 times their [weight]? And flowers. I love flowers. They're so colorful. I don't remember you." He says, "You made me." [God] says, "Show me what you do. Do somethin'. Show me what you do." And this is so brilliant. You know what he did? He did a soft-shoe. Man did a soft-shoe [*laughter*] up and down the stage. And when you think about it, the essence of man's grace is that soft-shoe. You never saw anybody do a soft-shoe you didn't smile and feel good.


# DAVID LETTERMAN

**David:** Here's what I think about, and this will never make the tape: Why is the spirit that you are in this being? Why aren't you the spirit of your next-door neighbor? Why isn't your spirit in me? Why isn't my spirit in that guy? Why is my awareness here?

**Jerry:** You want an answer?

**David:** Yeah.

**Jerry:** You picked it. You saw it, and you picked it. Did you ever see that George Harrison special that Scorsese did?

**David:** Yes. The three-parter?

**Jerry:** Actually, that's not the one I mean. The one—the *Concert for George*.

**David:** No, no. I didn't see that.

**Jerry:** Well, it starts with one of his Krishna things on the screen: "You have always been here and you will always be here." I had never thought of that, but I instantly believed it. Like this is—I don't want to get all Hindu on you—but this is this life. You picked it. There will be others. There were others before this. We're just moving through different things. You were here to do a certain thing, which I can tell you right now that you did. You accomplished what you set out to do here. And then you'll go back up there, back into the pool, and then you'll pick another one, and you'll do something else.

**David:** So how, mathematically speaking, how does that work with the fact that there are more people alive on this planet today than at any other time previous?

**Jerry:** It's getting more habitable. So more people are coming down to do it. It's easier to survive now than it was five hundred years ago. You had to be a heartier soul.

**David:** So everybody in here was in a state of dormancy, spiritually.

**Jerry:** Yeah. I mean, going through the whole [heart surgery] thing you went through, you must have some sense that your body is not really you. That you're in it and that you could leave it. You will leave it. When you went through that thing, you must have had some window of that, some glimmer of that, right?

**David:** Yeah.

**Jerry:** You don't want to leave this life. No one does. You're having a good life. You want to keep doing it. But you could check out, you could leave it. Did you have flashes of that going through that thing?

**David:** No. I'll tell you what I did become aware of was all my life I had to go to church every Sunday, and finally when I was sixteen I said to my folks, "I can't go to church every Sunday." So I stopped going. But I would always hear people refer to "oh, the spirit" and "this spirit" and "his spirit" and "his spirit will live forever." And it was only recently that I experienced that and have observed that and know it to be viable. Know it to be absolutely true.

**Jerry:** Oh, really?

**David:** Yes. The spirit of people lives forever.

**Jerry:** How did you get that?

**David:** It came to me in several forms, but most recently we had a very good friend of ours at the show pass away and—

**Jerry:** Anyone I know?

**David:** She did your makeup every time you were on the show.

**Jerry:** You're kidding? When did that happen?

**David:** About a year and a half ago.

**Jerry:** Wow, and she's young.

**David:** Yeah, in her forties and had three kids. She would stand next to me every show and put on my makeup. And she was there. Her spirit inhabits that room. It's palpable. And the theater. We will think about her and remember her and visualize her and it's . . . So to me that is a manifestation of that. I know it sounds simplistic, but it absolutely is meaningful for me. Her spirit will always be there.

> "This is the life. You picked it. There will be others. There were others before this."

## DON RICKLES

| | |
|---|---|
| **Jerry:** | Nobody knows what life is, Don. |
| **Don:** | Oh, Jesus. |
| **Jerry:** | We don't know what it is. |
| **Don:** | Oh, I do. |
| **Jerry:** | You do? |
| **Don:** | I could have been a damn good psychiatrist. That's what I do on the stage, it's a form of psychiatry. |
| **Jerry:** | I know, but what kind of life is that? Telling people— |
| **Don:** | Well, I don't do it. What kind of life is that? |
| **Jerry:** | That's not a fun life. |
| **Don:** | Hey, but if you do it and you're good at it, it might be great. |
| **Jerry:** | No. |
| **Don:** | But I'm saying I take it as a credit that I possibly could have done it, in my own mind. |
| **Jerry:** | Well, if you need delusions, that's your business. This is one of the reasons I do this show, because I love the people who really gave themselves to this profession. And this show is kind of my valentine to the people I love. |

## JUDD APATOW

| | |
|---|---|
| **Jerry:** | I didn't get the guilt gene. Despite my Long Island Jewish upbringing, I just didn't get it. |
| **Judd:** | Are you sure your parents were Jewish? |
| **Jerry:** | Guilt and worry . . . When I became friendly with George Wallace in my early twenties, I used to say, "I'm worried about this, I'm worried about that." He goes, "Why don't you just stop worrying?" |
| **Judd:** | Yeah. |
| **Jerry:** | I go, "How do you do that?" He goes, "Just stop." |
| **Judd:** | Wow. |
| **Jerry:** | And I did. And I never worried again. |
| **Judd:** | But how did you do that? People have said that to me for quite a long time. |
| **Jerry:** | You force yourself. |
| **Judd:** | Yeah. |
| **Jerry:** | You can do that. You want me to be your shrink? |

# GARRY SHANDLING

**Garry:** I wrote a joke that said, "I can meditate to the point where my mind is blank. But then there's no one to blame." So here's what happened. I did that joke onstage. And of course it's not really a joke, but then this is the luck of my life. Judd Apatow says to me, "Hey, I'm Skyping with Ram Dass tomorrow. Come on over." This is maybe a year ago. And I go over to Judd's house and there's Ram Dass, who lives in Hawaii. I said, "Ram Dass, let me tell you this joke." And I tell him that, and he laughs twice at it. He laughs, and then he thinks about it, and he laughs again, 'cause it's a joke for monks.

**Jerry:** I forgot the joke already.

**Garry:** One time I'm with Thich Nhat Hanh. He's got a monastery in San Diego and we're in a little hut, at a little table, just like in a movie. And Thich Nhat Hanh, you know, he's a genius. We're just sitting there and there's five monks standing against the wall—three of them are American and two of them are Vietnamese. Thich Nhat Hanh speaks broken English pretty good. He said, "So I understand you have some joke about the Buddha." And I said, "Well, Buddha never got married because his wife would have said, 'Are you going to sit around the house like that all day?' He was meditating and she goes, 'Why don't you meditate while you're taking out the trash?'" And there's dead silence in this little hut except for the three American monks who are laughing hysterically. [*laughs*] So then I explained to him the joke.

**Jerry:** That's funny.

**Garry:** Yes. And so the answer is in what we call nothingness. And that stillness. That's where all the answers are.

**Jerry:** You know, I met Steve Jobs a month before he died.

**Garry:** Tell me about that.

**Jerry:** I just was working up there, and I thought, "Let's call him." The same way you and I called Johnny Carson. And I know that's a very strong memory for you, as it is for me.

**Garry:** Yeah.

**Jerry:** We're standing—we can discuss this—we were standing on the stage at Radford [the CBS studio in LA]. And I said to you, "You know, one of these days, we're going to pick up that goddamn newspaper, and [Carson's] going to be gone. Why don't we call him?"

**Garry:** So I have to ask you—'cause you mentioned with David Brenner—I hope when Johnny died you didn't go, "There go those monologues. There goes that material."

**Jerry:** [*laughs*]

**Garry:** That is one of the funniest things to me—when David Brenner died, and I got kind of sad for a minute. I did know David. I've still got to go back over that. You know, "Now there's all that material . . ."

> *"The answer is in what we call nothingness. And that stillness. That's where all the answers are.'"*

| | |
|---|---|
| **Jerry:** | I didn't even finish the thought. |
| **Garry:** | What is the thought? |
| **Jerry:** | No, that was the thought. I was thinking, "Gee, all that material. He worked so hard on it. It's just gone. It doesn't mean anything to anyone anymore, and it took so much work to create it." |
| **Garry:** | That material, my friend, is purely a vehicle for you to express your spirit. And your soul. And your being. And that's why you're fantastic. So you keep reinventing that. |
| **Jerry:** | So it doesn't have any value beyond that? Beyond the end of this . . . |
| **Garry:** | It doesn't have any value beyond you expressing yourself spiritually, in a very soulful, spiritual way. It's why you're on the planet. God. Open up the sunroof. What year is this? |

# EPISODE INDEX

**101**
### *LARRY DAVID*
Larry Eats A Pancake

1952 Volkswagen Beetle

**102**
### *RICKY GERVAIS*
Madman In A Death
Machine

1967 Austin-Healey 3000
Mk III

**103**
### *BRIAN REGAN*
A Monkey And A
Lava Lamp

1970 Dodge Challenger T/A

**104**
### *ALEC BALDWIN*
Just A Lazy, Shiftless
Bastard

1970 Mercedes-Benz
280SL

**105**
### *JOEL HODGSON*
A Taste Of Hell From
On High

1963 Volkswagen Karmann
Ghia

**106**
### *BOB EINSTEIN*
Unusable On The Internet

1970 Mercedes-Benz
300 SEL

**107**
### *BARRY MARDER*
You Don't Want To Offend
A Cannibal

1966 Porsche 356 Dutch
Police Car

**108**
### *COLIN QUINN &
MARIO JOYNER*
I Hear *Downton Abbey* Is
Pretty Good . . .
1976 Triumph TR6

## 109
### CARL REINER & MEL BROOKS

I Want Sandwiches, I Want Chicken

1960 Rolls-Royce Silver Cloud II and 1970 Porsche 911S ("Henri")

## 110
### MICHAEL RICHARDS

It's Bubbly Time, Jerry

1962 Volkswagen Bus

## 201
### SARAH SILVERMAN

I'm Going To Change Your Life Forever

1969 Jaguar XKE E-Type Series II

## 202
### DAVID LETTERMAN

I Like Kettlecorn

1995 Volvo 960 Station Wagon

## 203
### GAD ELMALEH

No Lipsticks For Nuns

1950 Citroën 2CV

## 204
### DON RICKLES

You'll Never Play The Copa

1958 Cadillac Eldorado

## 205
### SETH MEYERS

Really?!

1973 Porsche 911 Carrera RS

## 206
### CHRIS ROCK

Kids Need Bullying

1969 Lamborghini P 400 S Miura

### 301

**LOUIS C.K.**

Comedy, Sex, And The Blue Numbers

1959 Fiat Jolly

### 302

**PATTON OSWALT**

How Would You Kill Superman?

1981 DeLorean DMC-12

### 303

**JAY LENO**

Comedy Is A Concealed Weapon

1949 Porsche 356/2

### 304

**TODD BARRY**

So You're Mellow And Tense?

1966 MGB Roadster

### 305

**TINA FEY**

Feces Are My Purview

1967 Volvo 1800S

### 306

**GEORGE COSTANZA**

The Over-Cheer

1976 AMC Pacer

### 307

**HOWARD STERN**

The Last Days Of Howard Stern

1969 Pontiac GTO

### 401

**SARAH JESSICA PARKER**

A Little Hyper-Aware

1976 Ford Country Squire

### 402
### *GEORGE WALLACE*

Two Polish Airline Pilots

1965 Buick Riviera

### 403
### *ROBERT KLEIN*

Opera Pimp

1967 Jaguar Mark 2

### 404
### *AZIZ ANSARI*

It's Like Pushing A
Building Off A Cliff

2012 Prevost X3-45

### 405
### *JON STEWART*

The Sound Of Virginity

1978 AMC Gremlin and
1968 AMC AMX

### 501
### *KEVIN HART*

You Look Amazing In
The Wind

1959 Porsche RSK Spyder

### 502
### *AMY SCHUMER*

I'm Wondering What It's
Like To Date Me

1971 Ferrari Daytona 365
GTB/4

### 503
### *BILL BURR*

Smoking Past The Band

1970 Ford Mustang
Boss 302

### 504
### *COLLEEN*
### *BALLINGER*

Happy Thanksgiving,
Miranda

1960 Austin-Healey Sprite

### 505
### *FRED ARMISEN*

I Wasn't Told About This . . .

1965 Saab 96 Monte Carlo 850

### 506
### *ALI WENTWORTH*

I'm Going To Take A Percocet And Let That One Go

1970 Mercedes-Benz 280SE Cabriolet

### 507
### *JIMMY FALLON*

The Unsinkable Legend, Parts 1 & 2

1956 Chevrolet Corvette

### 601
### *JULIA LOUIS-DREYFUS*

I'll Go If I Don't Have To Talk

1964 Aston Martin DB5

### 602
### *STEVE HARVEY*

Always Do The Banana Joke First

1957 Chevrolet Bel Air Convertible

### 603
### *JIM CARREY*

We Love Breathing What You're Burning, Baby

1976 Lamborghini Countach LP400

### 604
### *BILL MAHER*

The Comedy Team Of Smug And Arrogant

1979 Volkswagen Beetle Police Car

### 605
### *TREVOR NOAH*

That's The Whole Point Of Apartheid, Jerry

1985 Ferrari 308 GTB

### 606
### STEPHEN COLBERT
Cut Up And Bloody But
Looking Good

1964 Morgan Plus 4

### 701
### BARACK OBAMA
Just Tell Him You're The
President

1963 Corvette Stingray

### 702
### STEVE MARTIN
If You See This On A Toilet
Seat, Don't Sit Down

1954 Siata

### 703
### KATHLEEN MADIGAN
### & CHUCK MARTIN
Stroked Out On A Hot
Machine

1972 BMW 2002tii

### 704
### GARRY
### SHANDLING
It's Great That Garry
Shandling Is Still Alive

1979 Porsche 930
(a.k.a. 911 Turbo)

### 705
### SEBASTIAN
### MANISCALCO
I Don't Think That's
Bestiality

1969 Chevrolet Camaro Z28

### 706
### WILL FERRELL
Mr. Ferrell, For The Last
Time, We're Going To Ask
You To Put The Cigar Out

1970 Plymouth Road
Runner Superbird

### 801
### JIM GAFFIGAN
Stick Around For The
Pope

1977 Volkswagen Westfalia
Camper

### 802
### *MARGARET CHO*
You Can Go Cho Again

1967 Mazda Cosmo

### 806
### *JOHN OLIVER*
What Kind Of Human Animal Would Do This?

1959 Triumph TR3A

### 803
### *JUDD APATOW*
Escape From Syosset

1968 Pontiac Firebird 400 Convertible

### 901
### *KRISTEN WIIG*
The Volvo-ness

1964 Volvo 122S Amazon

### 804
### *J.B. SMOOVE*
Everybody Respects A Bloody Nose

1964 Studebaker Avanti

### 902
### *NORM MACDONALD*
A Rusty Car In The Rain

1958 Porsche Speedster

### 805
### *LORNE MICHAELS*
Everybody Likes To See The Monkeys

1955 Mercedes-Benz 300SL Gullwing

### 903
### *CEDRIC THE ENTERTAINER*
Dictators, Comics, And Preachers

1958 Bentley S1

### 904
### *LEWIS BLACK*
At What Point Am I Out
From Under?

1967 Cadillac Eldorado

### 905
### *CHRISTOPH WALTZ*
Champagne, Cigars, And
Pancake Batter

1957 BMW 507 Series II

### 906
### *BOB EINSTEIN*
It's Not So Funny When
It's Your Mother

2017 Acura NSX

### 1001
### *JERRY LEWIS*
Heere's Jerry!

1966 Jaguar E-Type Series
Roadster

### 1002
### *DANA CARVEY*
Na.. Ga.. Do.. It

Meyers Manx Signature
Dune Buggy

### 1003
### *KATE McKINNON*
A Brain In A Jar

1962 Fiat 600 Multipla

### 1004
### *ALEC BALDWIN*
Gyrating, Naked Twister

1974 BMW 3.0 CS

### 1005
### *BRIAN REGAN*
Are There Left-Handed
Spoons?

2005 Cadillac XLR

### 1006
### ELLEN DeGENERES
You Said It Wasn't Funny

1977 Toyota Land Cruiser
FJ40

### 1007
### ZACH GALIFIANAKIS
From The Third Reich
To You

1973 Volkswagen Thing
Dual Sport

### 1008
### JOHN MULANEY
A Hooker In The Rain

1969 Alfa Romeo Giulia
Super

### 1009
### DAVE CHAPPELLE
Nobody Says, "I Wish I
Had A Camera"

1973 Citroën SM

### 1010
### NEAL BRENNAN
Red-Bottom Shoes Equals
Fantastic Babies

1965 Porsche 356C

### 1011
### TRACY MORGAN
Lasagna With Six Different
Cheeses

1984 Ferrari 288 GTO

### 1012
### HASAN MINHAJ
Nobody Cries At A Joke

1992 Ferrari 512 TR

### 1101
### MELISSA VILLASEÑOR
The Museum Of Food

1991 Nissan Figaro

**1102**
### SEBASTIAN MANISCALCO

**My Wife Didn't Know The Extent Of It**

1960 Lambretta Li 150 Series 2 and 2018 Vespa Sei Giorni 300

**1103**
### SETH ROGEN

We Have The Meats

1976 Dodge Royal Monaco Sedan (the "Bluesmobile")

**1104**
### EDDIE MURPHY

I Just Wanted To Kill

2004 Porsche Carrera GT

**1105/1112**
### RICKY GERVAIS

China Maybe? Parts 1 & 2

2018 Rolls-Royce Dawn Convertible

**1106**
### MATTHEW BRODERICK

These People That Do This Stuff. They Stink.

2018 Lamborghini Huracán Performante

**1107**
### MARTIN SHORT

A Dream World Of Residuals

1982 Mercedes-Benz 300TD Wagon

**1108**
### BRIDGET EVERETT

Still Hot To The Touch

1961 Cadillac Series 62 Convertible

**1109**
### MARIO JOYNER

He Should Have Been Done That

1974 Volkswagen Thing

### 1110
### *BARRY MARDER*
Big Lots And BevMo!

1966 Porsche 356 SC

### 1111
### *JAMIE FOXX*
You Got To Get The
Alligator Sweat

1969 Maserati Mistral

# ACKNOWLEDGMENTS

**Comedians in Cars Getting Coffee** got started because Steve Mosko—who was head of Sony Pictures Television at the time—and I trusted each other so much. I remember him saying, "How about, I'll give you the money to make a few of these, and if it turns out to be something, we can figure out a deal then?" That's a lot of trust. And it is what eventually happened. A very, very rare show business occurrence and perhaps has never happened before or since.

I would also like to thank Ted Sarandos, who brought it to Netflix and gave the show a wide audience.

Tammy Johnston is the other most important person to *CCC*. She produced and poured her heart into it for years to make it work.

Special thanks also to Yossi Kimberg, Denis Jensen, and Melissa Miller, who were also essential players in the story.

Thanks to Jonathan Karp and Sean Manning for making this book so beautifully. And George Shapiro and Howard West for supporting me in every possible way.

And most important of all, my love and my life, Jessica Seinfeld, Sascha Seinfeld, Julian Seinfeld, and Shepherd Seinfeld. Thank you for showing me there's a whole gigantic world besides comedy clubs and coffee shops.

| | | | | |
|---|---|---|---|---|
| tey merial | Reenact Commercial | "This is where you got to coffee broil" | This is where Warren Beatty lives | Garry health |
| N on | Reflecting on their life phases | Introduction of Mitsy | George Wallace dog joke | Comedy Parking |
| auley now | Talk about Neon Signs | Issues with Mitsy | Garry tells girlfriend Story | Garry Story on |
| mint | Garry says he's just a guy from Arizona | Dennis Miller Story | Jerry can't find his photo | Finding names Outside |
| lon ew | Revisit losing material | RIP Robin Williams | "I forgot to ask her for coffee" | Reflection on complai |
| ch lo ve?" | Garry inventing Larry Sanders show style | Garry Not Feeling well (meter) | Boxing Ref at funeral (meter) | Going to lune |
| to in | Meeting to walk around lot | Walking down New York Street | Garry's jokes in Seinfeld | Script Gir |
| y to ete? | Blind Driver joke | Garry's suicide note | Why would Robin kill himself? | Explaining joke Dalai lan |

# CREDITS

**Behind-the-scenes photos courtesy of:**

Rutger-Jan Cleiren, Peter Holmes, Denis Jensen, Barry Marder,
Pete Souza, and John Taggart

BATMAN, SUPERMAN and all related character and
elements™ and © DC.